SUMMA OF THE CHRISTIAN LIFE

SUMMA OF THE CHRISTIAN LIFE

SELECTED TEXTS FROM THE WRITINGS OF

Venerable Louis of Granada, OP

THE EXISTENCE AND PERFECTIONS OF GOD
THE MARVELS OF CREATION

TRANSLATED AND ADAPTED BY

Jordan Aumann, OP

TAN Books,
North Carolina

NIHIL OBSTAT:	James R. Gillis, O.P., S.T.M. James J. McDonald, O.P., S.T.B.
IMPRIMI POTEST:	Edward L. Hughes, O.P., S.T.M. Provincial
NIHIL OBSTAT:	Thomas G. Kinsella, O.P. Censor Librorum
IMPRIMATUR:	Edward A. Fitzgerald, D.D. Bishop of Winona June 1,1954

Originally published in English by B. Herder Book Co., St. Louis, Missouri in 1954. Copyright © 1954 by B. Herder Book Co. Published by TAN Books in 1979. This translation was made from the Spanish edition of *Obra Selecta: Una Suma de la Vida Cristiana*, published by La Editorial Católica, Madrid, Spain, 1947, under the auspices of the Biblioteca de Autores Cristianos.

Cover design by Jordan Avery

ISBN: 978-1-5051-3519-0
Kindle ISBN: 978-1-5051-3599-2
ePUB ISBN: 978-1-5051-3598-5

Published in the United States by
TAN Books
PO Box 269
Gastonia, NC 28053
www.TANBooks.com

Printed in India

To Mary, Queen of the Most Holy Rosary

Contents ✠

BOOK TWO

THE MARVELS OF CREATION

Translator's Preface ✠

Louis of Granada stands without a peer among Dominican ascetical writers and his works are known and loved throughout the Christian world. Both as a writer and a preacher he dedicated himself with apostolic zeal to the task of transmitting sacred doctrine to the common people. He is par excellence a theologian for the laity.

The *Summa of the Christian Life* is not a mere anthology; it represents a careful selection of passages from the works of Louis of Granada. Moreover, in order to avoid a haphazard assortment of texts, the passages have been arranged in the order of the *Summa Theologica* of St. Thomas Aquinas, thus giving the entire collection a theological unity.

The Spanish edition of this work was compiled by Father Antonio Trancho, O.P., of Almagro, Spain, who was the first to realize the possibility of using the masterpiece of St. Thomas Aquinas as a framework for the spiritual writings of Louis of Granada. But Father Trancho did not live to see the fulfillment of his dream; with twenty-six fellow Dominicans he gave his life for God and for Spain when he was shot down by the Communists in the early days of the Spanish Civil War. The work was completed at last by the Most Reverend Francisco Barbado, O.P., Bishop of Salamanca and a son of the Dominican Province of Bética.

The present translation is made possible through the gracious permission of Bishop Barbado and the Very Reverend

Father Provincial of the Dominican Province of Bética in southern Spain. Although the original Spanish edition has been the basis of this English version, adaptations and deletions have been made with a view to the utility and benefit of American readers. The passages in the Spanish edition of the *Summa of the Christian Life* are taken from the critical edition of the works of Granada, made by Father Justo Cuervo, O.P., at Madrid, in 1906. For the convenience and satisfaction of the reader, the various passages which make up this *Summa* are identified in an appendix at the end of each volume.

JORDAN AUMANN, O.P.

Foreword ✠

THE VENERABLE LOUIS of Granada is one of the writers who has contributed most to the formation of the Christian character and spirit of the Spanish people. With clarity and precision he wrote of the most exalted doctrines of Christianity. No one knew as well as he did how to combine loftiness of thought and profundity of doctrine with a clarity and transparency of style that is within the grasp of all.

If the Spanish people merit the title of a theological race, it is not only because Vitoria, Cano, Bañez, and Suárez were Spaniards, but because the Spaniards are interested in the theological principles that govern the Christian life and for this they are greatly indebted to Louis of Granada. Without the diffusion of his books it is hardly probable that the *autos sacramentales* and the theological comedies of López, Lope, Tirso, and others would have enchanted the people with a poetry which today astonishes us by its profundity and theological precision. In spite of the greater human culture of our times, relatively few people are able to appreciate them.

That Louis of Granada wrote for the "wives of carpenters" was the unfortunate expression of disdain used by one who apparently had forgotten that the wife of the carpenter was full of grace and blessed among women. But the phrase that was intended to be an insult, contained within itself a lofty tribute. Even St. Paul, who wrote for those who were recently initiated in the Christian life, explained the most lofty mysteries of divine wisdom and attempted to place them within the grasp of all.

Like St. Paul, Louis of Granada aspired to bring the plenitude of the life of grace to the greatest number of souls, leading them by the hand in the ascent from virtue to virtue in their journey to the kingdom of heaven. There resounded constantly in his heart the echo of the words of the Apostle: "You are fellow citizens with the saints, and the domestics of God."[1] "Mind the things that are above, not the things that are upon the earth. For you are dead; and your life is hid with Christ in God."[2] "The mystery which hath been hidden from ages and generations, but now is manifested to His saints . . . is Christ, . . . whom we preach, admonishing every man, and teaching every man in all wisdom that we may present every man perfect in Christ Jesus."[3] "Let the word of Christ dwell in you abundantly, in all wisdom; teaching and admonishing one another in psalms, hymns, and spiritual canticles, singing in grace in your hearts to God. All whatsoever you do in word or in work, do all in the name of the Lord Jesus Christ, giving thanks to God and the Father by Him."[4]

It was the selfsame pedagogy of Christ, who made use of comparisons and parables to teach people the mysteries of the kingdom of God. This was not appreciated by those who reproached Louis of Granada, as they reproached his contemporary saints and friends, St. Teresa of Avila, Blessed John of Avila, St. Francis Borgia, and Blessed John de Ribera.

---

1 Eph. 2:19.

2 Col. 3:2–3.

3 *Ibid.* 1:26–8.

4 Col. 3:16–7.

The security of doctrine found in Father Granada leaves nothing to be desired nor is it necessary that one use a certain benevolence in order to give his expressions an orthodox sense. Those who are intent on finding mistakes, as a wise Master of the Sacred Palace once said, could find them even in the *Pater Noster*.

Moreover, Louis of Granada has the merit of combatting the spiritual exaggerations of his time, both those of the so-called intellectualists and those of the Illuminists. In much the same way, Francisco Vitoria combatted the influence of the Nominalists and the followers of Erasmus and established at Salamanca a glorious theological school. Granada, like Vitoria, possessed a brilliant intellect and a generous heart and he had mastered in an exceptional manner the great doctrinal synthesis of St. Thomas Aquinas. Louis of Granada is no eclectic; in his writings there are no affectations or adherences to the exaggerations mentioned above. He is firmly rooted in the principles of Thomistic theology and possesses a solid biblical, patristic, and metaphysical foundation.

Louis of Granada also overcame the tendencies to separate asceticism and mysticism, which were started in his day. Both aspects of the mystical life were evaluated by him and he coordinated them in such a way that both the ascetics and the mystics can look to him as a master. Undoubtedly, he gives greater emphasis to ascetical matters, for the simple reason that he directs his words in a special way to the great number of simple faithful who need above all to become enamored of virtue and holiness of life so that they will eradicate evil inclinations and rise steadily to a higher life. Granada attempted to lead souls to the threshold of contemplation and the mystical life, and because he himself lived that life intensely, his soul frequently soared to the regions of intimate communion with God and at times seems to move entirely in the planes of the mystical life.

Granada's vast classical and ecclesiastical culture, his absorbing spirit, and the perfection of his literary style, place him, together with Vitoria and Louis of Leon, among the creators of Christian Spanish humanism. With good reason has he merited the title of the Spanish Cicero. The dominant idea of humanism was a true evaluation of man but in some countries it was carried to the inadmissible extreme of a pagan anthropomorphism. For Granada, man is king of creation and attracts the glances of divine love and mercy and providence, but man is not to contemplate himself or take complacency in his own perfections; rather, he must direct himself to his Creator, returning love for love.

The appreciation that was expressed for Granada even during his lifetime is evidenced in many documents and written testimonies. In a benevolent and friendly letter, Pope Gregory XIII encourages the Dominican friar to continue his apostolate of the pen, especially now that his advanced age prevents him from sharing in the arduous labor of preaching. The letter is also a confirmation of the approval of the works of Granada which had been issued by the Council of Trent and countersigned by Pope Paul IV. St. Teresa of Avila, who had the astuteness to know and make friends with the holy souls that were her contemporaries, seeing that it was unlikely that she would ever meet Granada in person, at last decided to write to him and express her gratitude for the great amount of good he had done for souls through his writings. St. Peter of Alcántara held the *oración y Meditación* in such high esteem that he made a new edition and wrote a commentary on it.

St. Charles Borromeo, another contemporary of Granada, had frequent correspondence with him and asked him to send copies of his books as soon as they were published. So greatly did he esteem the works of Granada that he wrote a letter of commendation to the Pope, saying: "Of all those who have written on spiritual matters up to the present time and which I have known, there is no one who has written books in greater number or better selected and more profitable than Louis of Granada."

St. Francis de Sales likewise recommended the books of Granada to a bishop friend, saying: "I beseech you to hold fast to Louis of Granada in his entirety and let his works become to you a second breviary." Father Leonard Hansen, an English Provincial and biographer of St. Rose of Lima, states: "With equal diligence the glorious St. Rose of Santa María read and persuaded others to read the pious books that best treated of prayer, and among these she gave first place to the erudite work, *Oración y Meditación*, by Louis of Granada."

The high place that the works of Granada have held up to our own time is evidenced by the fact that they have passed through four thousand editions in various languages. In France alone there have been forty-eight editions of the complete works and in Italy there have been twenty-eight. It is evident from all this that the statement of the Spanish bibliographer, Nicholás Antonio, is a well-deserved tribute: "Our nation has never had a greater or more useful man and perhaps it will never again have one to equal Louis of Granada."

Francisco Barbado, O.P.
Bishop of Salamanca, Spain

General Introduction ✠

LOUIS OF GRANADA is the writer of the Spanish Empire. His life courses through a luminous arc which, with an almost mathematical exactitude, runs parallel to the greatest century of Spanish history. Born at a time when Spain began to advance steadily toward becoming a world empire, he reached his maturity in the days of the Council of Trent and the Battle of Lepanto, when Spain had reached the zenith of her imperial greatness. He died in 1588 when the splendor of Spain's golden century was beginning to pale. It was the year of the defeat of the Armada.

The exalted figure of Louis of Granada is bathed in glories. His works and his doctrine were the spiritual food of imperial Spain. Preacher, literary stylist, and spiritual writer: such are the three dimensions of his dynamism, a dynamism that has left a glorious path in Spanish and Christian culture. He is the preacher of Spain. He it is who brought the Spanish language to its classical perfection. He it is who began a new period in the history of Spanish spirituality, a period that produced St. Teresa of Avila and St. John of the Cross.

His influence throughout Europe and throughout the world is amazing; it is one of the most stupendous of historico-literary phenomena. His works have been translated into all languages; they have been read by princes and kings (Charles V and Philip II), saints and literary figures (St.

Teresa, Shakespeare, Molière), pontiffs and the ordinary laity, Protestants and pagans.

The Man

In the heroic impatience of Spain's reconquest, the city of Granada had become an epic dream of Spain. On the second of January in 1492 the lances that had been unsheathed for so many centuries were raised in exultant jubilation and the arrows of the Spanish Catholic rulers, Ferdinand and Isabella, now united under a common yoke of love, were placed point downward as a symbol of peace. It was the day of the conquest of Granada and with this conquest was re-established the geographic unity of Spain, which had been divided for eight centuries, since the Mussulman invasion of Andalusia in the year 711. In that same year of 1492, Christopher Columbus, commanding the three vessels, the Niña, the Pinta, and the Santa Maria, and invested with royal powers from the Alhambra, discovered the New World on the twelfth of October. In that year also the King and Queen created a school of humanities for the nobility and named Peter of Anglería its first rector.

These three facts are the key that opens the door to the golden century of Spain. But there were also other events of great importance. Ferdinand and Isabella, whose marriage had effected the political union of Spain, had achieved geographical unity of the nation by the reconquest of Granada. Their next objective was unity of religion. To that end, they founded new convents, reformed religious orders, and expelled the Jews, who were a constant threat of disintegration. They inaugurated the Inquisition to watch over the orthodoxy of the Catholic faith amidst the fanatical and proselytizing Jews and Moors who yet remained in Spain. They fostered enterprises of great political and religious significance, such as the discovery and expansion of the New World and the conquest of new kingdoms for Spain and for Christ.

The conquest of Granada was not only a joyous victory, but it also presented a problem: the problem of making the city Spanish once again. The difficulty was a complex one because at the same time that it was Christian, Granada continued to be in great part a Moorish stronghold. The rulers allowed the Moors to preserve their religion, their temples, their language and customs. The political, civil, and religious life of the city was reorganized under the double standard of Spanish and Moorish. But such a situation, if permanent, would have proved a constant threat to peace and unity. Consequently, Ferdinand and Isabella granted free entrance to any Spaniard from the provinces who desired to go to Granada and settle there. It was a great opportunity for citizens from poorer sections of Spain and it would at the same time hasten the blending of the Moorish population with the Spanish people.

Among the numerous immigrants was a young married couple from Sarriá, a hamlet in the province of Lugo. The Galician is by temperament and by necessity an eternal pilgrim, although forever after he carries in his heart a nostalgia for his own province. At that time the district of Lugo, like the rest of Galicia, had reached the peak of its poverty. The reconquered cities of southern Spain offered a magnificent opportunity for turning the wheel of fortune, and thousands upon thousands of *gallegos* played that wheel.

Shortly after settling in Granada, the two young immigrants from Galicia were blessed by the birth of a son in 1504 and they gave him the name of Louis. But fortune did not smile on that home. The father, Fancis Sarriá, died in 1509 and the little boy of five had to eat the bitter bread of a begging orphan. History would have forgotten those years if Louis himself had not had the great humility to recall them. In 1582 he wrote to his great friend and admirer, Cardinal Borromeo: "I was the son of a woman who was so poor that she lived on the alms that were given to her at the gate of the monastery." Louis also, barefoot and in tattered clothes, used to beg alms at the Dominican convent of Holy Cross.

Those years of suffering and privation had a great influence on the soul of Louis of Granada. He loved poverty as an eternal spouse, ardently, and like a Franciscan. He loved the poor like brothers and his great joy was to help them whenever he could. Even as a little boy, Louis acquired an ascetical sense of contempt for the world which was to be for him a norm of life and a stepping-stone to the higher world of the spirit where the passions do not challenge and fickle fortune does not deceive.

The sad years of orphanage and hunger that he endured with his beloved mother, whose name is unknown to us, were to end very shortly. The biographers have woven a colorful legend concerning the occasion on which fortune changed for the young orphan. Louis was fighting with a street urchin bigger than himself who had insulted Louis' mother. Nothing would have come of the fight had not the Count de Tendilla, Mayor of the Alhambra, passed by at the moment. As the Count approached, the bully fled but Louis stood his ground unafraid. When asked why he was fighting, Louis defended himself so ardently and with such courage that the Count was favorably impressed and took Louis under his patronage. Almost eighty years later, when a granddaughter of the Count, the Marquise de Villafranca, wrote to him from Naples for advice on the sanctification of her married life, Louis recalls the virtues of her "holy grandfather . . . who nourished me from tender years, giving me food from the very plate from which he himself ate."

Louis received his early training in the doctrinal schools founded by the first archbishop of Granada, Ferdinand de Talavera, formerly a professor in the University of Salamanca. The Archbishop had established these schools so that the children of both the Moors and Spaniards could be taught the rudiments of Christian doctrine, reading, writing, and music. The Archbishop had almost unlimited power in Granada and he had engaged a man to gather the children from the streets of the city and place them in the schools. Louis studied in such a school either before or after he had entered into the service of the Count de Tendilla as a page. He also became an acolyte in the royal chapel that had been installed provisionally in the Church of St. Francis of the Alhambra.

It is not certain that Louis studied the classical humanities under Peter Martyr of Anglería, as some biographers maintain. Although he gave evidence of a profound humanistic training, he could not have received it in the lecture hall of Peter Martyr because the master was not in Granada during the time that Louis devoted himself to these studies. However, the works of the famous master were available at the Alhambra and Louis and the sons of the Count must have spent many hours in delightful and formative reading. They also studied and practiced eloquence and Louis succeeded so well that he was given a prophetic nickname: the preacher.

As a result of his humanistic studies, a burning zest for the contemplation of nature was enkindled in Louis' fervent soul. It was a flame that would never be extinguished. Granada and its environs lay before his eyes like a vision in a dream. On the balconies of the Alhambra, deliberately placed so that they command a complete panorama of the city, Louis could pass delightful hours, feeding his spirit on a grace and beauty the like of which are to be found nowhere else in the world. Louis of Granada could be considered the creator of physical esthetics in Spain and one who knew best how to read the divine in the beauty of nature.

The hour came at last when Louis was faced with the problem of the choice of a vocation. At that time three professions beckoned to Spanish youth: the Church, the sea, or the barracks; that is to say, the clerical state, adventure across the seas in the New World, or service as a soldier of the king. Louis decided in favor of the Church and the religious life. To that convent where he had so many times begged "an alms for the love of God," he now went to ask "the mercy of God and the Order" and the black and white habit of a Dominican. He was, therefore, no stranger to the friars; poor of fortune, yes, but rich indeed in physical and moral qualities. On June 15, 1524, in the presence of the community and to the joyful tears of his beloved mother, he received the habit of a Friar Preacher. Few would wear it with as much dignity and triumph as he.

From that moment a new life began for Louis de Sarriá. The year of novitiate was lived under a rule of austerity and religious formation by a Father Master who instructed the novices in monastic observances and the exercise of religious virtue. The novices served the community in the refectory; they could not speak with strangers or even with the professed religious. It was a year of testing and preparation. The soul of Louis was nourished and enlarged by the Dominican spirit throughout that year and at its end he was judged suitable for profession, which he made into the hands of Fray Christopher de Guzmán, patriarch of the province and prior of Holy Cross.

At religious profession the Dominican enters into a new environment, that of the university; but it is an environment in harmony with his religious life. Constant study and a deep spiritual life: such is the theme of the Dominican student. Fray Louis was to pass four years as a student in Holy Cross Convent; years filled with dreams and labor.

The Convent of Holy Cross was founded by Ferdinand and Isabella shortly after the conquest of Granada, as a testimony of their great devotion to St. Dominic and a reward for the services of Fray Thomas de Torquemada. But it was also meant to be a stronghold from which the Dominicans, with their traditional vigilance, would watch over the orthodoxy of the Faith. By express will of the King, the convent belonged to the Congregation of Observance which, by means of study and religious observance, had reformed Dominican life in Spain. When Fray Louis was professed, the Convent of the Holy Cross was, intellectually and spiritually, one of the best in the Province of Andalusia. Known today as the Province of Bética, it had been separated from the Province of Spain in 1515 and the progress and vitality of the new Province were amazing. As frequently happens in new communities, it enjoyed great religious fervor and showed a keen interest in university studies. It expanded in many directions. The General Chapter of 1530, for example, records the foundation of no less than six new convents in Andalusia; its missionary zeal is attested by a rapid expansion in Africa; and the General Chapter of 1518 had annexed to Andalusia all the convents founded or to be founded in the Americas.

Holy Cross Convent in Granada was a House of Studies from the very beginning of the Province in 1515. Its first prior, Fray Albert de Aguayo, translator of Boethius' *De Consolatione Philosophiae,* imparted to the convent a vigorous university atmosphere. In surroundings so conducive to study and religious observance, Fray Louis reviewed Latin and then spent three years on philosophy and three years on theology. Such was the regulation of the Dominican *Ratio studiorum* at the time.

The texts used were the grammar of Nebrija, the *Summae* of Peter the Spaniard, and the works of Aristotle and St. Thomas Aquinas. Fray Louis was brilliant in scholastic disputations and had no equal in mental capacity, application to study, and exact observance of the monastic life. Consequently, it was no surprise when he was named for a scholarship at the celebrated college of St. Gregory in Valladolid.

Fray Louis was twenty-five years old when, in obedience to his superiors, he arranged his meager effects and began the tedious journey to Castile. At the beginning of June, 1529, he arrived at Valladolid, then the capital of Spain, and was received with fraternal warmth at the College of St. Gregory. For Fray Louis it was like arriving in a new world. Despite the cordiality of superiors and companions, he was completely disorientated and nostalgia struggled with obedience.

The day after his arrival, an older student was assigned to teach Fray Louis the statutes of the College and to acquaint him with the glorious history of those walls and lecture halls. The eight days of rigid apprenticeship were like the eight days of watching and vigil before being admitted as a knight of Thomistic truth. Always a good disciple, Fray Louis studied the statutes, page by page and word by word, and listened attentively as his pedagogue and companion recounted the history of the College.

St. Gregory's had been founded by Fray Alonso de Burgos, confessor of the King and Queen and Bishop of Córdoba, for the diffusion and growth of Thomistic doctrine. The College was completed in 1496 and was a marvel of plateresque architecture. The sensitive and contemplative soul of Fray Louis never wearied of admiring the cloister walk and the facade of delicately carved stone set against the austere and ascetical Castilian countryside. But all this was nothing when compared to the prestige that the College enjoyed as a center of learning. The lectures in theology and the arts were not surpassed by any other university in or outside of Spain. The pedagogue told all these things to Fray Louis very slowly so that the new student would never forget the responsibility and dignity of a student of St. Gregory's.

After the eight days of matriculation were passed, Fray Louis solemnly took the oath to the statutes of the College on June 11, 1529. With the taking of the oath, Fray Louis was formally invested in the College, a much coveted distinction but an honor laden with duties and obligations. In the mind of the young friar his first duty was worthily to represent Holy Cross Convent of Granada. Grateful for the confidence placed in him by his fellow religious of Holy Cross, he changed his name from Fray Louis de Sarriá to Fray Louis of Granada.

Let us reconstruct a typical day in the life of a student at the College of St. Gregory in 1529. We can do so by reviewing the statutes that governed the College, for they regulated the life of the students with a mathematical precision. The two most important occupations were study and prayer. All heard Mass daily, with the exception of the priest students who celebrated their own Masses. After Mass a prayer was recited at the tomb of the founder. Choral Office was fulfilled with rigorous regularity. Matins, Lauds, Vespers, and Compline were chanted in choir in a subdued voice; the minor hours and the Office of the Dead were recited in private. In the afternoon all attended the singing of the *Salve Regina* at the Dominican convent of St. Paul, which was adjacent to St. Gregory's.

The meals were another community act that no one was permitted to miss. The bell for meals was rung at eleven in the morning and at eight in the evening. Passages of Scripture were read at the noon meal; Dominican writings or excerpts from the *Moralia* of St. Gregory, at the evening collation. No one was permitted to enter the room of another student without permission and then the door was to be left open during the visit. Study was done by candlelight and lest a student fall asleep over his parchment books, one of the friars was appointed to go from cell to cell and extinguish all the candles that had not been put out within a quarter of an hour after Matins. The students rarely left the precincts of the College except for an occasional group walk.

There were lectures in logic, natural philosophy, moral philosophy, theology, exegesis, and cases of conscience. Moreover, there were public disputations in theology and public lectures in philosophy on every lecture day and the student had to assist at the one assigned by the rector. The official language was Latin, except on vacation days when Spanish could be spoken.

Fray Louis of Granada followed this schedule of life for five years. In the ascetical surroundings of Castile his spirit was gradually acquiring a temper of steel, the temper of the *conquistadores*. He was assiduous in scholastic disputations and solicitous in the fulfillment of his duties when it was his turn to officiate in choir, to read in refectory, to extinguish the candles in the cells, or to sweep the corridors. He was a religious without vainglory, possessing a great capacity for work and blessed with an open mind. Without seeking to do so, he won the admiration and sympathy of his fellow religious and professors. The fellow students of Fray Louis are almost entirely unknown to us save for Peter Sotomayor, who followed Dominic Soto in the professor's chair at Salamanca, Bishop Francisco Cerda, who attended the Council of Trent, and Melchior Cano.

What were the questions that interested the students and gave zest to collegiate life in the time of Fray Louis? Three trends dominated the intellectual life at St. Gregory's. The first was medieval scholasticism. Disputations were always held in the classical syllogistic form and the doctrine was always that of the great master, St. Thomas Aquinas. Secondly, there was the pious humanism that Vitoria had brought back from Paris, where he had taught from 1523 to 1526 and had initiated the attempts to modernize theological methods and apply theology to contemporary problems. The third trend was what we may call "Savonarolism" or a zeal for the apostolate. All three trends left a deep impression on the soul of Fray Louis.

In the Thomistic scholasticism that served as the framework for all the intellectual activities of the College, the figure of greatest prestige was that of the master, Astudillo, the Regent of Studies. A man of austere temperament and training and given entirely to speculative studies, he was a typical theologian of the Middle Ages by reason of his profound analysis, the ordered clarity of his exposition, and the dryness of his literary style. At the request of his students he agreed to publish his lectures and commentaries, and he entrusted the work of editing to Fray Louis of Granada. Not content with the merely material aspect of the editing, he adorned the work with two compositions: one in prose and another in verse, and both in Latin, wherein he sings the praises of Master Astudillo. The book was published in 1532 and is a commentary on Aristotle's *Physica* and *De Generatione et Corruptione*. In the first fruits of his pen, Fray Louis appears to us as one enamored of philosophy and an authentic man of the Renaissance as well as one capable of perfect Latin prose and verse. Astudillo had other manuscripts in theology and Sacred Scripture but he did not edit them. However, there is no doubt that under the tutelage of Astudillo, Fray Louis penetrated deeply into scholastic theology.

What Astudillo did for Fray Louis in the intellectual order, Carranza did for him in the spiritual order. Under Astudillo his vocation to be a man of letters was vivified, while Carranza evoked his apostolic vocation. His native goodness was a fertile field in which to plant the seed of aspirations and longings for a renewal of Christian society, a central theme in the life of Carranza. It was inevitable that there should be a struggle between the dry study of medieval parchments and the glowing zeal for the apostolate. Which would triumph? Ultimately Fray Louis prepared himself for a future apostolate of preaching—for which he had extraordinary ability—by means of study, prayer, and penances.

Five busy years passed, laborious years. The hour was approaching for the apostolate, but there would be disillusionment. Letters, scholastic disputations, much study—all serve to make one fruitful in the apostolate, but it is God who converts souls.

We now enter upon one of the most interesting periods in the life of Louis of Granada and yet it is the most obscure period for biographers. During his college days no one doubted that Fray Louis had magnificent qualities that fitted him for a life of teaching nor was anyone ignorant of his ardent longings and zeal for the apostolate. Fray Dominic Betanzos, on his return from America, had obtained permission to establish a Dominican Province in Mexico and he passed through Valladolid to recruit friars for the new foundation. Fray Louis was among those who stepped forward and generously offered themselves for the new venture. Louis had not yet completed his eight-year course of studies but he was willing to abandon the lecture halls.

On August 3, 1534, he was in Seville with twenty other Dominicans to inscribe his name as a missionary at the Office of Trade and Commerce with the Indies. King Charles V had given orders that the missionaries were to be provided for, both as to payment of passage and other necessities. On September 26 the boat was chartered that was to carry the missionaries to the New World. The departure was imminent. But when the time for embarking actually took place, Fray Louis remained on shore and another took his place.

What had happened? The privileges of volunteer missionaries had ceased. Pope Adrian VI had granted permission to all missionaries to go to foreign lands without doing any more than advising their superiors. The superior, under pain of excommunication, could not prevent the departure. But abuses had arisen in this regard and Pope Clement VII revoked the privileges in 1533. Consequently, the Dominican Provincial, Fray Michael de los Arcos, not wishing to lose a friar of such value, commanded Fray Louis to cancel his departure.

Another mission, more strenuous and bristling with difficulties, awaited him: the restoration of the abandoned convent of Escalaceli, near Córdoba.

The longing for the mission field remained a thorn in the soul of Fray Louis, but he accepted the sacrifice. Fifty years later, when his eyes were weary but his spirit still alert, the octogenarian Dominican friar would recall the days when he, too, had his foot on the gangplank of a ship bound for America and, overcome with this remembrance of disillusion and obedience, would take up his pen to write his *Catechism* for teaching religion to the Indians. "Seeing that in this age so many doors are opened for the spread of the faith among the Gentiles and desiring to have some small part in this work, . . . I wished . . . to serve with my small talents by writing this brief treatise in which I attempt to show how one can teach our holy faith to the infidels."

Escalaceli is a Dominican convent situated amid the pines and olive trees in the Sierra de Córdoba, about eight miles from the city. It was founded by Blessed Alvaro de Córdoba with the help of the King and Queen of Castile, whose confessor he was, in order to begin the reform of the Dominican Order in Spain after the general state of decadence that followed the repression of religious orders. There also he established the first outdoor *Via Crucis* in Europe, as a remembrance of his pilgrimage to Jerusalem. He filled that solitary place with biblical names and soon a life of sanctity began to flourish there.

A century later the spirit of the founder had been extinguished and the religious abandoned the convent to take up residence in a new convent in the city of Córdoba itself. By the spring of 1530 the abandonment of Escalaceli was complete. Some religious were not in favor of the move and instead of going to the new convent, they went to the Convent of St. Paul where the prior received them kindly. Later that same prior was elected provincial and it was he who gave Fray Louis the task of restoring Escalaceli.

Fray Louis was thirty years old when he embraced his assignment. In the spring of 1535 the Master General, Fray John Fenario, arrived and gave assistance to the task of Fray Louis. The material restoration of the sanctuary was effected through courage and sacrifice, but more important was the spiritual revival. With warm unction Fray Louis promoted devotion to Blessed Alvaro, whose remains rested in the church, and to the *Via Crucis* that he had established there. Escalaceli was converted into a center for pilgrimages and soon the faithful could be seen making the Stations of the Cross in the hills where Alvaro had erected them.

But the talents and zeal of Fray Louis were not restricted to the Sierra de Córdoba. He also dedicated himself to preaching and the direction of souls in other localities, first in Córdoba and its surroundings and later in all of Andalusia. The nobility vied with one another to secure his presence and in 1538 he was selected as the Lenten preacher in the cathedral of Córdoba.

Meanwhile, his former master, Astudillo, had died, but Carranza continued to triumph and in his glory he did not forget his beloved friend. In 1539, while attending the General Chapter of his Order in Rome, Carranza was granted the title of Master of Sacred Theology by express permission of the Pope. It was the opportune moment to realize a hope he had long cherished. He asked and obtained the assignation of Fray Louis to the College at Valladolid. But Fray Louis declined the honor. He did not wish the professor's chair. He preferred the theology of the heart to the theology of the mind.

As a result of his thwarted attempt to go to America as a missionary, a profound spiritual crisis arose in the soul of Louis of Granada. The writings of the famous Master John of Avila also had a great influence on the change of Fray Louis' attitude toward intellectual and spiritual problems. Fray Louis acquired a new appreciation and knowledge of the "mystery of Christ"; a knowledge that was not speculative but vital and concrete. He began to have a distaste for study because study gives no more than a skeletal knowledge of that mystery. Prayer, not study, is the way to understand and live the mystery of Christ in our souls. Fray Louis seems to believe that he had made a mistake in dedicating so much time to study heretofore. What really matters is to know our own nothingness and to know the supreme good that Christ has given us through redemption. To live Christ within us, as St. Paul teaches, and then to preach Christ.

The life of Fray Louis gradually acquired a strong orientation toward such ideas and in order to live them more fully, he withdrew as much as possible from the affairs of a world that so readily tempts a man with its vanities and vainglory and gave himself to prayer and meditation. A consequence of this new evaluation of life was the awakening in him of his vocation as a spiritual writer. He desired that the riches of the spiritual treasure should be imparted and shared by all and the means by which he would diffuse them was by preaching and writing.

The first literary fruit of this period is a small tract on the method of prayer, sent to a student at St. Gregory in Valladolid who, at the suggestion of Carranza, had written Fray Louis for advice. The little tract is entirely different from what

Fray Louis had previously written as a prologue to the works of Astudillo. The man has changed and also his style. The former was a Renaissance literary style; the latter is spirituality pure and simple. It is the first lecture of Fray Louis from the chair of Spanish spirituality. That same little tract was later to be transformed into a work that would make the name of its author immortal: *El Libro de la Oración y Meditación*.

Fray Louis was by this time advancing in giant strides in his fame as a preacher, a holy friar, and a man of administrative ability. Fray Augustine Salucio, a young Dominican of twenty-one who later became preacher to Philip II and whose sermons were especially liked by St. Teresa, never missed a sermon by Fray Louis. Later, in a book of advice for preachers, he was to give interesting details concerning the sermons of Fray Louis. At the Dominican Chapter celebrated at Osuna in 1544 Granada was granted the title of Preacher General. On this occasion Master Avila wrote him the first letter of their spiritual correspondence and it is one of the most beautiful letters ever written by Avila. In the summer of 1545, perhaps at the suggestion of the Duke of Palma, Fray Louis was named prior at Palma del Río, a beautiful town situated on the Guadalquivir river in a plain filled with lemon and orange groves between Córdoba and Seville. The city of Córdoba sent various commissions to the Dominican Provincial, begging that Fray Louis be left in that city, but to no avail. It is another proof of the high esteem in which he was held.

On September 21, 1546, at the suggestion of Fray John Alvarez, Cardinal of Burgos and formerly Bishop of Córdoba, Fray Louis was granted the privilege of going anywhere in Spain to preach in the company of a companion of of his choosing and no superior could prevent his preaching. Two months later the new Master General of the Order, Romeo di Castiglione, who assisted at the sessions of the Council of Trent, renewed the privilege.

In January of 1547 the Dominicans held a Chapter at Jerez de la Frontera. As prior of Palma del Río and a preacher general, Fray Louis took part in the Chapter. Likewise in attendance were Fray Augustine de Esbarroya and Fray Dominic de Baltanás, two great theologians, and Fray Alphonse de Montúfar and Fray Martin de Mendoza, later Archbishop of Mexico and Bishop of Córdoba respectively. The Duke de Medina Sidonia, accepted by the Chapter of Osuna in 1544 as a patron of the Province, was also in attendance. He was a descendent of the family of St. Dominic Guzman. Fray Louis preached the sermon at the Chapter and the Duke, completely captivated by the preacher, asked that he be sent as chaplain for his estates. Fray Louis accompanied him to Sanlucar de Marrameda, to Niebla, and to other castles of Andalusia. But other nobles also asked for Fray Louis; thus, the Marquis de Priego and the Count de Feria obtained permission from the Master General for Fray Louis to come to their estates.

Fray Louis did not spend much time with the Duke de Medina Sidonia. He did not like palace life and the Duke had to let him leave, in spite of his own wishes. Fray Louis was then prior at Badajoz. In that section of Estremadura, the home of the two great figures in the conquest of Mexico and Peru, Pizarro and Cortés, Granada dedicated himself to preaching, spending many days in the Castle of Zafra, the property and residence of the Count of Feria.

In his apostolic journeys Fray Louis frequently crossed the frontier into Portugal, for in those days there was no such thing as customs and visas and the Spanish language was spoken and understood by the Portuguese. The fame of the Dominican preacher had reached the ears of the Cardinal Infante, at that time Archbishop of Evora. The Prince Cardinal—son of Don Manuel I of Portugal—had heard him preach on a few occasions and eventually he selected Fray Louis as his confessor and preacher. The first time that we notice this is at the end of 1551 in autumn, when the Archbishop had asked him to explain to the people the vocation of the Jesuits, who had recently arrived at Evora. From that time on they were counted among Granada's friends.

Practically the rest of his life was spent in Portugal, with occasional return visits to Spain. At the invitation of the Cardinal, Fray Louis arrived at Lisbon and Queen Catherine, the sister of Charles V, selected him as her confessor and adviser. In the midst of such occupations, neither sought nor desired, Fray Louis never forgot that the pen is a mighty instrument in the apostolate. He continued to prepare his notes, to arrange his material, and to read the books of spirituality that came to his hands. In this way the little tract on the method of prayer that had originally been written for the student at Valladolid gradually became a book on prayer and was addressed to all. On August 21, 1553, the Bishop of Salamanca granted permission for the printing of the book, after it had been approved by Fray Peter Sotomayor, a former classmate of Fray Louis at St. Gregory's in Valladolid.

The success of the book was a complete surprise and the most surprised of all was Fray Louis. His success confirmed him in the vocation of a spiritual writer. From that time forward he dedicated himself with a divine impatience to writing on spiritual themes for all. In the serene brightness of Lisbon, situated on the banks of the Tajo River, and in a countryside that has constant springtime, he wrote and wrote. He wished to make the best possible use of his apostolate, leaving for a later time the final and best masterpiece from his pen. Hence the provisional character of some of his early writings. Between 1554 and 1559 Fray Louis published twelve books, one of them in Portuguese. For a man occupied with the duties of the pulpit and the court and later with the cares of a provincial, it was an extraordinary activity.

On the 14th of April, 1556, Fray Louis was elected Provincial of the Dominican Province of Portugal. The Master General, Father Usumaris, confirmed the election, but since Fray Louis was still formally affiliated with the Andalusian Province, the Master General assigned him to the convent at Evora and thus Fray Louis officially became a member of the Portuguese Province.

Louis of Granada was a model provincial in his diligence for the progress of the province. He founded two new convents, that of Montemayor and that of Ansede, and he laid the foundations for the convent at Setubal. All loved and revered him for his goodness and energetic spirit. He preached a great deal and wrote a great deal, although he had a secretary to assist him in the latter.

Fray Louis governed well. He had scarcely completed a year in office as provincial when Queen Catherine, who was acting as regent for the young Prince Sebastian, offered him the miter of the archbishopric of Braga, which would make him Primate of Portugal. It was a reward for his services to the court and a proof of the esteem in which he was held. Many clergymen aspired to this position, especially from among the nobility, and the Queen was so tired of their pleas that she once wrote: "God grant that during my reign all the prelates will be immortal so that I shall never again find myself in such difficulties." Nevertheless, she remained firm in her intention to give the miter to the humble and learned religious, although he was a foreigner. But Fray Louis did not aspire to the episcopacy and he suggested an alternate candidate, Fray Bartholomew de los Mártires. The Queen could not persuade Fray Bartholomew to accept the office and it was left to Fray Louis to settle the matter. He called Fray Bartholomew to the chapter hall and in the presence of the entire community he gave a sermon and issued a formal precept that Fray Bartholomew accept the office. The latter made a prostration and accepted. Very shortly he was to give evidence of his ability in the ruling of the archdiocese and as a member of the Council of Trent.

The Dominican Order celebrated an elective Chapter at Rome in 1558. As a provincial, Fray Louis had the duty to assist, but he did not go. It was easy for him to obtain a dispensation through the Court. Rome in those days did not have the power of attraction that it has today. A general decadence had reached even the Roman Curia and a phrase used by the Archbishop of Braga, Fray Bartholomew de los Mártires, while he was at Trent, became famous because of its sharpness and daring: "The most reverend and eminent Cardinals need a most reverend and eminent reform."

Meanwhile, the books of Fray Louis were receiving wide popular acclaim. Saints and sound theology were flourishing in Spain but there were also false sects of spirituality under the guise of mysticism. The Inquisition was established. Far away, over the Pyrenees, half of Europe was ablaze with the tragic fire of Protestantism. With Charles V there came to Spain a deluge of books with the message of a new spirituality that advocated a trend to the interior life, a disdain for all the external formalism of laws and ceremonies, an exaggerated insistence on faith for justification, and an almost complete nullification of good works. These exaggerations and errors readily infiltrated into the thought of some Spanish spiritual writers.

In 1525 the Inquisitor General, Alonso Manrique, published an edict against the Illuminists and a syllabus of false spiritual doctrines. Various cases were reviewed, but neither the edict nor the trials could destroy the evil seed. The Illuminists used various books as sources and some of the books by Fray Louis were found in their collections and libraries, for he was at the time the most popular spiritual writer. As a result, the name of Fray Louis was suspect.

To add to the mischief, the inquisitors knew very well that Fray Louis was an intimate friend of Carranza, now archbishop of Toledo, whose ruin they were seeking. The inquisitor, Valdés, charged Melchior Cano to censor the books of Fray Louis and the *Catechism* of Carranza. Cano, an irreconcilable enemy of Carranza, accused Fray Louis of heresy. Blinded by passion and prejudice, he could not distinguish between Christian perfection and the state of perfection and accused Fray Louis of attempting to make all Christians perfect, although all do not have the vows of religion. It was an unpardonable deviation for a theologian of Cano's stature, especially when it was a matter of judging his own brother in religion.

Fray Louis learned that his books were under censorship and were about to be placed on the Index. Knowing that Cano was the censor, the evil could not be remedied except by going to Valladolid. By the middle of August in 1559 Fray Louis was in Castile and he found the inquisitor, Valdés, resolved to place his books on the Index. But he was encouraged and heartened by the Princess, the ambassador of Portugal, and many admirers and friends, among them Francis Borgia. But the tempest was not to be quieted. Valdés signed the introductory letter to the catalog of indexed books and among the lists of condemned books were the works of Fray Louis.

A few days later the agents of Valdés arrested the Archbishop of Toledo, Fray Bartholomew Carranza, and brought him to Valladolid. He arrived in the city, riding on a mule and surrounded by archers and constables. He still wore his archbishop's hat but his eyes were a sea of tears and he aroused the pity of all who looked upon him. Among the crowds stood Fray Louis, convinced that nothing could be done, for there in Valladolid Cano and Valdés were omnipotent. Crestfallen, he prepared for his return journey to Lisbon.

In the eyes of the world Fray Louis continued to be suspected of heresy. He had seen the shipwreck of his books, which is equivalent to saying that he had witnessed the ruin of his vocation as a spiritual writer. But soon the dawn would break for the humble and apostolic Dominican.

Fray Louis was approaching the end of his term as provincial and was preparing his summary report on the state of the province and the account of his term as provincial. This done, he proceeded to Evora, where the Provincial Chapter was held on June 14, 1560. Fray Jerome de Azambuja, who had gained renown at the Council of Trent, was elected provincial and Fray Louis again took his place in the ranks.

But the labors of Louis of Granada were not to go unnoticed. On June 20, 1562, he received the title of Master of Sacred Theology by direct concession from the Master General. It was an unusual privilege and honor because Fray Louis had not fulfilled the requirements stipulated by his Order for the reception of this title: he had never taught. But at Trent and at Rome Fray Louis was evaluated in a manner far different from that in Valladolid. His book, *Libro de la Oración y Meditación,* was formally approved and the approbation was confirmed by Pope Pius IV. It was a well-deserved exoneration.

When the Chapter was ended, Granada fixed his residence at Santo Domingo in Lisbon. He could not live far from the Court because he was summoned there almost every day. It was the autumn of 1560 and Fray Louis was fifty-six years of age, although ascetical practices and the constant work of the pen and pulpit made him appear older than his years. His cell was poor and his possessions few: a wooden bed, a crude table, a few books, reams of colored paper (so that the eyes would not tire as he wrote), and a collection of various penitential instruments. Fray Louis could have lived in the palace but since childhood he was espoused of poverty and he disdained the delights and comforts of the world. He received many alms and he earned much money from his books, but all went to the convent or to the poor. He dressed in such poverty that he wore the same hat for forty years and his black cappa was worn and patched with twelve years of use. Although he was a frequent visitor in the royal palace, he paid no attention to the courtly atmosphere; his spirit rose above all the things that fascinate the worldly ones: gold, coaches, love, silk, and power. To subdue the rebellious flesh, he wore a penitential belt. He excelled in meekness, native and acquired humility, an exquisite distinction in his bearing, and good counsel for all who needed it.

Such is Granada's moral portrait. The physical portrait is given to us by one of his oldest biographers.[5] "He was of large and majestic stature, with a well-distributed weight. He had a face of angelic affability and his flesh was delicate and of good color. His eyes were happy but modest; his forehead, wide and serene; his teeth, white and in good order; his nose, stately and aquiline and somewhat large; his mouth, of good proportion; his head, large and somewhat bald. Most cordial in conversation, he was a friend to all, although no one became too friendly with him. He had an indescribable gravity in his appearance, as if he were always absorbed in spiritual contemplation."

This affable and simple religious, entirely given to the things of God, was very active and even dynamic. He rose at four in the morning and spent two hours in prayer. At six o'clock he celebrated Mass with remarkable solemnity and devotion. In those days priests were not accustomed to celebrate Mass every day but Fray Louis never omitted this spiritual banquet and stated that the best preparation for the celebration of Mass was to celebrate daily. After Mass he devoted himself to a lengthy thanksgiving and then returned to his cell where his secretary read to him for an hour. The reading completed, Fray Louis would begin to dictate as he paced up and down. His inspiration was fruitful and easy; the secretary wrote rapidly. At ten o'clock the secretary would be tired and Fray Louis would give him permission to leave. Then he would take up the pen himself and continue working, sometimes on a matter distinct from that which he had been dictating. At noon the bell summoned the friars to the refectory. Fray Louis would

5 Giovannini da Capugnano: *Vita del P. Fr. Luigi di Granata*, published at Venice in 1595.

go to eat and was not only content with the food provided, but would always leave a little for his friends, the poor. If the business of the Court prevented him from eating the common meal in the refectory, he would go to the second serving and as he ate, he had the material read to him which he had dictated in the morning so that he could correct and perfect it. After eating, he would visit the sick, chatting with them, inquiring about their health, and asking whether there was anything they needed. From the infirmary he went to the community recreation where he conversed affably for a half hour. The conventual bell would ring for solemn silence and the cheerful conversation was no longer heard in the cloister walks. Fray Louis would relax for fifteen minutes to half an hour and after this brief siesta, go to choir to chant Vespers with the community and remain some time in silent prayer. He would then summon his secretary and dictate until nightfall or Compline. He never missed Compline. The friars made the nightly procession to the statue of the Virgin Mary, singing the *Salve Regina*. Then they would say the concluding prayers and march in orderly fashion from choir to the refectory where there was a light collation or supper. Fray Louis remained in choir, wrapt in prayer. At ten o'clock in the evening, after the community had retired, Fray Louis would leave the church and go to his cell. For some time he worked by candlelight, writing or reading until his eyes would tire. In the season of fasting, he would then take the discipline rigorously; in the period of non-fasting, he would prepare a frugal meal for himself by candlelight. At eleven o'clock, after a brief period of prayer, he retired to a well-earned rest.

Fray Louis had now reached his zenith. He dedicated himself to the revisal and correction of the books that had been listed in the catalog of the Inquisition. He did it slowly and definitively. The confusion prevalent in spiritual matters had been clarified by the Council of Trent. Only then did the Inquisition release the books by Granada. The *Libro de la Oracíon y Meditación*, which reflected his most loved spiritual doctrine, was scarcely touched. The *Guía de pecadores* suffered a notable transformation. In addition, Fray Louis began new and difficult tasks: he wrote six volumes of Latin sermons, a work of ten years; he composed a book of rhetoric, apologetic works, and biographies of persons eminent in sanctity. In succeeding pages we shall analyze this array of varied writings. At this point we should like to delineate the three psychological phases in the life of Granada the writer.

The first phase is that of his years in Granada and Valladolid, years of study and love of letters, a period in which Fray Louis manifests himself—as is evident from the prologue that he wrote for the works of Astudillo—as a *homo sapiens*. The second phase begins with his departure from Valladolid and his futile missionary venture and ends with the Council of Trent. This period comprises the eleven years at Escalaceli, where he underwent a kind of spiritual conversion from intellectual interests and study to an appreciation for the "mystery of Christ." It is the beginning of an apostolate of preaching and writing that is nourished more by the spirit of prayer than by the cold speculations of the lecture halls. In this phase Granada is characterized as a *homo spiritualis*. The third and definitive phase extends until his death and here he reaches doctrinal and stylistic maturity. His spirituality grows in perfection, precision, clarity, and amplitude. Letters and the spirit give each other the kiss of peace. It is a period of synthesis between the *homo spiritualis* and the *homo sapiens*, between the *theologia mentis* and the *theologia cordis*. Now there is no struggle, only peace and tranquillity. There will always be letters and human science, Fray Louis confesses, and they will always be a great help in the apostolate. The *homo sapiens,* if he places himself under the guidance of the *homo spiritualis,* is not an enemy but a faithful collaborator in the life of the spirit.

The circumstances surrounding Granada's activities in the latter years of his life were harshly adverse. First, his health began to fail and he was incapacitated by almost total blindness; secondly, he was obliged frequently to intervene in worldly and religious politics and this was always a bitter cross for him. Fray Louis was not a man of the world; he did not want dignities; he had refused the much coveted office of an archbishop. In the last years of Granada's life St. Charles Borromeo and Cardinal Paleotti were most interested in seeing that this humble friar should receive the cardinal's hat, but he refused it. He was a contemplative at heart and his apostolate was the diffusion of sacred truth by word and writing. Nevertheless, a series of historical events obliged him to go out into the world and become embroiled in the affairs of men.

The first instance was a dangerous situation that arose in the Portuguese Court itself. Toward the middle of 1568 the Court intriguers provoked a serious discord by convincing the youthful monarch, Don Sebastian, that Catherine and the Cardinal Infante, Don Enrique, wished to usurp the royal power. Disgusted by such connivings and accusations, Philip II sent the Duke of Feria as an extraordinary ambassador to the Portuguese Court. His mission was fruitless, but he advised Philip II of the influence of Fray Louis at Court. Philip wrote to Louis and asked him to intervene. Granada went to the convent at Almeirín, which was near the Court, and eventually drew up an agreement and signed it in the name of the Portuguese royal family while the Duke of Feria signed in the name of Philip II.

Unfortunately, the rupture was not so easily healed; misunderstandings arose again and the pact was in danger of being broken. Catherine was prepared to flee to Castile and Philip II was ready to receive her in a manner befitting the sister of his father, Charles. But Pius V intervened and sent his nephew, Cardinal Alexander, as legate to Lisbon. He likewise sent a brief to Fray Louis, asking that he assist the Cardinal Legate in settling the dispute. Ultimately, through the conjoined efforts of the Cardinal and Fray Louis, the unpleasant matter was settled.

Another cross for Granada in his later years was a second attack on his *Libro de la Oración y Meditación*. It was the book best loved by Fray Louis. Formerly condemned by Cano and Valdés and later approved by the Council of Trent and Pius IV, it was once again in circulation and doing great good for souls. But in 1576 Fray Alphonse de la Fuente discovered a group of Illuminists or *alumbrados* in Llerena and he learned that a dominant factor in the growth of this heterodox movement was Granada's book on prayer. The news was immediately transmitted to Rome by the Nuncio, Ormaneto. Fray Louis intervened unwillingly but energetically by going to his friend, Zayas, the secretary to Philip II. The inquisitors at Llerena answered the interrogation of Zayas in a manner favorable to Fray Louis and the event passed without causing too much damage, although it disturbed his monastic peace and tranquillity.

But now more serious conflicts arose, more crosses for Fray Louis. Queen Catherine, a great admirer and protector of Fray

Louis, died on February 12, 1578. On the fourth of August of the same year, the youthful monarch, Don Sebastian, was cut down in the flower of his life during the fierce battle of Alcazarquivir in Africa. The Cardinal Infante was successor to the throne, but he was an old man of sixty-seven and his health was weak. Moreover, by reason of his ecclesiastical position he could have no descendants and the question arose concerning successors to the throne.

There were at the time three pretenders to the throne: Catherine of Braganza, who relinquished her claim; Anthony, the illegitimate son of Infante Louis and a converted Jewess whom the people maliciously called "the Pelican"; and Philip II, who was the legitimate nephew of King Emmanuel and had the greatest claim. Philip was determined not to surrender or lose his claim, but the Portuguese nobility was equally determined not to have a foreign king. The nobles asked the Cardinal to seek a dispensation from Rome in order to marry. They proposed it to him as a sacred obligation.

The Cardinal, a truly virtuous man, was sorely perplexed amid such insistence. His nephew, Philip II, sent an ambassador to persuade the Cardinal to ignore the outrageous request of the nobility. The ambassador, Christopher Moura, also had instructions to make full use of Granada's influence with the Cardinal King. After discussing the matter with Fray Louis, the ambassador wrote to Philip II: "I have had a long conversation with Fray Louis of Granada. He is, as we know, a holy man, and from all appearances he is withdrawn from the world and pays little attention to what goes on in it. He says that on certain feast days he visits the King [the Cardinal] and speaks of spiritual matters with him. . . . We spoke of this matter of the possible marriage of the King but Fray Louis does not believe that the King will do it, although some religious persons persuade him to do so. . . . Moreover, Fray Louis says he has not spoken to the King of this matter nor does he intend to do so. . . . He speaks with such simplicity that one can see that there is no duplicity in what he says."

A short time later a secret ambassador, Fray Hernando Castillo, arrived from Spain, ostensibly paying a visit to his fellow Dominican, but actually bearing instructions from Philip II. Again Fray Louis was obliged to speak of a matter so distasteful to himself. He recognized that Philip II had all the rights and claims to the throne but, being a Spaniard himself, Fray Louis could not declare such sentiments publicly. No solution was reached before the Cardinal's death on January 31, 1580, and nothing had been determined as to the succession. Anthony, the son of the *Pelicana,* proclaimed himself king at Santarem, and as a result Philip II commissioned the Duke of Alba to invade and conquer Portugal.

Crosses increased in number and weight as Granada approached his last years. Perhaps the greatest cross was the gradual ruin of the Dominican Province in Portugal, for which Fray Louis had labored so hard. The greater part of the religious were staunch defenders of Anthony's claim and they went about preaching a national war, saying that to fight against the Spaniards was to fight against the Lutherans. They disobeyed the prohibitions of their superiors, under the pretext that such commands were against the natural law of defending one's country. Many of the friars even took up arms and, what is even more censurable, became involved in political intrigue.

The principal victim was Fray Louis. At a moment when the situation was at its worst, they composed a false papal brief in which Granada was named Vicar Provincial. Philip II began to suspect Fray Louis and commanded him to appear at Court to render an account. The command was given under pain of death, but the Duke of Alba dared to intercept the order of the King and to plead in behalf of the old friar who was his confessor. Philip II listened gravely to the arguments of the Duke and finally conceded that Fray Louis was too ill to travel. Eventually it was discovered that the papal brief was a counterfeit and Fray Louis was exonerated. The humble Dominican wrote later to the Spanish King: "You can understand how easily one who knows not how to deceive can be deceived by others. I testify to your Majesty that although the brief had been in my hands a thousand years, it would never occur to me to think that a religious would falsify papal letters . . . and nevertheless continue to say Mass every day."

Fray Louis soon regained his good name and reputation. Philip II was convinced that the friar was easily duped because he was so good and simple. When he went to Lisbon, Philip honored the Dominican by visiting him in his cell and he invited him to preach in the royal chapel. Fray Louis accepted and Philip was so enchanted that he wrote to his daughters, the Infantas Isabel and Catherine: "Since it is late, I have no time to tell you more than that yesterday Fray Louis of Granada preached here in the chapel and he did very well, although he is old and has no teeth."

One last cross and a heavy one. A Dominican nun, prioress of the convent of the Annunciation in Lisbon, testified that she had received the stigmata on March 7, 1584. Even the Inquisition believed her and sent a memorial to Rome in order to inform the Pope. Gregory XIII then addressed a brief to Cardinal Albert, Archduke of Austria, Inquisitor General, and

Viceroy of Portugal. The case of the stigmatization aroused great wonder and admiration in Rome and no one doubted her sanctity. The Dominican Provincial commanded Fray Louis to write a biography of the nun and when Granada asked for documents, he received the accounts that had been written by the nun herself and her confessor, Fray Peter Romero. Granada wrote the biography and incorporated this material.

Later, in the autumn of 1588, it was discovered that the whole affair was a deception or delusion. Amazement was universal and the case has come down through history as an error on the part of Granada. He doubtless suffered a great disappointment, not for himself, but because of the great scandal to the simple and credulous faithful. This event occasioned the writing of his last sermon which, since it was written on a bed of pain and of death, can also be considered his spiritual testimony. It is a sermon on sinners in public life.

In Advent of 1588 Granada's health was unusually poor. Nevertheless, he prayed more, fasted every day, and took his discipline. In December he began to have serious attacks of nausea and vomiting which left him extremely weakened and by December 15 his fever began to mount steadily. On December 30 all hope for his recovery was abandoned. Death was imminent and the religious were deeply grieved at the inevitable loss of one they loved as a father.

On December 31, 1588, in the bare and humble cell at Santo Domingo, where monarchs of the world had visited him, Granada's lamp of life was extinguished. With tears of joy he had received the last sacraments. The novices knelt at the door to his cell for a last farewell, realizing that the inexorable gasp of death would come at any moment. Fray Louis also sensed its approach and he asked that they place him in the coffin. His life was failing, but without pain or effort. At nine in the evening he breathed his last and exchanged the counting of years for eternity.

Fray Louis of Granada had passed eighty-four years on earth and his death was considered one of the greatest losses to Christianity. Lisbon became a city of mourning. As soon as news of his death spread abroad, streams of people came to see him who in death seemed yet to be alive. He was buried at four in the afternoon and so many people were assembled that it was only with difficulty that the ceremony could be carried out. People surged to the coffin to touch his clothing, to kiss his hands, to touch his body with religious articles. As the body was carried out for burial, people tried to cut off pieces of his habit.

The General Chapter held in Rome in 1589 communicated to the entire Dominican Order the news of the death of Fray Louis and the following terse comment serves well as his epitaph: *Vir doctrina et sanctitate insignis et in toto orbe celebris.* Such was the earthly journey of Fray Louis of Granada, a journey filled with triumphs and crosses. He was, in the words of St. Teresa of Avila, truly a "man given to the world by God for the great and universal good of souls."

His Work and Doctrine

Fray Louis of Granada published his first work when he was fifty years old, a rather advanced age for a writer but nevertheless mature and balanced. His long life enabled him to dedicate himself to writing for thirty-five years and to leave us a legacy of works that have made him immortal. His works are numerous and we shall seek to classify them in a manner that is scientific, ordered, and practical.

Three standards of classification are available: linguistic, chronological, and thematic. The fact that Fray Louis wrote in Spanish, Portuguese, or Latin is accidental to our purpose, which is to give a general view of his work and doctrine. Therefore, we reject the basis of a linguistic classification. The fact that Granada published a work in a certain year has its importance for the historian and for a knowledge of the evolution of his spiritual thought, but it is not to our purpose to consider the chronological aspect of his works. Consequently, the criterion most suited to our purpose is the classification according to subject matter. But in order that we may not exclude entirely the other two criteria, in mentioning each work for the first time we shall also give the date and place of its publication. We shall not give the complete title of each work (which is of interest only to the specialist) but merely the principal title.[6]

Spiritual Theology

1. *De la manera de orar* (*How to Pray*), an expository letter written to Fray Louis de la Cruz in 1539; ed. by A. Huerga in *Hispania*, vol. X, pp. 331–35.
2. *Dos meditaciones para antes y después de la sagrada Comunión* (*Two Meditatións for before and after Holy Communion*), (Evora: 1555).

[6] In the days of Granada it was customary to give a double title to a book: the principal title, which was usually printed in large type and sometimes elegantly, and the explicative title, which was an explanation or brief description of the theme of the work. Bibliographers can find all these minutiae in the critical editions of the works. For the ordinary reader it will suffice to give the briefer title and the year of publication.

3. *Tratado de la Oración, Confesión y Comunión* (*Treatise on Prayer, Confession and Communion*), (Evora: 1555).
4. *Libro de la Oración y Meditación* (*Book of Prayer and Meditation*), (Salamanca: 1554; re-edited and augmented in 1555; definitive text in 1566).
5. *Tratado de la Oración* (*Treatise on Prayer*), (Lisbon: no date given; published under the name of Fray Peter of Alcántara).
6. *Recopilación breve del Libro de la Oración y Meditación* (*Brief Summary of the Book of Prayer and Meditación*), (Salamanca: 1574).
7. *Guía de pecadores* (*Sinners' Guide*), 2 volumes, (Salamanca: 1556–7; definitive text in one volume, 1567).
8. *Manual de diversas oraciones y espirituales ejercicios* (*Manual of Various Prayers and Spiritual Exercises*), (Lisbon: 1557).
9. *Manual de oraciones* (*Manual of Prayers*), (Lisbon: 1559).
10. *Compendio de doctrina cristiana* (*Compendium of Christian Doctrine*), written in Portuguese, (Lisbon: 1559).
11. *Memorial de lo que debe hacer el cristiano* (*Memorial of the Duties of a Christian*), (Lisbon: 1561).
12. *Tratado de algunas muy devotas oraciones para provocar el amor de Dios* (*Treatise on Certain Devout Prayers for Arousing the Love of God*), (Lisbon: 1561).
13. *Vita Christi* (*Life of Christ*), text in Spanish, (Lisbon: 1561).
14. *Memorial de la vida cristiana* (*Memorial of the Christian Life*), 2 volumes, (Lisbon: 1565).
15. *Adiciones al Memorial* (*Additions to the Memorial*), (Salamanca: 1574).

16. *Doctrina espiritual, en cinco tratados* (*Spiritual Doctrine, in five parts*), (Lisbon: 1587).

Apologetics

17. *Introducción del Símbolo de la Fe* (*Introduction to the Creed*), (Salamanca: 1583).
18. *Compendio de la Introducción del Símbolo de la Fe* (*Compendium of the Introduction to the Creed*), (Salamanca:1585).
19. *Breve tratado de la manera de proponer la doctrina cristiana a los nuevos fieles* (*Brief Treatise on the Manner of Expounding Christian Doctrine to Converts*), (Salamanca: 1585).
20. *Diálogo entre S. Ambrosio y S. Agustin sobre el Misterio de la Encarnación* (*Dialogue between St. Ambrose and St. Augustine on the Incarnation*), (Barcelona: 1605).

Hagiography

21. *Vida del Mtro. Juan de Avila* (*Life of Master John of Avila*), (Madrid: 1588).
22. *Vida de Fray Bartolomé de los Mártires, arzobispo de Braga* (*Life of Fray Bartholomew of the Martyrs, Archbishop of Braga*), (Valladolid: 1615).
23. *Vida del Card. D. Enrique, arzobispo de Evora y Rey de Portugal* (*Life of Cardinal Henry, Archbishop of Evora and King of Portugal*), in ed. Cuervo, *Obras Completas de Fray Luis de Granada*, vol. XIV, pp. 367–97.
24. *Vida de Sor Ana de la Concepción* (*Life of Sister Anna of the Immaculate Conception*), ed. Cuervo, vol. XIV, pp. 499–509.

25. *Vida de Doña Elvira de Mendoza* (*Life of Elvira de Mendoza*), ed. Cuervo, vol. XIV, pp. 411–22.
26. *Vida de Melicia Hernández* (*Life of Melissa Hernández*), ed. Cuervo, vol. XIV, pp. 423–34.
27. *Vida de Sor Maria de la Visitación* (*Life of Sister Mary of the Visitation*), unpublished.

Sacred Oratory

28. *Ecclesiasticae Rhetoricae sive de Ratione concionandi libri sex* (*Ecclesiastical Rhetoric*), (Lisbon: 1576).
29. *Partes que ha de tener un Predicador del Evangelio* (*Qualities of the Preacher of the Gospel*), (Madrid: 1588).
30. *Collectanea Moralis Philosophiae* (*Disquisitions on Moral Philosophy*), 3 volumes, (Lisbon: 1571).
31. *Silva Locorum Communium in Concionibus* (*Common Source Material for Sermons*), 2 volumes, (Salamanca: 1585).
32. *Trece Sermones de las principales fiestas del Señor y de la Sma. Virgen* (*Thirteen Sermons for the Principal Feasts of Our Lord and the Blessed Virgin*), (Lisbon: 1559).
33. *Concio de officio et moribus episcoporum* (*Sermon on the Duties and Qualities of Bishops*), (Lisbon: 1565).
34. *Conciones de tempore* (*Sermons for the Liturgical Year*), Volume I, from the first Sunday of Advent to Lent (1575); Volume II, Lent (1575); Volume III, from Resurrection to Corpus Christi (1576); Volume IV, from Corpus Christi to Advent (1576), (Lisbon).
35. *Conciones de Sanctis* (*Sermons on the Saints*), Volume I, from the feast of St. Andrew to the feast of St. Mary Magdalen (Lisbon: 1578); Volume II, from the feast

of St. Mary Magdalen to the end of the liturgical year (Lisbon: 1578).

36. *Sermón de las caídas públicas* (*Sermon on Public Sinners*), (Lisbon: 1588).
37. *Discurso de la Pasión del Salvador* (*Discourse on the Passion of the Savior*), ed. Cuervo, volume XIV, pp. 197–209.
38. *Sermón del Santísimo Sacramento* (*Sermon on the Blessed Sacrament*), ed. Robres, *Boletín Castellonense de Cultura*, XXIV, pp. 41–52.

Translations

39. *Contemptus mundi* (*Contempt of the World*), (Seville: 1536).
40. *Escala espiritual de San Juan Clímaco* (*Spiritual Ladder of St. John Climacus*), (Lisbon: 1562).
41. *Filomela del pseudo-Buenaventura* (*Philomela*, by pseudo-Bonaventure), (Salamanca: 1574).
42. *Comentarios de Astudillo a Aristóteles* (*Commentary of Astudillo on Aristotle*), (Valladolid: 1532).
43. *Suma Cayetana* (*Summa of Cajetan*), (Lisbon: 1557).
44. *Compendium doctrinae spiritualis* (*Compendium of Spiritual Doctrine*), (Lisbon: 1582).
45. *Stimulus pastorum* (*Exhortation for Bishops*), (Lisbon: 1565).
46. *Treinta y dos sermones sobre los mandamientos* (*Thirty-two Sermons on the Commandments*), (Lisbon: 1558).
47. *Meditaciones y homilías del Card. Enrique* (*Meditatións and Sermons of Cardinal Henry*), (Lisbon: 1574).

48. *Tratado de los Votos* (*Treatise on the Vows*, by Savonarola), (Lisbon: 1556).
49. *Carta de Euquerio* (*Letter by Euquerius*), (Lisbon: 1567).

We have given the list of the works of Fray Louis in the order of their publication. Hundreds of other works can be found which bear the name of Fray Louis but they are summaries or selections taken from his works. A few smaller works could have been added to the list but since they are unpublished and are not of great importance, we have omitted them.

Seen in its totality, the literary production of Granada is overwhelming both by reason of its quantity and the diversity of subject matter. One's admiration is increased when he reflects that the works of Granada have been translated into more than twenty-five languages and have gone through some six thousand editions. Let us consider briefly the literary style, the sources and documentation, the spiritual methods of Fray Louis, and his spiritual doctrine.

The basic reason for the success of the works of Fray Louis can be found in his masterly ability to coordinate many didactic and literary elements and put them at the service of a doctrine as robust as is the Thomistic doctrine. The austerity and rigor of the Scholastics is softened and vitalized by the pen of Fray Louis so that their doctrine appeals to every type of reader.

There are, in my opinion, three outstanding qualities in the literary style of Fray Louis: beauty, simplicity, and emotional tone. They are not separate entities, however, but are always united and mutually blended. The pen of Fray Louis was steeped in beauty and from it come some of the most brilliant metaphors to be found in rhetoric. His metaphors are so clear, so luminous, and so simple, that all readers understand them, both the learned and the ignorant. Fray Louis did not write for a select group of devotees, for he realized that the great truths can also be savored by the simple and unlettered.

Lastly, the prose of Fray Louis is so intuitive that the reader is captivated by the intimacy and fondness with which it speaks to him. It speaks to the heart. It is a prose that persuades and convinces. Fray Louis has such an affinity for souls that he becomes sorrowful when the soul requires it and lyrical when the soul begins to sing spiritually. The simple and emotional beauty of his style clothes a succulent and profound doctrine which is true spiritual theology. But Fray Louis does not consider literary style as an end in itself, as it is for the rhetoricians; it is nothing more than a means. He used it as such and he cultivated it with such energy that even in his lifetime he was considered the best of Spanish stylists.

Where did Granada get his inspiration? This is an interesting problem which we can only suggest. The honest writer is never content with his own opinions, his own observations on persons and things, his reasonings and findings. He seeks sources, books, authors, and he makes a judicious selection. Fray Louis was no exception. One of his biographers has made a detailed enumeration of the authors cited in the works of Granada and the result is truly astounding when one considers the possibilities of research in the fourteenth century.

Yet Fray Louis was not merely a voracious reader who read for the sake of reading, as do those who pass the time by perusing endless streams of novels. Fray Louis was very selective in his reading. No one has been more eclectic nor more facile than he in selecting the gems of classical and contemporary literature.

We can reduce to two general classes the sources used by Fray Louis: those which are basic or fundamental to the body of his doctrine, and those which are secondary and are used to give external adornment, to clarify some special point, or to give a modern setting to ancient and classical doctrines. Thus we find that Sacred Scripture is a basic source because it is the revealed truth of God. Fray Louis cites Scripture so often that he seems to know it by memory, and he transcribes its passages with such dexterity that one could say that he possessed an unusually fine critical sense. In difficult passages he usually had recourse to St. Jerome, the Doctor of Exegesis.

After Sacred Scripture come the Fathers of the Church. Of all the Spanish classicists, Fray Louis manifests the most profound love for those first theologians of Christianity. He strives to project himself into the mentality of the Fathers and into their age which, as he says, should be the model for modern times. He was especially partial to St. Jerome, St. Augustine, St. Ambrose, St. Gregory, St. Basil, St. Cyprian, and St. John Chrysostom.

But what gives solidity and stability to Granada's doctrine is his Thomistic training. He is faithful to the tradition of his Order. He is not a theologian of the lecture platform but a theologian of the people, yet the doctrinal basis of his writings is as secure and firm as a syllogism. The problems of the spiritual life are always viewed from the theological height of perennial principles and developed with an exactitude of concepts that astounds us today. Sacred Scripture, the Fathers, St. Thomas: such are the cornerstones of the inspiration of Fray Louis. Sacred Scripture as the revealed word; the Fathers and St. Thomas as the rational theology of the revealed word.

Among the secondary sources used by Granada we must mention St. Catherine of Siena, Savonarola, and Bautista de Crema as preferred authors. Fray Louis also studied the spirituality of the North: Tauler, Herp, and Louis de Blois, and he was interested in new biographies of spiritual persons and was familiar with most of those that were available. Before writing a book, he would acquaint himself as well as possible with what had been written on the theme and would select what seemed best to him and most suitable to his purpose. This was not servility or plagiarism, but good practical sense. Yet Fray Louis never adopted the spiritual methods of any of the other authors; rather, he was an innovator in spiritual methods.

Fray Louis wished to teach all the sublime truths of Catholic theology and to show that the life of Christ in souls is not a sweetmeat for the chosen few, but is meant for all the souls redeemed by Christ on Calvary's Cross. Departing from this fundamental principle, it was necessary to explore all the ways that lead to God. This is a basic theme in Granada's spiritual writings. Each book that he wrote fills some definite need and teaches a different method, thus opening new horizons to the soul for living the life of the spirit. Fray Louis realized that man is a creature wounded by sin and for that reason infirm, weak. Man does not always reach the goal to which his desires impel him. That should not be a source of discouragement, however, but one of confidence. "Do the best you can," Fray Louis would say, and in those five words we find a perennial and optimistic norm of action for the ascetical struggle.

We are not obliged actually to be perfect here and now, but to strive for perfection according to our powers and means. Grace perfects nature and if nature itself possesses a variety of ways for attaining its ends, how much more so will this be true of divine grace? The end is one and the same for all but the means to that end are multiple. Each Christian will seek the common goal by the means best suited to his temperament, his occupations, and his particular vocation.

Man is a creature made to the image and likeness of God and redeemed by Christ. In passing through this world, man merits by his actions either eternal salvation or eternal damnation. But life's journey is not the same for all. For some it is a pleasant walk, a journey without thorns; others find it a terrifying struggle in which man must conquer in order to emerge victorious. Some see the social life as a field of the apostolate, others see it as a danger to be avoided; some delight in a Christian contemplation of the beauty of the created world and see therein a reflection of the divine attributes, while others see in it nothing but danger and temptation. Fray Louis is familiar with the various ways of facing the spiritual problem. It is not feasible for all to travel by the same path; therefore, he does not deny to anyone the liberty of choosing that path which is most beneficial. He points out and explains all the possible ways, he shows how to conquer the difficulties in each one, and then he says with all confidence: "Now, make your choice."

The principal ways or spiritual methods expounded by Fray Louis are seven in number: 1) the direct way of prayer; 2) the positive and joyous way of virtue as opposed to the negative way of vice; 3) contempt of the world or the spiritual ladder; 4) contemplation of the works of God in the natural order and to ascend by them to the works of grace; 5) the royal and painful way of the Cross; 6) the simple way of the commandments and the sacraments; and 7) the example of the lives of the saints.

We should observe that the various ways or methods are closely interrelated among themselves, in spite of the fact that a superficial glance would reveal them as apparently diverse. The end that is common to all makes them blend and intermingle frequently, so that a Christian will rarely travel by only one path, to the exclusion of the others. When Fray Louis speaks of one way or method in particular, it is to give it emphasis but not to create an exclusion or dichotomy. They are simple ways by which the soul, cooperating personally and meritoriously with the impulse of grace, can arrive, joyful and trembling with love, at the end of the journey where he will receive the definitive laurel of glory.

Fray Louis has made the spiritual life attractive to all, both great and small, learned and simple. It was this fault—if one can call it so—for which he was censured in his day by some narrow souls. "He wants to make all Christians perfect!" exclaimed Melchior Cano. But we could ask him, in turn, "Is Christian perfection, then, the exclusive right of a select class?" "He is trying to make everyone live the Christian life! He is writing sublime truths for the wives of carpenters," was the sarcastic remark of the inquisitor, Valdés. But, as Fray Francisco Barbado, Bishop of Salamanca, points out, Valdés seems to have forgotten that "the wife of a carpenter" was full of grace and blessed among women.

We observe, finally, that Granada's solid doctrinal and theological formation enabled him to avoid the errors of contemporary spiritual trends, such as Quietism, the extravagances of the Illuminists, or the Protestant justification by faith alone without man's cooperation. Moreover, the fact that he himself lived an intensely spiritual life enabled him to avoid the cold intellectualism found in other writers on spiritual subjects.

Fray Louis is all fire and affection because he lives what he writes. His doctrine is not a humanistic or literary writing; if it is anything, it is life. Nevertheless, Fray Louis could appreciate and rightly evaluate all the good qualities of Humanism to give color and attraction to his doctrine. In this respect he is modern, psychological, and an astute observer of human nature.

Perhaps the best synthesis of the spiritual doctrine of Fray Louis is this *Summa of the Spiritual Life*. It is not merely a collection or anthology of selected passages, but a practical and spiritual exposition of the *Summa* of St. Thomas Aquinas, almost article by article. Only after reading this work can one appreciate the full sweep of the spiritual doctrine of Fray Louis. He has written a spiritual theology that is within the comprehension of all and has treated of theological questions which range from the nature and attributes of God, the mystery of the Trinity, and the creation of the world and man, to man's last end and the means to that end. His doctrine, therefore, gives muscle and bone, color and beauty, emotion and tears to the skeleton of St. Thomas' dogmatic and moral theology. Some questions he does not treat because they are purely speculative and matters of the School, but in other more practical questions he shows an advance over the teaching of St. Thomas, as when he links devotion with prayer.

Thomistic exhaustiveness and orthodoxy: this is what we wish to emphasize as characteristic of the spiritual doctrine of Fray Louis of Granada. We would add that the fact that he wrote for all classes of people sometimes clips his mystical wings. Undoubtedly he lived a profoundly mystical life but he seldom brings the reader beyond the gates to the mystical way. He leaves the soul there, for then the Holy Ghost is the Master who leads souls onward. Fray Louis makes no attempt to explain the phenomena of the mystical union between God and the soul, for not all are capable of understanding these things. Nor was the *milieu* of his time propitious to such a treatment, given the ill-will that had arisen against mysticism because of the abuses and errors of certain pseudo-mystics who called themselves *alumbrados*. Nevertheless, mystical touches and passages are not totally lacking in the works of Fray Louis. When they occur, they are luminous and rapid as a lightning flash and almost spontaneous and unconscious, for he quickly recovers himself and returns to the purely ascetical attitude. But the way is prepared—and souls also—for the flowering of Spanish mysticism which was especially personified in St. Teresa and St. John of the Cross.

The theme of the ascetical writings of Fray Louis is ever the same: that the Christian lives the life of Christ and is identified with Him through the grace that He merited for us by the redemption and is communicated to us through the sacraments. It is a development of the Pauline concept that the true Christian lives in and for Christ. To be a genuine Christian it does not suffice merely to profess the Catholic faith passively and indifferently; it is not enough to believe dogmas; one must also practice the virtues. Our profession as Christians is a militant profession; we are knights of the Lord.

Consequently, Fray Louis attempts to awaken and arouse the Christian from the state of lethargy and to convert him to God, leading him little by little to a life fully lived in the mystery of Christ. To accomplish that, the first thing to be done is to win the good will of the Christian so that he will truly desire to live in conformity with his title as a Christian; the second is to teach him what he must do to arrive at the perfection of the supernatural life; the third, to teach him the sources from which the soul acquires the power to overcome the world and the passions, and the means placed at his disposal for advancing in the spiritual life.

Let us observe the way in which Fray Louis develops his magnificent program of the spiritual life. The first step, we have seen, is to convert the Christian. Presupposing grace, conversion is effected through a consideration of contrasts. On the one hand, there is the mystery of man's earthly existence, vexed by the seven arrows that cause the seven wounds of human life: brevity, uncertainty, fragility, inconstancy, deceit, sorrow, and death. Human life is like a flower that opens its bud in the morning and then languishes little by little, to die at the close of day. Death is a fact that no one can avoid; it approaches us as inexorably as a naked sword. This truth should provoke in the soul a deep nausea for all things earthly.

On the other hand, one considers the numerous divine benefits given to man by God, benefits that reach their culmination in the work of redemption through which Christ offers us eternal life and a happiness that can begin even in this life through the intimacy of the soul with God. Here is a grand and consoling truth that gives wings to the soul and courage to the heart of a man. Confronted with these truths—the frailty of our earthly existence and the love of God that elevates us to a new life—the shock is tremendous. The Christian man determines to bid farewell to the world and its deceitful pleasures and, encouraged by hope, takes refuge in the cross of Christ, where peace, love, and salvation can be found.

The second step is to teach the newly converted Christian what he ought to do to live the Christian life. It does not suffice for him to remain in a state of sterile passivity; the world would soon draw him again into its whirlwind. He who has resolved to be a Christian in very truth must begin to fulfill with exactitude the commandments of God and the Church and to practice the virtues. It is characteristic of Fray Louis that he always touches the inner core of a man and his insistent longing for happiness. But true happiness is not to be found in pleasures, power, or the vanities of the world; it is to be found in God, and Christ has merited that divine happiness for us through the Cross. Therefore, mortification and penance—the cross of life—are necessary if we are to identify ourselves with the Redeemer, so that the temptations of the world will not overcome us and grace will encounter no obstacles in its sanctifying work.

The third step is to teach the converted Christian the sources from which his soul can acquire the strength to overcome the obstacles encountered by a human nature corrupted and weakened by sin. The primary source is grace, which heals and elevates nature and was merited for us by Christ. Fray Louis never tires of repeating this fact; it is, as it were, the central theme and cardinal truth of his doctrine. Grace is given to us in the sacraments, especially in the Eucharist, which makes us vital and physical participants in the mystery of Christ.

Another efficacious means for progress in the spiritual life is the practice of prayer. Prayer begins by being vocal, asking God for the necessary favors and mercies and, above all, uniting the heart with Him and raising man to the divine presence. Then it becomes mental and recollected as it ponders the divine benefits. But whether vocal or mental, it soon becomes a prayer that is devout, affective, and effective, arousing in the soul a promptness for the fulfillment of the divine and ecclesiastical precepts and the exercise of the virtues. But even this does not suffice. God's love for man is not restricted to assisting him with His grace and promising a reward for all the good works meritorious of eternal life. God gives us something more; He gives even in this life an anticipation and foretaste of the perfect happiness of glory. Therefore, prayer should also be unitive. The soul should arrive at an intimate union with God through that ecstatic prayer which is a prelude to the eternal embrace which God will give the soul in the happiness of heaven.

"Prayer," says Fray Louis, "is the rising of the soul above and beyond itself and all created things, to unite itself with God in a deluge of infinite sweetness and love. Prayer is an emptying of self to receive God when He comes in a new grace, bringing Him into the soul as to His kingdom and placing Him there as in His temple, to possess and love and enjoy Him. Prayer is the soul's presence in God and God's presence in the soul; God gazing on the soul and the soul gazing on Him. . . . Prayer is a spiritual chair where the soul, seated at the feet of God, hears His doctrine and receives the sweet impulse of His grace. . . . Prayer is a festival between the bridegroom and the spouse, a spiritual sabbath on which God rests in the soul. . . . Prayer is a royal gate through which the soul enters into the heart of God; a foretaste of the glory to come."

In the above passage, Granada has become enraptured in a spiritual canticle which is pure mysticism. This is the goal to which he desires to lead all souls. Then they can say that they are true and perfect Christians. This paragraph, which is one of the most beautiful mystical passages in all Christian literature, was suppressed by Fray Louis when he was told that it did not please Melchior Cano and the Inquisitors. Nevertheless, it compares favorably with the degrees of prayer outlined by St. Teresa, who was an assiduous reader of the works of Granada.[7]

We should not be surprised that Fray Louis gives such importance to prayer, for in a wide sense it is nothing other than the conversation of the soul with God, a communication that admits of various degrees as the soul passes from the purgative to the illuminative way and from the illuminative to the unitive way. In truth, Fray Louis is one of the most profound writers on prayer in the entire history of Christian spirituality.

In the list of Granada's literary works we can easily distinguish between those that pertain strictly to spiritual theology and those that treat of it only in a wide sense or are somehow connected with it. However, we are interested only in those works of Granada that can be called masterpieces of spiritual theology. These are four in number: *Libro de la Oración y Meditación*, *Guía de Pecadores* (in its definitive redaction, for in the first edition of two volumes it was written provisionally and even Fray Louis did not consider it a finished work), *Memorial de la Vida Cristiana* and the additions to this work, and *Introducción del Símbolo de la Fe*.

The first work, *Book of Prayer and Meditation*, was conceived in the solitude of Escalaceli where Blessed Alvaro had erected the first outdoor *Via Crucis* in the West. It has a marked autobiographical character and an internal structure

---

[7] In her *Life* St. Teresa treats of meditation, the prayer of quiet, of recollection, the sleep of the faculties, the prayer of union, of rapture, and flights of the spirit. In her *Way of Perfection* she repeats the same doctrine. In the *Interior Castle* she perfects and clarifies her doctrine, distinguishing between vocal prayer, mental prayer or meditation, the prayer of recollection, the prayer of quiet, and the prayer of union, which eventually terminate in the mystical marriage.

remarkable for its theological orthodoxy and luminous clarity. It has served as a manual of prayer for countless souls. St. Peter of Alcántara confessed: "It is the best book that I have read in our language because it best expounds the practice and exercise of prayer. It contains good meditations and helpful counsels for beginners, the advanced, and the perfect." It is also renowned for its literary beauty, so that Azorín could say of it that "the Spanish language has never reached such fierceness or such angelic suavity" as it does in this work.

The second work, *The Sinners' Guide*, is a work of Aristotelian symmetry, possessing a structure as harmonious as that of a classical palace. Doctrine prevails over the empirical and the autobiographical elements. It is without a doubt the most scholastic work of Fray Louis. Its title reminds us of a similar work by the Spanish Jew of Córdoba, Moses ben Maimón: *Guía de Descarriados (Guide for Heretics)*. Maimón wrote his book to lead the erring Jews back to the law of God, as Moses had led them through the desert to the Promised Land. Fray Louis wishes to lead the sinner—another errant—from the sad bondage of sin to the sweet way of virtue, which is the straight road to the promised land of heaven. Although there is a certain likeness in the books by the Dominican of Granada and the Jew of Córdoba, there is a radical difference in method and doctrine. Maimón is a rationalist and a narrow-minded skeptic; Granada is all peace and sweetness and theological hope. The only real similarity between the two books is the general theme; all else is essentially different.

The third work, *Memorial of the Christian Life*, is of a definitely Platonic flavor both in its title and method of development. The author aims to do no more than to remind the Christian of his obligations, leading him through seven enjoyable tracts to the true spiritual life which corresponds to the name Christian. Later, Granada added two more tracts called the *Additions,* the second of which is a treatise on the love of God and is of such Platonic beauty that Menéndez y Pelayo says that it surpasses everything that has ever been written in Spanish. It is so exquisite a doctrine on love that St. Francis de Sales remarks in his *Theotimus* that it is all that could be said or that one could wish to say.

The fourth and last masterpiece, the *Introduction to the Creed,* is a gigantic work. Fray Louis wrote it in his old age but it manifests the youthfulness of his soul. It is a work that shows his preoccupation with the conversion of the Jews and Mohammedans. Fray Louis knew the Oriental mind very well. While his book on prayer is a lament over the miseries of life and a spiritual contempt for the world, the *Introduction to the Creed* is a canticle of praise. Its schematic structure is most beautiful. Beginning with the doctrine of creation, he leads men to a knowledge of God, whose goodness and providence are manifested through the works of His hands. This method is justified in Sacred Scripture and in the writings of the Fathers of the Church. After demonstrating that God is the Creator and is provident and wise, he concludes in the second part that only the Christian religion can give Him due worship. In the third part he passes from the work of creation to the work of redemption and shows that only the Catholic religion can plumb the depths of this mystery. This third part is a tract in rational theology; the fourth part is a tract on the positive and Biblical theology of this mystery. This is undoubtedly the most admirable book of Fray Louis and modern literary critics never cease to be amazed at the genius that produced it.

Influence of Fray Louis

To Fray Louis is very rightly applied the title "Catholic," a title that we prefer above all others in classifying him in the history of culture. He merits this title in the double meaning that the word connotes: firm orthodoxy that never deviates from true dogma, and universality. With the appearance of his first book, he easily crossed the frontiers of national lines to become first a European author and then, through many translations, a universal author. Both by extension and penetration his influence in the world of the spirit is a phenomenon of extraordinary value in the history of Christian spirituality. An analysis of this historical phenomenon would require a work of such amplitude as would exceed the limits of this introduction; nevertheless, we shall give a synthesis and summary of the world-wide influence of Fray Louis.

The great men of the world visited the cell of Fray Louis to seek counsel, to satisfy their curiosity, or to admire the humble friar who lived the vocation of a religious and a writer and was completely detached from the things that fascinate the world: bishops' miters, royal palaces, riches, and fame. Philip II, monarch of the world, could not resist the urge to visit the Dominican whose writings had become the event of the century. We have already seen how he at one time suspected Fray Louis as the cause of the political intrigues that arose at the time of the disputed succession to the Portuguese throne, but after that period the sympathy and admiration of the Emperor for the Dominican friar were increased more than ever. When the Emperor first came to Portugal, he paid a surprise visit to Fray Louis and afterwards asked him to preach the sermons in the royal chapel. A year later, confined to a bed of suffering which was also to be his deathbed, that monarch on whose empire the sun never set, meditated on the brevity of life and the vanity of earthly glory by reading Granada's *Book of Prayer and Meditation*. We know also that Emperor Charles V prepared himself for death by retiring to the monastery at Yuste and reading the works of Fray Louis.

But it was not only Philip II who disturbed the monastic silence and solitude of the religious. The young King, Don Sebastian, had visited the cell of Fray Louis, as had John Andrea Doria, the admiral of Philip II. The Duke of Alba, captain general of the Spanish regiments, chose the Dominican as his spiritual director. Fray Louis later closed the eyes of the Duke in death and then wrote to the widow one of the most beautiful panegyrics in existence.

Scarcely a legate, ambassador, nuncio, or important person neglected to visit Fray Louis while in Lisbon. So great was the fame that had come to him through his writings that everyone wanted to meet the humble religious who could write so beautifully and whose life was so much in conformity with his doctrine. The great Teresa of Avila, whose sandals had been covered with the dust of most of the main highways of Spain and whose spirit dwelt in mystical heights, felt the strong desire to meet Fray Louis personally. Since she could not do so, she took her pen and wrote to him: "Of the many persons who love Your Reverence in the Lord . . . I am one. I am convinced that for no work or effort would I have desisted to try to see him whose words would be such a comfort to me, if it were in conformity with my state and my being a woman."

Italy also was filled with the renown of Fray Louis. St. Charles Borromeo, the model of prelates and the genial promoter of Catholic reform, was one of the most sincere admirers of Granada. On March 7, 1582, he wrote a letter to Pope Gregory XIII in which he stated: "Of all those who up to our time have written on spiritual matters . . . it can be stated that no one has written books either in greater number or of greater selection and profit than Fray Louis of Granada. . . . In fact, I do not know if in matters of this type there is today a man more beneficial to the Church than he is." At the request of St. Charles, the Pope directed a brief to Fray Louis and it is one of the most eulogistic that the Pontiff wrote during his reign. "Beloved son," he says, "health and apostolic benediction. Your extensive and continuous labor has always been very acceptable to Us. . . . You have preached many sermons and published many books filled with doctrine and devotion. . . . How many souls have profited through your sermons and writings! . . . How many sons have been engrafted on Christ! You have done them much more good than if, they being blind or dead, you had obtained for them from God sight and life."

As is to be expected, Spain was the first beneficiary of the writings of Fray Louis and that from the very first moment. His first work, *Book of Prayer and Meditation,* went through eight editions in the first year. Since that time the presses of Lisbon, Amberes, and Salamanca have not ceased to give to the world new editions of the works of Granada. A historian of those times tells us: "Water girls carried his books under their arms and the market women read them as they waited to sell their merchandise." Kings read them, and the richly ornamented volumes were looked upon as the best and most profitable nourishment of the hearts and minds of the members of the royal families. Nuns were greatly attached to them and in reading them were inflamed with a greater love of God. In some religious rules and constitutions they were mentioned as almost obligatory spiritual reading for the novices.[8]

Everyone read the books of Fray Louis. St. Teresa read them and commanded her nuns to do the same. Fray Louis of León, while working at Salamanca on one of the best of all Castilian books, *Los Nombres de Cristo,* fed his spirit with the words of Fray Louis of Granada. Years later, confined to the prison of Valladolid, he asked for no other books than those of Fray Louis because they brought a ray of light in the midst of such human bitterness.

The literary and educated people likewise read Granada's books and were often inspired by them, as were Quevedo and Espinosa. Especially did orators read his works, for Fray Louis is an outstanding figure in Spanish sacred oratory. It is not strange, therefore, to find great sections of Fray Louis

---

[8] The reading of the books of Fray Louis is mentioned in the instruction for the Discalced Carmelite novices which had been approved by St. John of the Cross. The statutes of the collegiate students at Valencia, redacted by Blessed John Ribera state: "All the time that students are eating, both at dinner and at the evening collation, one of the students will read to them from some book. We especially desire that the books of Fray Louis of Granada have first place because of the devotion we have had and do have for the doctrine contained in his books."

The regulations that govern the famous choir school at Montserrat—where one can hear the most beautifully sung *Salve Regina* in the world—command that the young students read the works of Granada in order to keep aflame the fire of the spirit. The same is true of the Hermits of Córdoba and of the desert of Tardón where the Basilian fathers live. Likewise, the synodal rules of the Archdiocese of Santiago de Compostela commanded, in the year 1579, that the books of Granada be read. There was no bishop in Spain in the seventeenth and eighteenth centuries who did not eulogize, recommend, and even grant indulgences to those who read the works of Fray Louis.

in the sermons of Cabrera, Salucio, Lanuza and others. And when Spanish oratory began to become pompous and ornate, once again Fray Louis was taken as the model to remedy the extravagances.

It is also worth noting how much Fray Louis of Granada has contributed to the theological and Christian formation of the Spanish people. Before the sixteenth century the Spanish theater was profane and worldly and the priest had no part in it except in the role of a buffoon or comedian. But toward the end of the sixteenth century and through the eighteenth century the Spanish theater was perhaps the best in the world. The theater was by that time profoundly theological. It was the age of the *autos sacramentales,* allegorical plays based on religious themes, written by such great literary and dramatic figures as Calderón, Lope, Tirso, and others. Even today they amaze one with their dramatic beauty and theological profundity. Did the generality of the Spanish people of the time grasp the meaning of these *autos sacramentales?* Yes; and the proof lies in the clamorous success of their presentations. It is not possible to gauge exactly the influence that the works of Fray Louis had in those plays, but he was the theologian of the people and the fact of his influence is undeniable.

Even Spanish heretics and atheists were admirers and readers of the works of Fray Louis. It is true that in Spain the heretics have never risen "two inches from the ground," as Gavinet states so graciously and ironically, either because they had been completely overwhelmed or because no one paid any attention to them. If they wished to prosper, they had to go to a foreign country. So the famous Quietist, Molinos, in his *Guía espiritual,* made use of citations from the works of Granada to give special weight to his unorthodox doctrines.

More notable yet is the case of Marchena, atheist, revolutionary, liberal, and the sworn enemy of all spiritual writings. On one occasion the bookseller, Fauli, went to Marchena to reprimand him for corrupting his son with his revolutionary and atheistic ideas. Entering the room of Marchena, he found him reading Granada's *Sinners' Guide*. He could not repress a gesture of astonishment. Marchena noticed it and then made this extraordinary confession: "Do you see this volume, which by its tattered condition seems to have been as used and read as much as an old breviary which the priests use every day? Well so it is, because I have carried it with me for twenty years and not a day passes but that I read some part of it. It accompanied me in the time of terror in the prisons of Paris, it followed me in my sudden flights, it came with me to the shores of the Rhine, to the mountains of Switzerland, and all over. This book has a power over me that I cannot explain. I cannot read it nor can I stop reading it. I cannot read it because it convinces my understanding and moves my will in such a way that while I am reading it, I feel as much a Christian as you or any nun or as the missionaries who go to die for the Catholic faith in China or Japan. I cannot stop reading it because I know of no book more wonderful in our language."

In the present-day Catholic and cultural renascence of Spain, after the tragic obscurity of the centuries, the figure of Louis of Granada is being re-evaluated. Formerly his books were praised with well-deserved panegyrics, but today we are witnessing the beginnings of a truly scientific study of his works. Azorín, one of the most worthy contemporary figures of Spanish letters, has dedicated voluminous essays to the subject; Laín Entralgo has written a masterly monograph on the anthropology of Granada's works; Llaneza has constructed a monumental bibliography; Cuervo has edited a critical edition of his works in fourteen volumes; and the *Biblioteca de Autores Católicos* has published the *Suma de la Vida Cristiana*. All this has served to make educated people realize, as Pemán observes, that Fray Louis is "in some ways the creator and in every sense the exponent and greatest reflection of Spanish devotion and piety. The *Summa of the Christian Life* is not merely a beautiful solo, it is a great Spanish chorale, made up of the voices of the children who chant the catechism answers, the pastors who preach in the rural districts, the old women who attend evening devotions, and the canons who dispute in the seminaries. Spain praying and speaking and manifesting itself as thoroughly Catholic, that is Father Granada."

Analogous to the influence of Fray Louis in Spain is that which he had in Portugal. There he spent the most fruitful days of his apostolate. He was a counselor at the Court and the adviser of kings but he was above all a spiritual educator of the people. A Jesuit of the time wrote to Rome that the people were visibly moved by the preaching of Fray Louis. The same success met his books in Portugal as in Spain and we need not look for a historian to tell us that they were carried under the arms of children and market women. Fray Louis himself states that the first edition of the *Memorial of the Christian Life* appeared in Lisbon in 1561, "with the favor of our Lord and her Highness [the Infanta Doña Maria to whom it was dedicated], and was so well received that in the city of Lisbon alone almost the whole edition was exhausted." Although the people read and understood Spanish, Fray Louis was also able to write in Portuguese. Thus, his *Compendium of Christian Doctrine* was written in Portuguese and printed at the expense of

Queen Catherine. In the rural sections of Portugal it was read at Sunday Mass.

Martins has proved that a work attributed to the famous nobleman and ascetic, George de Silva, is for the most part a translation of selections from Granada. Father Getino has studied Granada's influence on Portuguese writers and orators and has compiled a series of comparative texts wherein it is clearly shown that Hector Pinto, Mendoza, and Coutiño drank from the limpid stream of the writings of Fray Louis.

The enormous influence that Fray Louis had in France deserves a study from a triple point of view: the divulgation of his books among the French people, his influence on the spiritual writers who gave France her glorious pre-eminence in spirituality during the seventeenth century, and the debt that the great French orators, with Bossuet at their head, owe to Fray Louis. As to the divulgation of the works of Granada in France, Llaneza lists 500 editions of the works of Fray Louis in French. Naturally, this means that they were read in that quantity because books that are not read are not sold and books that are not sold are not published. The historians of French spirituality are in accord in stating that Granada was for many centuries the irreplaceable master of the spiritual life. "French literature of the seventeenth century," says Father Getino, "has a Granadine scent and can be taken as the most notable example of personal influence in all literary history." Such was the general diffusion and popularity of Fray Louis that not even the masters of French literature or French spirituality had as many editions as he did during the golden age of France in the seventeenth century. It is curious to note that Granada was quoted or referred to even in the theaters. Thus Molière has Sganarelle recommend the reading of the *Sinners'*

Guide to his daughter in order to cure her of sentimentality and frivolity.

Secondly, in regard to the influence of Granada on the French masters of spirituality, we can safely say that there is no French spiritual writer in the seventeenth century who did not read Granada. Bremond, in his history of religious sentiment in France, relates a beautiful anecdote that touches on this point. John Baptist Romillon was the son of a Calvinist and, moved by the religious-political zeal of that sect, he took up arms. What could be expected from a youth who becomes a soldier to defend heresy, but every kind of vice proper to his age—vices fomented by war and authorized by his error? Thus he lived, a victim of his passions, vicious as a soldier and blasphemous as a heretic, until the age of twenty-seven. Then he had occasion to visit a relative, Madame Chateauneuf, and after the customary polite greetings, he revealed the sadness of his soul, weighted with sin and disillusioned by heresy. Madame Chateauneuf advised him to read the *Book of Prayer and Meditation* by Louis of Granada and actually gave him a copy which her husband had just brought from Paris. This, comments Bremond, is an interesting detail that gives us a glimpse of the France which the historians of the religious wars do not know: a man who brings from Paris a book of devotion for his wife and she, instead of wearying her nephew with words of controversy, gently offering him the book. So John Baptist Romillon meditates, sometimes on the book of Fray Louis, sometimes on the *Institutions* of Calvin. Page by page he compares the teaching of the two authors. In 1579 he publicly adjures his heresy before the Bishop in the church at Cavaillon. Thanks to the iron quality of his provincial mind, he later became a priest and then the founder of a religious institute.

Among Catholics the reading of Fray Louis was more fruitful still. St. Louise de Marillac, an outstanding example of the blending of the contemplative life and apostolic action, had a profound love for the books of Granada; the reformer of Montevillier, Louise de Hospital, read Granada in his own tongue for she knew Spanish very well; St. Vincent de Paul preferred him above all spiritual authors and today his sons, the missionaries of Saint Lazare in Paris, make their retreats from the books of Granada; Cardinal Berulle, founder of the Oratory, held Granada as a master unsurpassed.

St. Francis de Sales, Bishop of Geneva and Doctor of the Church, published his *Introduction to a Devout Life* in 1608. From a literary aspect it is often called an introduction to the French language; as a spiritual work it is the most widely read of all the books by St. Francis de Sales. This work was to a great extent inspired by Fray Louis, for the meditations in the first part and the content of numerous chapters in the second part are taken from the *Memorial* of Fray Louis. This is not surprising if we remember that St. Francis de Sales, on June 3, 1603, wrote to Anthony Revol, Bishop-elect of Dol: "I urge you to have on hand the complete works of Fray Louis of Granada and to use them as a second breviary. In my opinion you should begin by reading the *Sinners' Guide*, secondly the *Memorial*, and then all the rest. But to derive profit from them, they should not be read rapidly and in gulps, but you should ponder over them and savor them, chapter by chapter, meditating in your soul with much attention and prayers to God. They must be read with reverence and devotion as books that contain the most useful inspirations."

Thirdly, we must mention the influence of Fray Louis on French orators. As we know, Fray Louis was a great orator—the best in Spain—and he also wrote much concerning oratory. His *Ecclesiastical Rhetoric* was composed in Latin and had gone through sixteen editions in France when Joseph Climent, Bishop of Barcelona, had it translated into Spanish in 1770. The didactic character of the work and its diffusion in France show that the French knew how to profit from it more than the Spaniards did. It contributed efficaciously to the flowering of French oratory in the seventeenth century, as Climent tells us. The literary ideal that Granada proposes in his *Rhetoric* is the same as that of Bossuet. Actually, Bossuet, Fenelón, and Bourdaloue often quote Granada and the French themselves admit that in the works of the French orators sermons of Granada can be found, copied word for word.

The Italian spiritual writers, Savonarola, St. Catherine of Siena, Crema, and Fermo were sources of inspiration for Granada. But he paid back in abundance what he had received from Italian writers and became, in turn, a spiritual master in Italy. The editions of the works of Granada, says the bibliographer, Toda, were the most numerous of all the Spanish spiritual works published in Italy. In the very year of the appearance of the *Book of Prayer and Meditation,* two Jesuits, Gaspar de Loarte and James de Guzmán, who lived in Italian colleges, were busily occupied with its translation. Bernard and Bremond point out that in the early days of the Society of Jesus the works of Fray Louis exerted a greater influence than did the *Exercises* of St. Ignatius. The first edition of the works of Granada appeared in Italy in 1556, while in Spain the works were banned because of a temporary ordinance of the Inquisition. In Italy also appeared the first biography of Granada. Thomas á Kempis was translated into Italian, not from the Latin text, but from a Spanish version redacted by Granada.

Father Gianetti collected all that Fray Louis had written on the Rosary and in 1572 published a book entitled *The Rosary of the Glorious Virgin Mary*. It met with tremendous success and very shortly passed through twenty editions. Two other books based on selections from the works of Granada are: *Instructions for Pilgrims who go to the Madonna of Loreto and other Holy Places* and a life of St. Clement, taken from the *Introduction to the Creed.*

The most devoted admirers and friends of Granada among the Italians include Bascape, Spaciano, Doria, Cardinals Riario, Alessandrino, and Paleotti, and St. Charles Borromeo. The last-named, in imitation of St. Francis de Sales, frequently preached from the books of Granada. Of the religious congregations founded in the sixteenth century special mention should be made of the affection that the Barnabites had for the works of Fray Louis. Their rule states that they should strive diligently to provide good books for their subjects and especially the books by Fray Louis of Granada. In the section that treats of the instruction of novices, it is advised that their principal study should be the books of Fray Louis.

Three Spanish authors have awakened a lively interest in England: Guevara, Louis of Granada, and Cervantes. The appreciation for Cervantes, however, did not develop until almost the eighteenth century. By the sixteenth century the most widely read Spanish author in England was Antonio de Guevara, whose writings are colloquial, jesting, and ironic. But when the works of Granada appeared in the middle of the sixteenth century, he became the preferred Spanish author. The *Book of Prayer and Meditation* was especially popular among English Catholics. Selections from this work immediately passed into the sermon books of the age, prayer books, and books of meditation. As in France, the ideas of Granada were reflected even in the theater. In the scene of the burial of the beautiful and tragic Ophelia in *Hamlet*, ideas and phrases are repeated from the *Book of Prayer and Meditation*.

The English refugees in the Low Countries and in France exercised a tremendous influence on the profane and religious literature of their country. In 1579 religious, priests, and laity began a period of great translation which lasted until the end of the seventeenth century. The outstanding among them are Stephen Brinkley, John Fenn, Thomas Lodge, and above all, Richard Hopkins, who published his translations of the Spanish mystics at Louvain, Brussels, Liége, Ambert, and Douai. His versions were as faithful as they were literary and were read and admired in Great Britain not only by Catholics but also by Protestants. His translation passed through fifty editions in less than a century. Even Puritan ministers, such as Francis Meres, who translated the works of Granada, did not find it paradoxical to dedicate their translations to outstanding Protestants such as Thomas Egerton, the Lord Keeper of the Great Seal of England. The Granadine influence is more surprising because it was prevalent, not in a period of Catholic reaction, as happened during the passing influence of the Stuarts, but at the very moment when Elizabeth and her ministers, Buckley and Walsingham, were using every means to rid England of all traces of Catholicism. It is not necessary to explain this attraction to Granada by the English love of rhetoric and the heroic; it can be explained by the fact that in spite of the political and religious upheaval, the souls of the English remained essentially Catholic.

The works of Granada were also translated and diffused in the Low Countries. Despite the fact that the Protestant Revolt later ignited the flame of rebellion and obliged the Spanish troops of the Duke of Alba to unsheathe the sword, many translations of Granada's works were made into Dutch and Flemish. In Germany the Protestant Revolt made the diffusion of the works of Granada very difficult. At the end of the sixteenth century the Jesuits petitioned Rome for permission to establish colleges in Germany and to translate the works of Granada. In spite of the difficulties encountered, more than seventy German editions of Granada's works finally appeared. It is worth mentioning that the most beautiful editions of the Latin version of the complete works of Granada were made by the Germans, especially in Cologne, Mainz, and Frankfurt.

Even more limited was the diffusion of the works of Granada in Poland, a nation which is Catholic by essence and a martyr by the tragic destiny of its history. In the midst of so much suffering and the brutal assaults of her enemies, Poland kneels at the sanctuary of her patroness, the Virgin of Czestochowa. We have record of a fairly large number of Polish versions but we know nothing more than that, and a curtain of darkness now prevents one from making further investigation.

In central Europe, especially in Czechoslovakia and the country of St. Stephen, Hungary, we know that there are editions and readers of Granada's works. In Greece, also, we find a beautiful edition of the *Sinners' Guide*. But of necessity our information on these countries must be scarce and partial, as is the information on the works of Granada in Arabic, Persian, Turkish, and Syrian. However, the Vatican Library possesses a rare and precious Syrian version of Granada's tract on Communion and confession, printed in two tones of ink. The biographer Diago and the bibliographers Galiana and Llaneza also report a translation of the *Book of Prayer and Meditation* in Turkish. As to Persian, Fray Augustine de Gobea, O.S.A., states in his *Viaje de Persia* that he saw the King of Persia receive a translation of the *Introduction to the Creed,* richly bound in calfskin. Father Buck gives much information on Arabic translations and describes various editions in that language.

In the Orient it was principally the missionaries who made the works of Granada known. Fray Santa Cruz, O.P., the founder of the missions at Tonkin, translated many of Granada's books for his Christians. More recently a new translation of the *Sinners' Guide* was made into Anamite. There are also versions in Chinese as well as Tagalan, the language of the natives of the Philippines.

But the Oriental versions of Granada's works that are most interesting are those in Japanese and they have aroused great curiosity on the part of bibliophiles. Many translations are extant and it is probable that many more are buried beneath the dust and forgetfulness of time. It is known from tales brought back by the missionaries themselves that the Japanese version of the *Sinners' Guide* did much to preserve the faith of the Christian Japanese when the fierce winds of persecution were blowing over the entire Japanese empire. A modern Jesuit missionologist, Father Bayle, has said: "It fills one with a holy joy to see that the *Sinners' Guide* was one of the bulwarks that sustained a hidden but vital Christianity for two centuries, while both in Europe and Japan it was believed dead." The Portuguese Jesuits had brought the works of Granada to Japan and to them falls a good measure of the glory for the good that this book has worked in souls, nourishing the flame of their faith and heroism when persecution had deprived them of all priestly ministration.

Latin America has always manifested a great admiration for the books of Fray Louis. Some of Granada's books were almost always to be found in the modest and frugal equipment of the early missionaries. There were also editions of his works in the cargo of the ships that set out from Seville for the New World. But many missionaries, filled with a divine impatience, did not wish to wait until the Indians had learned Spanish; they translated some of Granada's works into the native dialects.

Among the Latin-American readers of Fray Louis we must mention the Flower of the Americas, Rose of Santa María, known as St. Rose of Lima. Father Leonard Hansen, O.P., her biographer, relates the following anecdote: "Sister Rose of Santa María always had at hand the books of Fray Louis of Granada and of them all, she preferred the *Book of Prayer and Meditation*. In one of her struggles with the devil-tempter—a true phenomenon that frequently happened in the lives of the saints, as St. Teresa of Avila tells us—she protected herself by reading this book. Once the devil became very furious and snatched the book from her, tore it apart, and threw it on a rubbish heap. Rose remained unmoved, certain that the Lord would return it to her, as He did."

As regards North America, I admit my inability to speak of the diffusion of Granada. In the Library of Congress in Washington there are many editions of Granada but the major part of them were published in England. Before the flowering of its own magnificent presses and publishing houses, the United States received most of its books from England, as Canada did from France. But some translations have been made in the United States with greater or less success. However, a few Americans have written brilliant doctoral dissertations on Granada. One of them, by R. Switzer at the University of

Columbia, treats of the Ciceronian style of Granada; another, by M. B. Brentano at Catholic University in Washington, treats of nature in the works of Fray Louis. At the present time there are several others in preparation.

Epilogue

The century, the sixteenth; the empire, Spain; the writer, Granada. The dawning of the sixteenth century appeared on the horizon of history with a sign of complex problems. The harmonious synthesis of medieval theological thought had been rent by the destructive attack of Nominalism and the inertia and indifference of a Scholasticism that was lost in a maze of byzantine disputes. There was metaphysical anarchy in thought, social anarchy in nations, and religious anarchy in monasteries. Two movements, Humanism and the Protestant Revolt, burst forth like flowers of evil from the chaotic decadence of Europe. Reform! The cold and rebellious cry pierced Europe to its marrow while the doctrine of external justification sought to smother the true interior life of the soul.

The Protestant Revolt overran middle Europe with its anti-Roman fanaticism; Humanism, like a draft of poisonous air, penetrated the very head and members of the Church. A unanimous voice throughout Christendom begged for Catholic reform. The rhetorical attempts of Erasmus and his humanistic evangelism were inefficacious; more futile still and dangerous was the attempt to effect a compromise or concordance between radically opposed doctrines and dogmas. The literature of the controversialists answered as best it could but it did not produce the desired effects. Some even attempted a Catholic reform without Rome's guidance or approbation.

The plan was absurd and doomed to failure. True reform would have to be a work of the Church herself.

The infamous sacking of Rome in 1527 brought the Curia a bitter taste of the chastisement of God's wrath. Pope Clement VII expelled his cardinals. The true reform of the Church had begun and Catholicism, faced with the moral indignity of its deserters, stoutly and robustly defended itself. The Church manifests herself as mistress of truth in the Council of Trent; she shows the holiness of her head and members in St. Pius V and the legion of saints who flourished during the time of Trent; she knows how to oppose the humanistic evangelism by reviving the old religious orders and establishing new congregations. The Church has a compassionate heart for those who suffer (St. John of God); she does not, like the mercenary shepherd, abandon her sheep (the pastoral zeal of St. Charles Borromeo, Fray Bartholomew de los Mártires, St. Thomas More), but goes out in search of erring souls (St. Francis Xavier in Japan and St. Turibius in South America). The Church is founded on a rock and has the divine assurance that the enemy will not prevail; she suffers, she struggles, but in the end she conquers. When the storms and battles are over, the Church appears more beautiful, more brilliant, more joyous, and more secure than ever before. At the end of the sixteenth century, listen to the angelic music that St. John of the Cross sings on the summit of Mount Carmel; it is the Church singing in her heart.

In that same century we find Spain close to the Church. Spain lives and keeps vigil as a defensive vanguard of the Church. She is the "evangelizer of half the world, the hammer of heretics, and the light of the Council of Trent."

The Catholic Kings, Ferdinand and Isabella, have unified Spain geographically by the taking of Granada; politically, by their bond of matrimony; religiously, by the expulsion of the Jews. Spain rapidly becomes the first power in Europe. The sword of the great captain is invincible in Italy, Columbus discovers a new world, the Spanish battalions command Flanders and conquer the Protestant army of the Elector of Saxony. At San Quentin, the Spaniards defeat the French; at Lepanto, they overwhelm the Turkish might that had been a constant and terrifying threat to the Church. Thanks to the labors of Spanish missionaries, the Church obtained a kind of recompense or indemnity for the Protestant break. All Spanish America, the Philippines, and other Spanish dominions were converted to Catholicism. It is a sin which the intransigent pacifists have never forgiven Spain.

It is of minor importance to note that the sun never set on the Spanish Empire; it is much more important to realize that it was starred with figures of great magnitude. We recall Fray Francis Vitoria, who modernized theological methods and introduced international law into the lecture halls of Salamanca. His disciples then carried his teachings to the Indies and to Trent, to give a new period of splendor to Catholic theology.

We recall Fray Louis of Granada, the spiritual writer of the Spanish Empire. Born in Granada of a humble family, his life develops along most interesting channels that run parallel to the cultural and psychological problems of his time. From Lisbon, then the center and watchtower of the Spanish Empire, radiate the figure, the word, and the work of Fray Louis to all the known world. Through translations into most of the languages of the civilized world of his time, his books circle the globe. Together with St. Teresa of Avila and Fray Louis of León, Fray Louis of Granada has justified the famous phrase of Charles V. "Spanish is the language made to speak with God."

The mortal remains of the humble Dominican friar rest at Lisbon, near the sea, but neither the world nor forgetfulness will ever bury his fame.

Alvaro Huerga, O.P.
Regent of Studies
Convent of the Holy Cross
Granada, Spain

BOOK ONE

The Existence and Perfections of God

Prologue ✠

JUST AS THERE is a diversity of tastes and opinions among authors, so also is there a variety of subjects and themes which they treat. Some are enchanted by the beauty of eloquence and, consequently, they attempt to create the perfect orator, taking their pupil in his earliest years and leading him through all the steps and phases of this art until they place him at its very summit. Others use the same method to fashion a perfect prince, a great captain, a courtier, and so forth. Thus each writer strives to clarify and illustrate whatever he esteems most highly.

But it is certain that of all human vocations there is none more lofty than that of the perfect Christian who, being ordained to a supernatural end, lives a life that is likewise supernatural. For that reason the saints call such a person a celestial man or an angel on earth. Now if authors have most diligently taught whatever is required for those other vocations in life, which are so much the less noble as their ends are less noble, how much more necessary it is to do the same thing as regards the Christian vocation which, since it is so much more lofty than the others, is much more difficult to attain.

The Apostle wrote to the Colossians[9] that the words and doctrine of Christ should be preached abundantly among them and that they should teach and admonish one another concerning their respective duties. If there is no occupation, however lowly, that does not require rules and regulations in

[9] Cf. Col. 3:16.

order to be well done, how much more is this true of the greatest of all occupations, which is to serve and please God, to conquer the kingdom of heaven, and to prevail against the powers and deceits of the enemy.

How will the uneducated man know what this occupation demands if he is not reminded of God's promises and warnings and the weighty obligations that he has of serving Him? How will he be able to confess correctly if he is not taught the parts of the sacrament of penance and how to perform each one of them? How can he have sorrow for his sins and a purpose of amendment if he is not reminded of the reasons and motives for lamenting them? How can he receive Communion worthily and profitably if he is not taught the things required for this? How will he be able to regulate his life, cultivate virtue, and flee from sin if he does not know the means by which he must seek the former and avoid the latter and does not recognize the temptations and snares of the enemy? How can he formulate a prayer that will be fruitful and accompany it with the necessary conditions and virtues if he has not the doctrine for this? How can he ever reach the love of God if he knows not the means by which it is attained, as well as the things that impede it? We need enlightenment in all these matters, for we did not receive them in the womb of our mothers before we were born. Hence, with good reason are we likened to that man in the Gospel who was born blind from his mother's womb.

For many years I have desired to see a book that would treat of the formation of the perfect Christian and would be a *summa* of all that pertains to the Christian vocation. Good workmen strive to have at hand all the tools that are necessary for their labor and those who study any art or science seek some book in which is compiled all that pertains to their subject. It would seem profitable to do the same in regard to this art of arts and science of sciences. Possessing such a compendium, those who truly desire to serve God would easily find doctrine and light for their life, while preachers and confessors zealous for the good of souls would have something from which they could readily dispense to their hearers whatever is necessary for the fulfillment of the Christian vocation.

I am well aware that there is no lack of books on sound Catholic doctrine, but most of them treat of some particular aspect and do not attempt to treat of everything in a brief space. Furthermore, although the various catechisms, which are syntheses of Christian doctrine, treat of everything that pertains to the Christian life, they state merely the bare substance of doctrine and only that which is necessary for a clear understanding. They are more speculative than practical, for they are meant to enlighten the understanding rather than move the will to the practice of the virtues. For this reason I have decided, with the help of the Lord and the writings of the saints, to compile this book wherein all these matters will be treated. My purpose is the formation of the perfect Christian and I shall lead him through all the steps and exercises of the Christian life from the beginning of his conversion to the summit of perfection.

The project that we are here attempting—the formation of the perfect Christian—is properly the work of the Holy Ghost, but just as grace does not preclude our own industry but rather concurs with it, so also neither does the interior instruction of God exclude the exterior teaching of men, but necessarily demands it. This office belongs especially to the priests and ministers of the Church to whom God commits us so that they may teach us and inform us of His law.

So important is this office that Moses reserved it for himself alone, at the advice of Jethro, his father-in-law, who told him to refer all temporal matters to other judges but to keep for himself whatever touched upon religion and divine worship.[10] And because certain priests were later careless in this office, God spoke to them through a prophet, saying:[11] "Because thou hast rejected knowledge, I will reject thee, and thou shalt not do the office of priesthood to Me." Again, through the mouth of Isaias,[12] God threatened them with a severe chastisement, saying that because of their attachment to their sins He would punish them with a terrible scourge in which wise men would lose their wisdom and the understanding of the prudent would be obscured. If the lack of wisdom in the elders was considered a great and terrible chastisement, the same is true if wisdom be lacking in the Church's ministers, for without the light of the intellect which guides and regulates the whole Christian life, what can be expected but blindness, irregularity, and other serious evils?

Although it is the office of preachers to cure this blindness with the light of God's word, preachers are not always available nor do they always treat of the matters that are most necessary. Neither are they able, as a rule, to descend to the particulars that moral doctrine demands, for this requires individual instruction which is not usually given from the pulpit. Therefore the reading of good books is highly profitable, for books are mute preachers that neither weary us because of their length, for we can always put them aside, nor leave us

---

[10] Cf. Exod. 18:13–27.

[11] Cf Os. 4:6.

[12] Cf. Isa. 29:14.

wanting because of their brevity, for it is within our power to continue reading as long as is necessary.

Although spiritual reading has always been necessary, it is even more so at the present time. In the ancient days of the primitive Church pastors and priests were so fervent and conscientious in the ministry of the word of God that preaching was of itself sufficient to preserve and promote the virtue of the faithful. Today, however, many priests think that nothing more is required of them than the administration of the sacraments and the celebration of Mass at specified times, and they content themselves with this. Therefore, the greater the lack in preaching, the greater the necessity of supplying for this deficiency by means of good books.

The fruits of the word of God, who can expound them? For His word is the light that illumines our understanding, the spark that inflames our will, the hammer that softens the hardness of our hearts, the knife that cuts off the excesses of our passions, the candle that illuminates all the steps of our lives, and the seed that bears fruits of eternal life. It is a food and nourishment that sustains us and a delight that enlarges and fortifies our souls in God. Whoever reads books on sound doctrine is able to partake of and enjoy such fruits.

So great is the light and fruit of spiritual reading that we know from experience many persons who have changed their entire lives by this means. When asked the root and cause of such a change, they responded that after reading such and such a book they resolved to amend their lives. So also the treasurer of the Queen of Ethiopia was reading the prophet Isaias while riding in his chariot and God converted him through St. Philip, who took as the text of his instruction the very passage that the eunuch had been reading.[13] Moreover, the remarkable and heroic works that King Josias performed during his reign, whence did they proceed but from the reading of a sacred book that had been sent to him by the priest Helcias, as is related in the Book of Kings?[14] And the astounding conversion of St. Augustine, did it not also begin with the reading of a holy book?

So sublime are the mysteries that the Christian religion proposes to man and so powerful for moving hearts that I would not be surprised if they effected a great change in anyone who attentively considers them. Moreover, spiritual reading serves not only to arouse those who are sleeping but also to safeguard those who are already awake. For that reason the word of God in Scripture is called bread or nourishment, because it sustains and preserves souls in the spiritual life just as material bread sustains the body in its corporeal life.

This is not a business to be hurried, but one that requires great deliberation, for it concerns the government of your entire life and what follows after. How insistent you are that your worldly affairs be carefully sifted and examined. You are not content with only one opinion concerning them, but you consider and review your case in numerous conferences with experts lest you make a mistake. But in this business of your Christian life you are not dealing with things of earth, but of heaven, nor of external affairs and interests, but of yourself. Realize, therefore, that the discussion of it must not be accompanied by dozing and yawning but with utmost attention. Therefore, do not read this book rapidly, as you would any

---

[13] Cf. Acts 8:28.

[14] Cf. II Paralip. 34:14 ff.

other kind of book, scanning the pages hurriedly in order to reach the end. But sit down as a judge in the tribunal of your heart and listen to the words in silence. If up to this point you have erred, take care that you make a fresh start. Be sensible; cut the thread of your mistakes and begin to wind it in the other direction.

Which of you will say now that you believe me and will listen with attentive ears and later, like a good judge who has heard the allegations and proof, will pass sentence on yourself? What a blessed enterprise! What an effort well expended! I know well that I am attempting a great deal and that no amount of writing is sufficient to realize this task. For that reason, at the very outset I entreat Him who is the virtue and wisdom of the Father, to be present here and give spirit and life to my words so that they will move the hearts of those who read them.

Therefore, Christian reader, receive this little work which in a short time and with a little effort on your part will partially supply your needs. It will serve as a preacher, exhorting you to live well, and will furnish you with doctrine that will teach you how to live well. It will serve as a guide in your examination of conscience, as a preparation for the reception of Communion, as an impetus to prayer, and as a fruitful source of meditation. If this book has any merit at all, it is because it treats of everything that pertains to all Christians, whether they be beginners or proficients in the Christian life. Finally, if it has required great diligence and effort to compile all this material and present it in a smooth and easy style, all will be considered well spent if the fruitfulness of the book is equally as great, for no physical labor can begin to compare with the least spiritual benefit.

CHAPTER 1 ✠ *God's Existence*

THE FIRST THING proposed for our belief among the articles of faith is that there is a God, for it is necessary to know that there is a ruler of the universe, a first truth and goodness, and a first cause on which all other causes depend and which itself depends on no other. This is the very foundation of our faith and the first thing which must be believed. Therefore the Apostle states: "For he that cometh to God, must believe that he is, and is a rewarder to them that seek him."[15]

This truth is so manifest to the natural light of reason that it can be acquired through an evident demonstration, as was done by many philosophers and is still done today by all wise men who, from a knowledge of the effects existing in the world, rise to a knowledge of the first cause from which they proceed, namely, God. For that reason St. Thomas says that learned men do not have faith in this first article because they possess evidence of its truth, and evidence is incompatible with the obscurity which is annexed to faith. But the ignorant do not possess such evidence and therefore they have faith concerning this article. They believe it because God has revealed it and the Church has proposed it for belief.

It may seem that one could be excused from discussing this question among Christians because they all profess this article of faith. So they do; but in spite of that, we have seen and still see daily men who are so impudent, so impious, and so perverse that although intellectually they confess that there is

[15] Heb. 11:6.

a God, they deny Him in their works. They do not live any differently as a result of believing in Him than if they did not believe in Him at all. For such as these, who keep the light of faith so hidden and forgotten, it will be beneficial to show clearly by the light of reason that there is a God. Perhaps this will give them a sort of jolt so that they will look to themselves. In addition to this, there is another and greater benefit which is common to all, namely, that the very things that proclaim God's existence likewise declare many of His perfections and especially His wisdom, omnipotence, goodness, and the providence by which He rules and governs all things.

Let us now see what principles the philosophers used in order to attain this truth so that we shall embrace with greater joy what our faith teaches. For when faith is wed with reason and reason with faith, the one attesting to the other, the soul enjoys a most lofty knowledge of God which is firm, certain, and evident. Faith strengthens us with its firmness and reason gladdens us with its clarity. Faith shows God to us covered by the veil of His greatness, but reason partly removes this veil so that God's beauty may be seen. Faith teaches us what we ought to believe; reason enables us to believe with joy.

These two lights together dissipate all darkness, calm the conscience, satisfy the understanding, remove doubts, and make us sweetly embrace the sovereign truth. Hence, we have two teachers: Sacred Scripture and creatures, both of which aid us greatly in the knowledge of our Creator. Therefore, let us consider some of the principles and arguments that the philosophers used for attaining the truth of God's existence. I say some, because we shall treat only of those that are most clear and best accommodated to the capacity of the laity, leaving the more subtle ones for the schools of theology.

Of all these arguments Cicero places great importance on the following: Among the many and varied nations in the world there is none so barbarous or savage that, although it may not know the true God, it will not at least understand that a God exists and honor Him with some type of veneration. The reason for this is that apart from the beauty and order of this world, which give constant testimony that there is a God who governs it, the Creator Himself has imprinted on the hearts of men a natural inclination to love and reverence God as the universal Father who sustains and governs all things. From this inclination proceeds that outward expression of religion which we see in all the nations of the world. And so strongly is this inclination impressed on human hearts that in its defense one nation will battle against another without having any other reason for fighting, as happened between the Christians and the Moors. For each side believes that its religion is the true one wherein God is fittingly honored and feels obliged to speak out in behalf of God and to wage war on those who do not honor Him as they believe He should be honored.

Moreover, each day we see men pass over from diverse sects to our religion, sometimes making great sacrifices to embrace the true religion. So also in the days of Esdras, when the children of Israel returned from the Babylonian captivity, those who had married women of Gentile lineage abandoned them, together with their children, in order not to break the law of God which forbade such marriages. From this we can see how deeply the Creator has planted the affection for religion in our hearts, for it prevails and conquers man's greatest natural affections.

The philosophers state yet another proof of God's existence which is based on the natural inclination of which we have spoken. Whenever men find themselves in some great and extraordinary conflict or danger, they naturally and instinctively raise their hearts to God and ask for help. This movement is so spontaneous that it precedes any reasoning process; it flows from the very nature of man. For this recourse to God is the voice and testimony of man's very nature confessing that there is a divine Ruler who sees and foreknows all things and is present in every place. It is an admission of His providence, His goodness, His mercy, His love for men, and His desire to assist them. God Himself, when He created man, implanted in him this natural inclination which would move him to have recourse to God as to a true father in all his trials and afflictions.

Another motive which the philosophers, and indeed all men, have for acknowledging the Divinity is the structure, order, beauty, and grandeur of this world. Nothing can be found in the administration and government of the world, says Cicero, that could be justly criticized, and if there be anyone who would like to change something already made, he will either make it worse or will not be able to change it at all. But if it is true that everything in the world is so made that it could not be improved upon as regards the needs of life nor made more beautiful to look upon, let us see whether such things could be made by chance or could remain in the state in which they are if they were not governed by a divine providence.

If the works of nature are more perfect than the works of art and yet the works of art are made according to reason, then it follows that the works of nature cannot be lacking a reason for their existence. For who, after seeing a well-painted picture, does not realize that it is a result of art, or on seeing a boat plying the waters afar off does not realize that this movement is caused by reason and art? Would he then dare to say that the world, which produced these very arts and artists, is lacking in reason and art?

But let us raise our eyes to greater things. In the heavens shine forth the lights of innumerable stars, the greatest of which is the sun, which illumines all things and is many times larger than the earth. Yet these great fiery masses never do harm to the earth or the things upon it; rather, they help it in every way. Yet if they were to change their places and positions, the whole world would very likely be consumed by fire.

Let us imagine, says Cicero, a heavy darkness such as that which is said to have proceeded in times past from the fires of Mount Etna and obscured all the surrounding region. And let us imagine further that for a space of two days no man was able to see another. If, then, on the third day the sun were again to brighten the world, it would seem to these men that they had risen again. And if, as Aristotle says, men dwelt beneath the earth in subterranean palaces and had never seen the earth, although they had heard by rumor that there was a Divinity in the outer world; and if the bowels of the earth were suddenly to open and these men were to come forth and see the earth and sea and heavens, the grandeur of the clouds, the velocity of the winds, the beauty and efficacy of the sun, the phases of the moon, and the variety of the stars, without a doubt they would know that the rumor was true and that there was in the universe a sovereign Divinity on whom all things depend.

But since they are accustomed to see such things every day, men do not marvel at their beauty nor try to understand the reasons for things. As if the novelty of things should move us more than their grandeur to inquire into their causes! Yet who would consider him a reasonable man who, after seeing the relation and fitness of all these things, would say that they were all made without prudence or reason and that these things which no intelligence can comprehend were due entirely to chance? When we observe the movements of a clock or any mechanical figures, do we not realize that there is some art and cause of these movements? And seeing the remarkable regularity of the movements of the heavenly bodies, are we not forced to acknowledge that all this is done according to an intelligence, indeed, an excellent and divine intelligence?

But putting aside the subtleties of arguments, let us look upon the beauty of the things that have been made by divine providence. First, let us consider the solid earth which is held together by its own spinning movement, clothed in flowers, grass, and trees, and peopled with an incredible multiplicity of things so varied and different that they cause unending pleasure and delight. Add to this the perennial fountains of refreshing springs, the clear waters of the rivers, the green garments of their banks, the height of the mountains, and the smoothness of the prairies.

Moreover, what great diversity we find among animals, both tame and wild; what flights and songs of birds; what expansive pastures for herds and numerous forests for the life of wild animals. And what shall we say of the races of men who have been placed on this earth as laborers and cultivators? They have not let it be taken over by the wild beasts nor become a wild entanglement of trees and shrubbery, but by their industry they have made the fields and islands and river banks resplendent with houses and cities. Consider also the beauty of the sea: what a multitude and variety of islands are in it; what freshness and delight on its shores; what diverse species of fish, some in the depths of the sea itself, others swimming just beneath the surface or leaping among the waves. Or consider the air that alternates between day and night, how it vaporizes and ascends on high as clouds above the ocean and then how these clouds are moved from place to place by the winds before they condense and irrigate the earth with rain. This same air supports the flight of the birds and gives all animals the elements by which they are sustained and conserved. Finally, consider the heavens that gird the earth and enfold all things as the ultimate terminus and extremity of the universe. See how the glimmering lights of the stars follow their orderly course and how the sun, with its rising and setting, is the cause of day and night, so that the earth is saddened at its absence and gladdened at its coming. See how the moon lightens the earth with the light it receives from the sun and passes through its various phases from a crescent to the full moon. Consider also how the planets trace their courses through the heavenly space and how the fixed stars are arranged in such a manner that they portray certain figures according to which they are named, such as the Dipper and the Ram, and which serve as guides for those who sail the seas. If we were to see all these things in one glance of the eye, as we now picture them in our imagination, none of us could doubt the existence of divine providence.

All these observations were made by Cicero and arguing from the construction, beauty, and benefits of the lower world and the order and invariable constancy of the heavenly planets, he proves that things so great, so beneficial, so beautiful, and so well-ordered could never have been caused by chance, but must come from a most wise Creator and Ruler. For who would say that a large and excellent painting of many beautiful colors and designs had been made by the chance blot of paint that happened to fall on a canvas? And what painting is more grand and more beautiful than this universe? What colors more vivid and pleasing than those of the meadows and trees in the springtime? What forms more exquisite than those of the flowers and the birds? What could be more resplendent than the starry heavens? Who, then, will be so blind as to say that they are all the result of chance?

In addition to the above arguments, there is yet another no less forceful for the proof of God's existence, a very palpable reason which is easily understood by every intellect, however uneducated. This argument proceeds from the observation of the skills possessed by all the animals regarding the things necessary for their preservation, defense, cure of sickness, and production of offspring. In all these things they do no less than they would if they actually possessed perfect reasoning powers. Thus, they fear death, they flee from dangers, they seek what is beneficial to themselves, they know how to make their nests and care for their young, even as do men gifted with reason. More than this, from among the multiple varieties of herbs in the fields, they know which ones are fit to eat and which are not, which are beneficial and which are poisonous; and however hungry they may be, they will never eat of the latter. The sheep fears the wolf even if it has never seen one, but it does not fear the mastiff, which greatly resembles the wolf. The chicken does not fear the turkey, though a very large bird, but it is afraid of even the shadow of a hawk, a much smaller bird. The chicks fear the cat but not the dog and this even before they know from experience the harm that may come from contrary things.

All the animals lack reasoning power, for in this respect they differ from men, but they do all things that pertain to their preservation as perfectly as if they possessed reason. Therefore, we must confess that there is an infinite reason and perfect wisdom which so assists all these creatures and so governs and directs them that they act just as they would if they possessed reasoning powers. For by the same act that the Creator formed them and willed that they should be and live, He likewise gave them everything necessary for the preservation of their existence. Otherwise He would have created them in vain and without reason.

If we were to see a child of three years speak with the discretion and eloquence of a great orator, we would say that another person was speaking in that child, for at that age a child is incapable of such eloquence and discretion. So also when we see that all the creatures that lack reason perform their actions in accordance with reason, we are forced to confess that some universal reason exists, some lofty wisdom which, without bestowing reason on them, gives them inclinations and natural instincts that will effect in them what reason does in man. The philosophers recognize this clearly when they say that the works of nature are works of an intelligence that does not err, meaning that they are works of a supreme wisdom that labors with such perfection that no defect can be found in its effects. The consideration of created things moved St. Augustine to say that he would more readily doubt that he possessed a soul in his body than to doubt that there is a God.

Now tell me, if you carefully consider the beauty of the royal house of this world and the structure and provision of all things that are in it; if you consider the great vault of the heavens, painted with a variety of stars; and if you consider the table of the earth, filled with diverse meats and fruits and other edibles, with its shady nooks and gardens and fountains, its expanses of green grass across the mountains and valleys and meadows, the illumination it receives by day and by night from the tapers and fires in the heavens, the gold and silver and precious stones that are in the veins of the earth, the various dwelling places it affords—the waters for those that swim, the air for those that fly, and the earth for the rest—and finally, if you consider how all the things in this royal house are ordered to the service of the prince, who is man, how could you believe that all this came about by chance? How could you fail to see that all this had and has a powerful and wise Maker?

Therefore, the beauty and grandeur of the world and its unity amid variety moved not only the philosophers but all nations to believe that things so great and beautiful and well-ordered could not have been made by chance but that they had a most wise and powerful Maker who created them by His omnipotence and governs them by His wisdom. That is why David exclaims: "The heavens show forth the glory of God, and the firmament declareth the work of His hands."[16] In other words, the beauty of the heavens, adorned with so many lights, and the marvelous order of the stars with their movements and courses, preach the glory of God and make all nations praise Him, marvel at His grandeur, and recognize Him as the Maker and Lord of all things. Likewise, the order of the days and nights, their lengthening and shortening, so suitable to the needs of our life, preach and testify that works so great and well-ordered cannot be attributed to chance or fate but that there is in the universe a sovereign ruler who in the beginning created all things and now conserves them by His providence. But these admirable works do not speak or

---

16 Cf. Ps. 18:1.

testify to this truth in human voices, which could never reach the ends of the universe. Their speech and testimony is their invariable order, their beauty, and the art with which they are so perfectly made. This type of language is heard in all lands and it draws men to the worship and veneration of the Creator.

CHAPTER 2 ✠
The One God

HAVING DEMONSTRATED THAT there is a supreme Lord of the universe and Governor of all creation, whom we call God, it is now necessary to show that there is only one God and impossible that there be many. Briefly, it can be proved by the following argument: If there were two Gods, distinct from each other, one would necessarily have to possess something by which He would be differentiated from the other. Now, if that possessed by one and not by the other were an imperfection, then the first would not be God because there can be no imperfection in God. But if it were a perfection, then the second would not be God because he would be lacking some perfection. For God is eminently perfect and to such an extent that there cannot be anything else more perfect.

The same truth is also confirmed by the following example: We see that in any good government there must be one head by whom all else is governed and maintained in peace and concord. Likewise, in any army there is a supreme commander who controls all, in a kingdom there is a king who rules all, in a city there is one mayor who governs it, and in a home the father of the family is obeyed by all. Even in the human body there is but one head which exerts its power on all the members. Whence, just as it would be a monstrosity were a body to have two heads, so it would also be if there were two governors with equal power over the same republic. Inevitably dissensions and factions would arise, some persons following one side and others another. So the Savior said that every kingdom divided against itself will be destroyed.[17]

We need not look far for examples. Although Romulus and Remus, the founders of the city of Rome, were both carried in the same womb, they could not be contained in the same city; Caesar and Pompeius, who were father-in-law and son-in-law, could not be contained in the whole world. But what better example could we find than the bees, in whom the Creator has implanted the instinct to follow but one queen wherever she goes. They are so loyal to her that when she dies, all the other bees gather around her and were they not removed, they would remain there without food until they themselves died. And if two queen bees should strive for the rule of the hive, the other bees will kill one queen and remain with the other. Admitting that all good government proceeds from one head and seeing that this world is actually perfectly governed, it follows that the world is controlled by one supreme Lord and Ruler and not by many.

Another argument, no less convincing, can be added to the foregoing. We know a multitude of diverse things cannot be reduced to unity and concord except by one, just as in music various voices together could not produce sweetness and harmony if there were not some musician to direct them so that

[17] Cf. Luke 11:17.

their voices would sweetly blend. Otherwise they would produce only dissonance and discord. The same unity and concord is evident in the many things of this world. All of them, from the least to the greatest, unite in the service, sustenance, and preservation of man so that nothing in the heavens, on the earth, or in the sea and air is exempt from this service. Seeing how things so varied and different (many of them even contrary to one another) are all reduced to the one purpose—the service of man—we must necessarily admit that there is one supreme Governor who has reduced this great variety to unity and concord and that this is the one God who, as He created the visible world not for Himself or the angels but for man, so also He ordained all things with such order that they would be of service to man.

CHAPTER 3 ✠

God, Incomprehensible and Ineffable

WHEN ONE CONSIDERS the divine perfections, great wonder and admiration arise in the soul. For God is immense, infinite, incomprehensible, and ineffable and whatever could be said or imagined concerning His greatness is as nothing when compared to what remains to be known. Whatever any creature, even an angel, can know is finite, just as the creature itself is finite, but God's greatness is infinite. Therefore, there is no proportion between what is understood and what remains to be known. For that reason David says that God "made darkness His covert, His pavilion around Him,"[18] signifying that no created intellect can comprehend the loftiness of the divine essence. The same truth is conveyed when the Psalmist states that God "ascended upon the cherubim, and He flew; He flew upon the wings of the winds,"[19] meaning that even those sovereign spirits in whom are deposited the treasures of divine wisdom are lowly in this knowledge and they lose sight of Him who flies on the wings of the winds. This is symbolized in Isaias by the two seraphim who covered the face and feet of God with their wings, thus signifying the incomprehensibility of God, for they do not see Him from one extremity to the other nor comprehend all that He is.[20]

What has been said up to this point prepares the way for the negative theology of which Dionysius is the great master. In this life we have two types of knowledge concerning God: one affirmative and the other negative. Affirmative knowledge scans the perfections and beauty of the heavens, the earth, and all creatures and enables us to know how much more perfect and beautiful is the Creator who made them, for in Him all these things are contained in an infinitely eminent manner. We call this knowledge affirmative or positive because it affirms and confesses that all these perfections exist in God.

Negative knowledge is that which presupposes the lowliness and finiteness of all our concepts and hence denies all perfections of God as conceived according to our mode of understanding. In other words, it states that God is not great or beautiful or wise or powerful in the way in which our minds

---

18 Ps. 17:12.

19 Ps. 17:11.

20 Cf. Isa. 6: 1–2.

conceive these perfections, because He is all these things in a much different manner which created intellects cannot comprehend. In this way we praise and glorify Him the more because we confess that His grandeur is infinite, immense, incomprehensible, and ineffable.

To form some concept, however confused, of that sublime being, we must take as our starting point a principle stated by Dionysius, namely, that in every creature there are three elements: being, power, and activity. These elements are so interrelated that through knowing one we know the others. Thus, in knowing a thing's activity we are able to know the extent of its power, and knowing its power, we can know a thing's essence or being. These same three attributes—being, power, and activity—can be considered in relation to God, but in Him all three are one and the same. Through the grandeur of His works we know the greatness of the power from which they proceed and through the immensity of this power we know the excellency of His being. Yet from our viewpoint, the one is not exactly equivalent to the other because God's being is much more extensive than is manifested to us by His power. With the same ease with which He created this world, God could, by His word alone, create a thousand other worlds as great or greater than this one. Let us imagine, then, what must be the being of Him who possesses such admirable and amazing power. What comparison can there be with any created power, none of which is able to create even an ant?

Once having understood the infinite distance and difference between the power of the Creator and every created power, we shall also understand the difference between a created being and the being of the Creator. Consequently, we say that the divine substance is infinitely removed from every other substance. It possesses a different mode of being, power, grandeur, wisdom, beauty, and other infinite perfections that no created intellect can comprehend.

Therefore, in order to know something of God as He is in Himself, we must leave behind all the creatures of heaven and earth and soar far beyond all that can be sensed, imagined, or humanly understood in order to arrive at that substance which surpasses all sensation and understanding and infinitely surpasses all created things. It has neither figure nor quantity nor quality nor any other accident; neither does it admit of composition or change; therefore it is not subject to division or diminution. It neither perceives by means of any corporeal sense nor is it perceived by any corporeal sense. It is not a soul nor any potency of the soul; neither is it a body or any form of the body. It cannot cease to be nor ever be more than it is because it is already the plenitude of being. It is not reason or intellect (at least, not in any way that we can understand), though it is another type of reason and intelligence and life. It is not great nor good nor wise nor powerful nor beautiful in the way that we would imagine because God is all these things, but in a very different manner.

For that reason not only Dionysius but also Plato, who preceded him, used the following terms when treating of the divine perfections: supergood, superpowerful, super-beautiful, superwise, thus giving to understand the eminence and loftiness of the divine perfections as best our intellects are able to grasp them. For God is the one substance above all substance and the one life surpassing all life. He is the one light beyond all light, which our eyes cannot see; the one beauty surpassing all beauty, which our intellects cannot grasp; the one sweetness above all sweetness, which is beyond the reach of our senses, and not only ours, but also those of all the angels and cherubim and seraphim.

Consequently, as understood by created intellects, the perfections of the Creator are so lessened that it is truer to negate them of God than to affirm them. Ecclesiasticus teaches this in the following words: "Blessing the Lord, exalt Him as much as you can; for He is above all praise. When you exalt Him put forth all your strength, and be not weary; for you can never go far enough. Who shall see Him and declare Him? And who shall magnify Him as He is from the beginning? There are many things hidden from us that are greater than these: for we have seen but a few of His works."[21]

When the pious soul considers this and realizes that no title, no name, no attribute, no praise can fittingly express what is owing to God and that all the praise of men and of angels is infinitely insufficient to explain what He is, it then desists from using those names and understands that there is an immense abyss of incomprehensible grandeurs yet unknown. So the soul remains in a holy silence and terrible awe. Not understanding, it understands and not knowing, it knows, because it realizes that the Lord is incomprehensible and ineffable.

Thus the soul praises God more in this way than by all the names and excellencies it could attribute to Him. This was expressed by the royal prophet when he said: "Thy praise in Sion, O Lord, is silent,"[22] giving to understand that the most perfect praise of God is that holy silence and awe wherein the pious soul remains absorbed in great admiration for such incomprehensible majesty.

---

21 Ecclus. 43:32–36.

22 Ps. 64:1 (version according to St. Jerome).

This is the theology so often repeated by Dionysius. In one place he says that the obscurity and darkness in which God is said to dwell is a light inaccessible which, as the Apostle says, no man has ever seen nor can see. Yet, by the very fact that man neither sees nor knows, he is more intimately united with that Lord who surpasses all understanding. In another place Dionysius states that this holy ignorance is true knowledge of that Lord who is beyond every intellect and every substance. Whence, this eminent theologian concludes by saying that we venerate the great secret of the sovereign Deity, who transcends all intellects, by a sacred reverence of the soul and a chaste silence. By chaste silence he means that which rejects all curiosity of understanding and remains in admiration and awe of the divine Majesty who ties the tongue and binds the understanding, leaving it submerged in the abyss of His bottomless grandeur. Then does the soul sing with the prophet: "Thy praise in Sion, O Lord, is silent."

All that has been said up to this point enables us to understand to some degree the immensity and grandeur of our sovereign God and Lord before whom the seraphic spirits who assist at His throne are prostrate, adoring Him with holy awe.

For this reason we read in the Book of Job[23] that the pillars of heaven (which are those sovereign spirits who govern the world) tremble in the presence of such great majesty. Yet this fear is neither painful nor servile, but filial and reverential, because knowing the immensity of that grandeur, they understand that just as the greatness of God's goodness calls forth supreme love, so the height of His majesty awakens reverence and fear.

---

[23] Job 26:11.

CHAPTER 4 ✠
Devout Meditation on God's Incomprehensibility

O MOST HIGH and clement God, King of kings and Lord of lords! O eternal wisdom of the Father who, seated above the seraphim, dost penetrate the incomprehensible with the clarity of Thy vision so that there is nothing which is not open and naked before Thy eyes! O Lord, so wise, so powerful, so holy, and so great a lover of all that Thou hast made, especially of man whom Thou didst redeem and whom Thou hast made master of all things, turn Thy most clement eyes and open Thy divine ears to the supplications of this poor and lowly sinner.

O my God, my soul desires nothing more than to love Thee, for there is nothing else more worthy of Thee and nothing more necessary for me than this love. Thou hast created me to love Thee and hast placed my happiness in this love. Thou hast commanded me to love Thee and hast taught me that therein is merit, virtue, sweetness, liberty, peace, happiness, and all true good. This love is a brief compendium which contains all the good that there is on earth and a good portion of that which is to be expected in heaven.

Thou didst likewise teach me, my Savior, that one cannot love Thee without knowing Thee. We naturally love our parents and benefactors, our friends and those to whom we bear any similarity, and all goodness and beauty. But knowledge is always presupposed so that from it love will be born. But who will enable me to know Thee and understand how in Thee alone are all the reasons and causes of love? Who has more goodness than Thee? Who is more beautiful, more perfect? Who is more of a father, a friend, and a more generous benefactor? Finally, who save Thee is the spouse of our souls, the port of our desires, the center of our hearts, the last end of our life, and our final happiness?

What shall I do, my Lord, to attain this knowledge? How can I know Thee when I do not see Thee and how can I see Thee when my eyes are so weak and Thy light is inaccessible? Who will give me wings like a dove so that I may fly to Thee? What shall he do who cannot live without loving Thee and yet Thou art so difficult to know?

All our knowledge is born of the senses, for they are the gates through which the images of things enter our souls and through those images we know the things themselves. But Thou, O Lord, art infinite and canst not enter by such narrow gates nor can I form any image of so lofty a being. How, then, shall I know Thee? O lofty substance! O noble essence! O incomprehensible majesty! Who shall know Thee?

All creatures have finite and limited natures and powers, for Thou didst create them all in number, weight, and measure. Thou didst give them their limitations and assign the boundaries of their powers. Thus fire is active in heating and the sun in illuminating and their powers extend widely, but these created things have restrictions and limits beyond which they cannot pass. For that reason we can scan them from end to end and comprehend them because each is contained within the limits of its power. But Thou, O Lord, art infinite and there is no boundary that contains Thee. No intellect can attain to the ultimate reaches of Thy substance because it has none. Thou art above every genus and species and every created nature, and since Thou dost not acknowledge anything superior to Thyself, neither is Thy power restricted. A man can travel around the whole of this great world which Thou hast created because, although it is very large, its greatness is nevertheless finite and limited. But Thou, O bottomless ocean, who can traverse Thee? Thou art eternal in duration, infinite in power, and supreme in authority. Thy being neither began in time nor does it terminate in the world. Thou art before all time and Thou dost command the world and things beyond the world.

Since Thou art so great, who can know Thee? Who can understand the loftiness of Thy nature when he cannot even comprehend the lowliness of his own? The very soul by which we live, whose functions and powers each one of us experiences, has never been comprehended by any philosopher, for it is made according to Thy image and likeness. Since our ignorance is so great, how can we ever hope to arrive at a knowledge of Thy sovereign and incomprehensible nature?

But in spite of all this, my Savior, I cannot nor ought I desist in this endeavor, because I cannot nor do I wish to live without this knowledge which is the beginning of love. There is no other wisdom save in knowing Thee; there is no rest apart from Thee; there are no delights except those that are experienced in gazing upon Thy beauty.

And though there is little that we can know of Thee, yet it is of much greater worth to know a little about lofty things, however obscurely, than a great deal about lowly things, however clearly. If we cannot know Thee completely, we shall know all that we are able and we shall love all that we know. Our souls will be content with this, for the bird is satisfied with what it can hold in its beak, though it cannot exhaust all the water in the fountain.

Even more, Lord, Thy grace will aid where nature fails, and if we begin to love Thee a little, Thou wilt give us for this little love another which is much greater, with greater knowledge of Thy glory, as Thou hast promised through the Evangelist: "He that loveth Me, shall be loved of My Father: and I will love him, and will manifest Myself to him."[24]

Our holy faith and Sacred Scripture also aid us, Lord, wherein Thou didst deign to reveal to us the marvels of Thy grandeur so that this lofty knowledge would arouse in us a love and reverence for Thy holy name. We are further aided by the university of creatures which tell us to love Thee and teach us why we must love Thee. For Thy beauty shines forth in their perfections, and in their use and service is manifested Thy love for us. Thus, in every way they prompt us to love Thee, both because of what Thou art in Thyself and what Thou art to us. What is all the visible world, Lord, but a mirror that Thou dost hold before our eyes so that therein we may contemplate Thy beauty? For it is certain that just as in heaven Thou shalt be a mirror in which we shall see all creation, so in this life creation is a mirror in which we are able to see Thee.

The entire visible world is a great and marvelous book which Thou hast written and offered to the eyes of all the nations of the world, the Christians as well as the pagans, the wise as well as the ignorant, wherein they may study all things and know who Thou art. What are all the creatures of this world, so beautifully and perfectly made, but so many illuminated letters that declare the beauty and wisdom of their Author? And since Thy perfections, Lord, are infinite and cannot be fully represented by any one creature, it was necessary to create

---

[24] John 14:21.

many, so that fragmentarily each one could proclaim something of Thy perfections. Thus the beautiful creatures manifest Thy beauty; the strong, Thy strength; the great, Thy grandeur; the works of art, Thy wisdom; the brilliant, Thy clarity; the sweet, Thy suavity; the well-ordered and governed, Thy marvelous providence.

Thou art proclaimed by so many and such faithful testimonies! Who will not believe so many witnesses? Who will not delight in the harmonious music of so many and such sweet voices which with a wide variety of tones preach to us of the greatness of Thy glory? Surely, Lord, he is deaf who does not hear such voices and blind if he does not see such marvelous splendors. He who sees all this and does not praise Thee is likewise mute; and he who does not recognize the nobility of the Creator in so many testimonies is ignorant.

It seems to me, Lord, that all the fault is ours that in spite of so many testimonies of Thy greatness we know Thee not. What leaf of a tree, what flower in the field, what worm however small, if we closely examine its structure, will not display great marvels? But how is it that, surrounded as we are on all sides by such wonders, we do not know Thee? How is it that we do not praise and proclaim Thee? Why do we not have minds properly instructed to know the Master through His works, clear eyes to see His perfection in His handiwork, nor ears to hear what He says through them? The splendor of Thy creatures is pleasing to our eyes and their structure and beauty delight our understanding, but our minds are so myopic that they do not gaze higher to see the Maker of that beauty and the Giver of that delight.

We are like children before a book ornamented with gilt letters; they take pleasure in looking at it and playing with it, but they do not read what the letters say nor understand what they signify. We are even more childish than children, for Thou hast placed before us this marvelous book of the entire universe so that by means of the creatures in it, which are so many living letters, we might read and know the excellency of the Creator who made them and realize the great love that prompted Him to make such things for us. But we do no more than take delight in the sight of such beautiful things and do not realize what Thou dost wish to signify by them.

O perverters of the divine works! O children and more than children! O liars and destroyers of the plans and counsels of God! Alas for those, says St. Augustine, who delight in gazing upon God's symbols and forget to look for that which He wishes to teach them, which is the knowledge of the Creator.

Do not Thou permit in me, my dearest Savior, such ingratitude and blindness to Thy infinite goodness. Enlighten my eyes so that I may see Thee; open my mouth so that I may praise Thee; awaken my soul so that I may know Thee in all Thy creatures and love and adore Thee and give Thee thanks for all these benefits. I desire not to fall into the sin of ingratitude because it is written in the Book of Wisdom that on the last day the whole world will fight against the unwise.[25] And thus the very creatures that have been given us for our use will become our chastisement.

Thou, O Lord, who art the way, the truth, and the life, guide me by Thy providence, teach me by Thy truth, and give life to my soul with Thy love. It is a long journey to ascend by creatures to the Creator and a difficult occupation to know how to look at the works of so great a Master and through

---

[25] See Wisd. 5:21.

them to know the counsel and wisdom of the Maker. He who is not able to understand the art of a small sketch made by the hand of some great artist, how will he be able to understand the art of so great a painting as this universe? It happens to all, my Lord, when we set ourselves to consider the marvels of this work, as to a rustic woodsman who for the first time enters a large city or a royal house filled with gorgeous furnishings. He is intoxicated with the beauty of the edifice. He forgets by which door he entered and gets lost in the house. He knows not where to go or which way to turn, unless someone leads and directs him.

But, Lord, what are cities and royal palaces but so many swallow's nests when compared to this royal palace of the universe which Thou hast created? And if a creature of reason is lost in that small nest, what will he do in a palace of such variety and grandeur? How can one swim in this deep ocean of marvels if he would drown in a small stream? Therefore, guide me, Lord, on this journey. Take this rustic woodsman by the hand and with the finger of Thy spirit point out the marvels and mysteries of Thy works so that in them I may recognize and adore Thy wisdom, Thy omnipotence, Thy beauty, Thy goodness, Thy providence and may bless Thee and praise Thee and glorify Thee forever and ever. Amen.

CHAPTER 5 ✠
The Divine Perfection

THE PERFECTION OF God will be clearly seen if we consider the immense difference between uncreated being and all created things. All creatures had a beginning and can have an end and one creature is subordinated to another, but God neither recognizes any superior being nor does He depend on any other. All creatures are variable and subject to change, but God admits of no change or variation. All creatures are composites, each according to its nature, but in God there is no composition whatever, only perfect simplicity, for if He were composed of parts there would have to be some maker who preceded Him, and that is impossible. All creatures could be more than they are, have more than they have, and know more than they know; but God cannot be more than He is because He is the plenitude of being, He cannot have more than He has because He is the abyss of all treasures, He cannot know more than He knows because His knowledge is infinite and by reason of His eternity all things are present to Him.

For that reason Aristotle calls God pure act, which means ultimate and consummate perfection. He does not suffer any addition because He cannot be more than He is and it is impossible to imagine anything that He would be lacking. All creatures march under the banner of movement so that, poor and needy as they are, they can move to seek what they lack; but God has no need to move because He lacks nothing and is ever present in all places.

In all created things, since they have diverse parts, some parts are distinct from others; but because of God's utter simplicity, there can be no distinction of parts in Him. His existence is His essence; His essence is His power; His power is His love; His love is His will; His will is His intellect; His intellect is His understanding; His understanding is His being; His being is His wisdom; His wisdom is His goodness; His goodness is His justice; His justice is His mercy. Though these last two perfections have effects which differ (to pardon or to punish), in God they are one and the same thing, so that His mercy is His justice and His justice is His mercy. Thus, in God are found all works and perfections, even those which to us seem mutually exclusive. He is most hidden and most present; not circumscribed by place, yet present in all places; invisible, yet all-seeing; immutable, yet changing all things; ever working and ever at rest; filling all things, yet never contained; foreseeing all things, yet never distraught; immense, yet lacking quantity; good, yet lacking quality.

Finally, since all created things are restricted to singular essences, their power is likewise limited, as are the works which they perform. They reside in certain places; they have proper names by which they are signified, particular definitions by which they are declared, and specific categories according to which they are classified. But that sovereign substance, since He is infinite in being, is also infinite in power and all things else. Therefore He is not expressed by any definition, no genus can contain Him, no place can contain Him, no name can signify Him by a proper concept. Rather, as Dionysius says, since He has no name, He possesses all names because He contains in Himself all the perfections signified by those names.

Whence it follows that all creatures, being limited, are comprehensible, but the divine being, since He is infinite, is incomprehensible to every created intellect. As Aristotle says, what is infinite lacks limits, and therefore it cannot be comprehended by any intellect save that of an infinite being. What else is signified by the two seraphim whom Isaias saw on either side of the majesty of God, each angel having six wings, two of which covered the face of God and another two covered His feet, but that not even those sovereign spirits who have the highest place in heaven and are closest to God are able to comprehend all that God is, although they clearly see His essence and beauty?

Just as he who stands on the seashore truly sees the sea but is not able to fathom its depth or expanse, so also those sovereign spirits and all the elect who dwell in heaven truly see God but cannot comprehend the abyss of His greatness or the duration of His eternity. For this reason it is said that God is seated above the cherubim and in Him are hidden the treasures of wisdom. He is above them because they cannot attain to Him nor comprehend Him.

This is the darkness which God made His covert, as David says,[26] and which the Apostle states yet more clearly when he says that God dwells in light inaccessible.[27] But David calls it darkness because it prevents the sight and comprehension of God. For, as the philosopher has well said, just as there is nothing more clear and visible than the sun and yet nothing is less clearly seen because of its excessive brightness and the weakness of human vision, so there is nothing more intelligible

26 Psalms 17:12.

27 See I Tim. 6:16.

in itself than God and yet nothing less clearly understood in this life, and for the same reason.

Therefore, he who would in some manner know God, should realize that after arriving at the last of the perfections that he can understand, there yet remains an infinite road to traverse, for God is infinitely greater than man has been able to understand. And the more he realizes this incomprehensibility, the more will he have understood God. Hence, St. Gregory, in commenting on the words of Job: "Who doth great things and unsearchable and wonderful things without number,"[28] says that we speak with greater eloquence of the works of divine omnipotence when, remaining enraptured and astonished, we are silent about them. Thus, man fittingly praises God by being silent about that which cannot be expressed by words.

Dionysius counsels us to honor the secret of the sovereign deity with sacred veneration of the soul and an ineffable and chaste silence, realizing our inability to understand and confessing the incomprehensibility of that ineffable essence whose being is above all being, whose power is above all power, whose greatness is beyond all greatness, and whose substance infinitely surpasses every other substance, both visible and invisible.

Accordingly, St. Augustine says, "When I seek my God, I do not seek the form of a body, nor temporal beauty, nor the brilliancy of light, nor the melody of song, nor the perfume of flowers, nor honey nor manna delectable to the taste, nor anything else that can be touched or grasped by the hands. None of these things do I seek when I seek my God. Rather, I seek a light above all light, which the eye cannot see; a voice above

---

[28] Job 5:9.

all voices, which the ear cannot perceive; a perfume above all perfumes, which the nose cannot detect; a sweetness above all sweetness, which the tongue cannot taste; an embrace above all embraces, which the sense of touch cannot perceive. For this light shines where there is no space; this voice sounds where there is no air to carry it; this perfume is detected where there are no breezes to diffuse it; this savor delights where there is no palate to taste it; and this embrace is enjoyed in such wise that it is never ended."

If you wish to conjecture something of God's incomprehensible greatness, cast your eyes on the structure of this world which is His handiwork, so that by means of the effect you may know something of the nobility of the cause. Presupposing first of all what Dionysius says, that as a thing's being is, so is its power and as its power, so also its operation, see how beautiful, well-ordered, and great is this universe. See how densely populated it is with the variety of things that live on the earth and in the sea and air. This great and admirable machinery of the world, as St. Augustine says, was created by God in a moment, snatched from non-being to being. All this without any material from which it was made, no ministers to assist, no tools, no external models from which to copy, and no space of time in which to complete the work. By a simple expression of His will, this great universe and the army of many things came forth. Even more, consider that with the same facility with which He created this world, God could create, if He so wished, hundreds of thousands of worlds, greater, more beautiful, more densely populated than this and having done so, with the same ease He could annihilate them without any difficulty.

If, then, as Dionysius supposes, by the effects and works we can know the power of things and by the power we can know the being itself, what must be the power from which this work of creation proceeded? And if this power is so great and incomprehensible, what must be the being that manifests such power? Without doubt it surpasses all understanding.

There is even more to be considered: that works so great as these, those which are as well as those which can be, do not equal or exhaust the greatness of the divine power. Rather, they are infinitely lowly because the divine power could extend to infinitely more. Who, therefore, would not be amazed and astonished when he considers the greatness of such a being and power? For although it cannot be seen with the eyes, at least one can conjecture how great and incomprehensible it is.

Returning now to our subject, you can understand to some extent what must be the perfection of God, for it is necessary that it be such as is His being. Thus Ecclesiasticus speaks of God's mercy: "For according to His greatness, so also is His mercy with Him."[29] And equally great are His goodness, His benignity, His majesty, His clemency, His wisdom, His sweetness, His nobility, His beauty, His omnipotence, and His justice.

Thus God is infinitely good, infinitely tender, infinitely loving and lovable, infinitely worthy of being obeyed, feared, and adored. And if the human heart were capable of infinite love and fear, infinite obedience and reverence, then according to the law of justice, they would be owing to the dignity and excellency of God. For if the greater the excellence and nobility of a person, the greater the reverence due, then it necessarily

[29] Ecclus. 2:23.

follows that since God's excellence is infinite, there is owing to Him an infinite reverence. Whence it also follows that whatever falls short of an infinite measure in our love and reverence for God, also falls short of that which is due the dignity of His grandeur.

Chapter 6 ✠
The Divine Beauty

Not only goodness but also true beauty greatly moves the heart to love. For this reason some learned men have said that the object of our will is the beautiful, because they saw with what force it attracts all wills to itself. But if created beauty is so lovable, how lovable must Thou be, O Lord, who art an ocean of infinite beauty and the fountain from which all other beauty proceeds? The beauty of creatures, Lord, is particular and limited but Thine is universal and infinite, for in Thee alone are contained the beauties of all that Thou hast created.

Just as the sun is more clear, more resplendent, and more beautiful than all the stars in the heaven together and of itself gives more light than all the others, so also Thou alone art infinitely more beautiful than all Thy creatures and more suited to gladden and enrapture their hearts. The sun and the moon are astonished at Thy beauty and the angels are never satiated with it because they see therein all the perfections and beauties of creatures more perfectly than in the creatures themselves.

What is all the beauty of this visible world when compared with that of the invisible world? What is all the beauty of bodies when compared with that of the angelic spirits? It is like a star compared to the sun. St. John tells us that in his great revelation he saw an angel of such clarity and beauty that he would have adored him had not the angel himself prevented it.[30]

But if the beauty that surpasses all visible beauty is so great, what must that be which contains in itself all the beauty of invisible things? We shall be able to understand it to some extent if we consider the multitude of angels and the grades and order of their perfections. The angels are so numerous that they surpass the multitude of all corporeal species and although they are not infinite, they are innumerable, and no one can count them save Him who numbers the stars and calls each by name.[31] Yet in spite of the fact that they are so numerous, the angels are so perfectly ordered that the second has all the perfections of the first and more in addition by which he differs from the first, just as in the grades and dignities of the Church the superior dignity has all the perfection of the inferior and a grade more by which it differs from the lower. This same order which is evident in the hierarchy of the Church militant is to be found in the angelic hierarchy of which the first choir is that of the angels, the second, that of the archangels, and thus through all the nine choirs to the last, which is that of the seraphim, who are closest to God. The seraphim possess all the perfections and powers of all the other angels, just as man possesses all the powers and essential perfections of all the other animals which are inferior to him.

---

30 See Apoc. 19:10.

31 See Ps. 146:4.

But now, Lord, I wish to ascend by the ladder of creatures and see something of the inestimable beauty which is Thine. In the first place, it is clear that Thou dost possess the beauty of all visible creatures as well as that of all invisible creatures. In addition to this, Thou dost possess other infinite beauties that are not communicated to any creature. The sea is great not only because of the waters of all the rivers that empty into it, but also because of the water which it has of itself and which is greater beyond compare. So also Thou, O Lord, art an ocean of infinite beauty, for not only dost Thou possess all the perfections and beauties of all created things, but Thou hast other infinite beauties which are proper to Thee alone and not communicated to others, though in Thee there are not many beauties, but one most simple and infinite beauty.

Since this is so, how can we ever comprehend Thy beauty? It is a mirror of all things and an abyss of all graces, for Thou dost incorporate into Thyself all other beauties as well as those that are proper to Thee. It is said that a certain painting of Queen Helen was exceedingly beautiful because the painter used as models six maidens of perfect proportions, taking from each one what seemed to him most beautiful. But if the finished picture was so beautiful because it was a composite of the perfections of all six of the maidens, what must be the beauty of Him who contains in Himself all the perfections of all creatures and also His own? Neither the language of men nor of angels can expound this.

O brightness of eternal light! O stainless mirror of God's majesty! O paradise of all delights! What will it be, my God, to see Thee face to face? What will it be to see that light with Thy light? O blessed day when I shall see Thee, when Thou shalt reveal Thy face to me and manifest to me all Thy beauty!

O day well worth the price of all the torments and labors of the world!

So great is Thy beauty that the mere sight of it is sufficient to gladden the sovereign spirits of heaven and completely fill their capacity for love. Perpetually inflamed by Thy infinite beauty, they love Thee with all their strength and never tire of this love. For Thy infinite beauty, which is ever present to them, draws to itself all their powers so that they cannot cease to be ever actually loving Thee. And this is what St. John signifies when he says that the four holy creatures that were before the throne of God "rested not day and night, saying: Holy, holy, holy, Lord God almighty, who was, and who is, and who is to come."[32]

The saints also, while yet on earth, experienced something of the same. We read of the virgin, St. Clara, that after receiving a visitation from God after the feast of the Epiphany, her soul remained so absorbed in God and so enraptured by the divine sweetness which she had tasted that for many days she could not be attentive to anything that was said to her. All her senses were alienated and translated to God.

What is more, the same divine beauty that gladdens the choirs of angels and enraptures the saints also delights the Lord Himself, who has no other happiness than to see and enjoy His own beauty. It is clear, says Aristotle, that the supreme good is free from human occupations such as sleeping, eating, drinking and the like. Accordingly, there remains no other activity for Him save to contemplate. But what does He contemplate? Does He, perhaps, find His happiness in the contemplation of something outside Himself? Evidently not,

---

[32] Apoc. 4:8.

for if such were the case, that thing would be better and more noble than Himself, for the mere sight of it would suffice to make Him happy. Then that thing would be God and not He Himself. It is thus proved that if God's activity is to contemplate, and if in contemplating He is happy, then He Himself is the object of His own contemplation.

What, then, must be that beauty, the mere sight of which suffices to make God happy and fills His infinite capacity for happiness? What must be that beauty on which the Lord from all eternity is ever gazing and will continue to gaze upon for all eternity without ever tiring of it? Rather, He will continue to receive from it an incomprehensible joy to which all created joy is as nothing in comparison.

Let us now make the following application. It is evident that all the beauties of this world and of the next, when compared with God's infinite beauty, are like a drop of water compared to the ocean or a spark compared to the sun. Indeed, they are much less than that, because these things are all created and finite and can be compared to one another. But what proportion can exist between two extremes of which one is finite and the other infinite?

From this small drop of created beauty let us take one in particular: that of any human creature. We see the extremes to which some men go when they think that they are in love with another person. They neither eat nor drink nor sleep for thinking of the one they love, and sometimes they even lose their health and reason and life itself. Little less than this is what happened to Amnon, the son of David, for love of Thamar.[33]

[33] See II Kings 13:2.

But if these persons suffer so much for such a little spark and shadow of beauty, what would they do if they were offered a beauty wherein are contained all the beauties of the visible and invisible world, together with the supreme beauty of God? Is there any kind of calculation that could measure it? Is there any intellect that could comprehend it? Is there any patience that would suffer that such extremes be endured for the vain shadow of beauty and yet so little be done for that which is true and infinite beauty? If men endure so much for a little dust and ashes and for a flower that blooms today and withers tomorrow, why do we not run after Thee, O Lord? Why do we not love Thee with all our strength? Why do we not swoon away for this divine love as did the spouse in the Canticles?[34] How can we eat or drink or sleep for thinking of Thee?

Therefore, let me love Thee with all my soul, O infinite Beauty. Open my eyes that they may see Thy beauty and close them to all things else. Let all creatures, Lord, be a mirror in which I contemplate Thee, an image in which I see Thee, a ladder by which I rise to Thee, and a book wherein I read of Thy grandeurs.

Open my eyes, O Lord, and anoint them with the balm of Thy grace so that I may see some small spark of Thy splendor. Arouse in my heart so great a thirst for Thee that I may say with the Psalmist: "As the hart panteth after the fountains of water; so my soul panteth after Thee, O God. My soul hath thirsted after the strong living God; when shall I come and appear before the face of God?"[35]

---

[34] Cant. 2:5.

[35] Ps. 41:2.

Come, then, all ye lovers of God. Come to this fountain and drink of this divine liquid. Be insistent in this demand and importune with the Psalmist, saying: "My heart hath said to Thee: My face hath sought Thee; Thy face, O Lord, will I still seek. Turn not away Thy face from me; decline not in Thy wrath from Thy servant. Be Thou my helper, forsake me not; do not Thou despise me, O God, my Savior."[36]

Chapter 7 ✠
The Divine Goodness and Mercy

When, Lord, by Thy infinite goodness Thou shalt deign to carry us to Thy heavenly mansion where we shall clearly see the beauty of Thy glory, we shall no longer need the mirror of creatures but shall see Thee as Thou art in Thyself and shall know Thy infinite goodness. But now, while we travel through this vale of tears, exiled from Thy presence and Thy sweet company, we cannot know Thy goodness save through Thy works, which give testimony of the fountain of goodness from which they proceed.

But it is most fitting, Lord, that even now we should know as much as possible about Thy goodness, because goodness is the principal motive of love. Thou who hast created all things didst infuse into each one its laws and nature and Thou hast created our will so that its natural inclination should be to love

[36] Ps. 26:8 ff.

the good. Therefore, as color is the object of sight, and sound is the object of hearing, so the object of our will is goodness. So intimate a union exists between goodness and the will that this faculty never extends the arms of its affection to anything else. And if sometimes, by embracing evil, it commits adultery against goodness, it is because it has been deceived by some false and apparent good.

But if the object of the will is goodness and if a thing possessing more goodness is deserving of greater love, how great should be my love for Thee, who art infinitely good and whose very nature is goodness! Thy goodness, Lord, is as vast as Thy being and since Thy being is infinite, so also is Thy goodness. True it is that we have never seen the greatness of Thy goodness as it is in itself, and yet we find some manifestation of it in Thy works, both those of nature and those of grace as well as those of glory.

For what are the works of creation and divine government, of man's redemption, justification and glorification, but testimonies of Thy goodness? What is it to have created all things and to have bestowed Thy perfections on them so generously, each according to its measure, but proof of Thy divine liberality? What is the care by which Thou dost provide each thing with all that is necessary for its maintenance, defense, and well-being, but further proof of Thy goodness? Of the countless number of fish in the sea and birds in the air and animals on the earth, there is none so small and despicable that Thou art unmindful of it. Even the tiniest bird does not fall into the snare without Thy permission.

The greatness of Thy goodness shines forth most sweetly in the happiness and contentment which Thou dost give to even the lowliest creatures of the earth. I see the lambs skip and jump with remarkable lightness and joy in the retirement of their pastures. I see with what gaiety puppies or kittens play and scurry among themselves, and the pleasure and joy which this gives them. I hear the nightingales and other birds sing joyfully, filling the air with their songs as proof of their contentment. From all this I understand what must be the tenderness of Thy heart, for Thou, Lord, art He who provides them with such happiness. Not content with furnishing sustenance to all Thy creatures, Thou dost also fill them with all the happiness and joy they are capable of receiving. This is signified by the Psalmist when he says: "The eyes of all hope in Thee, O Lord, and Thou givest them meat in due season. Thou openest Thy hand, and fillest with blessing every living creature."[37]

What greater proof of goodness than to see that a Lord of such great majesty, without any self-interest but only out of goodness and liberality, extends His providence even to the little birds and fishes and, not content with this, provides them with their recreations and play by creating in them inclinations for such joys? Just as Thou, O Lord, dost possess not only being but perfect happiness, so Thou desirest that all Thy creatures, however lowly, should participate in Thee according to their own manner and thus enjoy both the one and the other, having not only being but happiness.

Who is not amazed at this marvel? Who does not see here the infinite tenderness and sweetness of the divine heart? For what man would be concerned as to whether or not the ant, the fly, or the mosquito are contented, whether they are happy or sad? Who, then, will not marvel that the Lord of such majesty, in comparison with whom the whole world is little more than

---

[37] Ps. 144:15.

an ant, should take such particular care, not only of the life of these little animals, but also of their recreation and pleasures?

O marvelous goodness! O inestimable sweetness! O my God, what great things must be stored in Thy heavenly mansion for Thy faithful friends if Thou art so concerned about the happiness of these little creatures! How can I fear that Thy providence and mercy will be lacking to men redeemed by Thy precious Blood if they are not lacking to the animals of the fields?

And if all this proclaims to us the greatness of God's goodness, which is to show mercy without expecting any return, how much more manifest is it when we see that He continues to bestow benefits even when He has been offended? Many nations in the world pay no heed to the glory and obedience that they owe Thee, Lord, but dishonor and blaspheme Thy holy name. What is even worse, some, instead of adoring Thee as the Creator, worship sticks and stones. Yet in spite of all this, Thou dost bless these regions with abundant fruits of the earth, animals in the fields, fish in the sea, rich mines of gold and silver and precious stones, and a host of other things that serve for the provision and adornment of those who continually offend Thee. Such is the goodness and magnificence which Thou dost declare to us through the Evangelist, saying that Thy Father makes the sun rise upon the good and the bad and rains upon the just and the unjust.[38] Who will not recognize the richness and magnificence of Thy heart when Thou art so benign even to the ungrateful and the sinners? Who will not love Thee, Lord, with all his powers? Who will not put all his hope in Thee? Who will not forget himself for Thee? Who will not run after Thee in the odor of these ointments?

---

[38] Matt. 4:45.

And if, Lord, the works of nature so greatly manifest Thy goodness, how much more the works of grace? If Thy care for brute animals preaches to us of Thy goodness, how much more the care which Thou hast for men, especially for those who are poor and lowly. For true greatness lies in being a protector to the little ones; true power, in being a defense for those who cannot protect themselves; perfect goodness, in doing good for others without any self-interest or hope of a return.

Who could ever explain the care that Thou hast and dost command us also to have for the poor, the afflicted, the needy, and all unfortunate persons? How frequently in the Old Law and in the Gospel Thou dost repeat this command! What great rewards for him who does this and what terrible punishments for him who is unmindful of it!

How could the care of the poor and the needy and the works of mercy be more highly recommended than to make them the basis on which to judge on the last day whether or not one is deserving of the kingdom of heaven?[39] With what words could these things be more highly extolled than when Thou sayest, Lord, that one who does these things to the least of Thy little ones, has done it to Thee? If words and work are indications and testimonies of the heart, what must be the heart from which such words and works have proceeded? And as if all this were little, Thou Thyself, O Lord, whose title is King of kings and Lord of lords, dost add to these titles another no less honorable, which is that of Father of orphans and Judge of widows.[40]

O great goodness! O true grandeur! O bowels of infinite pity! How much more lovable and admirable does this title

39 Matt 25:34.

40 Ps. 67:9.

make Thee than the others. The others declare the greatness of Thy majesty, but this one shows forth the immensity of Thy goodness, and for that reason Thou dost treasure it more than all other titles, however lofty they may be. For it especially pertains to Thy goodness to favor the little ones, to protect the oppressed, to provide for the orphans, to look after strangers and travelers, and to see that justice is done them, ever casting Thy eyes, not where Thou canst expect a return, which Thou dost not seek, but where Thou canst bestow more goodness.

But the greatness of Thy goodness is manifested even more by Thy mercy toward sinners, whom Thou dost suffer with such meekness and await with such patience. They have offended Thee, but Thou callest them to forgiveness; they have injured Thee, but Thou invitest them to peace and dost offer them satisfaction. How easily Thou dost let them find Thee; how prompt Thou art in hearing them; how tenderly Thou dost receive them; and with what largess Thou dost pardon them. So great is Thy goodness and mercy that, as one of Thy saints has said, Thou dost not reject or despise anyone, save him who in his folly abhors Thee. And even then, although angered, Thou dost not castigate him immediately, for Thou art patient and merciful.

My God and my salvation, wretch that I am, I have angered Thee and done evil before Thee. I have provoked Thy wrath and merited Thy fury. I have sinned, but Thou didst bear with me patiently; I have offended Thee, but Thou didst see me to penitence. When I repented, Thou didst pardon me; when I returned to Thee, Thou didst receive me; and if I delayed in returning, Thou didst wait for me. Thou dost direct the erring soul, call back the rebellious soul, await the slothful soul, and embrace him when he returns. Thou dost teach the ignorant, console the sorrowful, raise up the fallen and sustain him after his rising. Thou dost give Thyself to him who asks for Thee, let Thyself be found by him who seeks for Thee, and open the door to him who knocks.

But if, Lord, Thy treatment of sinners so greatly manifests Thy goodness, how much more is this true of Thy treatment of just souls, who are Thy sons and friends and the heirs of Thy kingdom and in whom the image of Thy goodness shines forth in a special manner? This is one of the arguments that most clearly proves the greatness of Thy goodness. Since it is characteristic of the good soul to love all other good souls and to despise evil as such, it necessarily follows that the better one is, the more he will love goodness and abhor evil. And since Thou, O Lord, art substantially and infinitely good and, indeed, art goodness itself, what must we conclude save that Thou hast an infinite love for the good soul and an infinite hatred for the evil soul so far as it is evil?

Love is the first and greatest of all blessings and the root and source of all others. Thy love for those who are truly good and in whom the image of Thy goodness and sanctity shines forth is so great that the magnitude of the favors and blessings which Thou dost bestow on them is inexplicable. Without a doubt it surpasses anything that could be imagined. It will be understood by one who has experienced it but neither he nor anyone else could ever put it into words. For who could ever explain Thy providence and paternal solicitude for Thy friends: how Thou dost hear their prayers, how Thou dost console them in their tribulations, how Thou dost sanctify and purify their lives, how Thou dost visit them and gladden them in the house of Thy prayer, and how Thou dost honor them both in life and in death?

The favors and blessings that Thou dost bestow on pure souls greatly move other hearts to love and serve Thee, for just as men are prompted to serve a great prince if they know that he is considerate, liberal, and faithful to all his servants, so those who read the lives of the saints or deal with spiritual and devout persons and see the many favors and blessings that the Lord bestows on them, are confused at seeing that they themselves are so far from such a state. As a result, they are greatly moved with a desire to love and serve a Lord from whom they will receive the same blessings if they seek Him wholeheartedly, for He is not an accepter of persons nor does He deny Himself to those who seek Him. He who wishes to know about the providence and care that God has over His own should read the psalms, the prophets and the sacred historical books. Thus, Ecclesiasticus says of divine providence: "The eyes of the Lord are upon them that fear Him; He is their powerful protector and strong stay, a defense from the heat and a cover from the sun at noon; a preservation from stumbling and a help from falling. He raiseth up the soul, and enlighteneth the eyes, and giveth health and life and blessing."[41]

What more could be said? What else is there that the human heart could expect or desire? Who will not consider as rich and blessed those who are included in this universal and great blessing? And who would not desire to be of this number and thus be entitled to a share in such a treasure? For God's providence is such that He Himself declared and promised through Zacharias: "He that toucheth you, toucheth the apple of My eye."[42] Could there be anything else to promise? It

41 Ecclus. 34:19–20.

42 Zach. 2:8.

is as if God had said: "He that touches you, touches Me," and it would seem that nothing more could be added to this. But God did find something to add when He said: "He touches the apple of My eye."

Nor are the words of the Psalmist less tender: "For He hath given His angels charge over thee, to keep thee in all thy ways. In their hands they shall bear thee up, lest thou dash thy foot against a stone."[43] In another place David says: "The Lord keepeth all their bones, not one of them shall be broken";[44] and we read in the Gospel: "Are not two sparrows sold for a farthing? And not one of them shall fall on the ground without your Father. But the very hairs of your head are all numbered. Fear not, therefore; better are you than many sparrows."[45] No providence more special or minute could be imagined and yet this is what is promised to us in Sacred Scripture. Who would not wish to die for love of a Lord who takes such care of His friends? Who will not strive to be one of them?

Although the historical books of Scripture are filled with examples that clearly manifest the fulfillment of these promises, one of the most remarkable of all is that of Tobias, for whose consolation and assistance the Lord sent an angel from heaven in the guise of a fellow-traveler to accompany him on a long journey. The angel remained with Tobias during the entire journey and they passed from inn to inn and from city to city, eating and drinking together and conversing amicably as one traveler to another. And after the marriage of Tobias the young man took two camels of the father-in-law, Raguel, and went to Rages to collect the money that Gabelus owed to

---

43 Ps. 90:11–12.

44 Ps. 33:21.

45 Matt. 10:29–31.

Tobias. Then the wealthy Tobias was led back to the house of his father, who was cured of his blindness when Tobias annointed his eyes with the gall of a fish. Tobias also was cured of his holy blindness which prevented him from knowing Raphael as an angel and he was made joyful and given peace for the rest of his days.

Who does not see here the great love that God has for His servants and the paternal care that He exercises over them? And who will be so blind and such an enemy to himself that he will not strive to love this Lord with all his heart and to live in such a manner that he will merit to be under the wings and protection of such providence?

But if Thy goodness and providence, Lord, cannot be fittingly expounded, who will ever be able to explain that which Thou dost reserve for those who are maltreated and abused because of their service to Thee? The service that they render Thee in such circumstances is greater and their need more urgent, and since it is proper to the true and faithful friend to give assistance in the time of need, it is here that Thou dost bestow the greatest favors and helps.

The Apostle teaches this very clearly when, after having passed through great tribulations, he testifies: "Blessed be the God and Father of our Lord Jesus Christ, the Father of mercies and the God of all comfort, who comforteth us in all our tribulation, that we also may be able to comfort them who are in all distress, by the exhortation wherewith we also are exhorted by God. For as the sufferings of Christ abound in us, so also by Christ doth our comfort abound."[46]

---

[46] See II Cor. 1:3–5.

In the same tone David says: "According to the multitude of my sorrows in my heart, Thy comforts have given joy to my soul."[47] And in another place: "But the salvation of the just is from the Lord, and He is their protector in the time of trouble. And the Lord will help them and deliver them; and He will rescue them from the wicked, and save them, because they have hoped in Him."[48]

He who has read the accounts in the historical books of the Bible and would desire to know yet more of this divine providence should read about the ordeals of the martyrs. There he will see the grandeur and marvel of God's providence. There he will witness the goodness, the tenderness, and the fidelity of the Lord. He will see that God not only strengthened those who suffered with incredible fortitude and constancy, but He also assisted them by evident miracles. Sometimes He quenched the flames of fire and tamed lions and other ferocious beasts; at other times He illumined the martyrs' prisons, healed their wounds, restored amputated or lacerated limbs, covered their naked bodies, gave them power to work miracles, sent angels to staunch the blood that flowed from their wounds. What is more marvelous still, through such wonders He sometimes converted the very persecutors who were tormenting them.

Thus we read that after Josias had accused the apostle James before King Herod, he led the prisoner off to behead him. Along the way to execution the apostle performed a miracle, as a result of which Josias was converted to the true faith and was so constant in it that he suffered death together with the

---

[47] Ps. 93:19.

[48] 36:39.

apostle. Here is splendidly manifested the goodness and mercy of our Savior who infused faith and the spirit of martyrdom in one who had merited great punishment.

And who will read of the sufferings and martyrdom of the thirteen-year-old St. Agnes and of the eighteen-year-old St. Catherine of Alexandria, and not be amazed at the marvels that the Lord worked through these virgins during the struggle of their martyrdom? He sent a dove bearing food to St. Catherine while she was in prison and later her Lord and Spouse visited her to encourage her in her sufferings. He shattered the wheel of torture on which she had been placed and with a voice from heaven He promised special favors to those who would honor His passion. When St. Catherine was finally beheaded, He caused milk to flow instead of blood, thus manifesting the whiteness of her virginal purity, and He commanded the angels to carry her body to Mount Sinai for burial. Later, a healing oil trickled from her sepulcher.

But what is even more remarkable, He gave St. Catherine such wisdom and eloquence during her lifetime that the tyrant who caused her martyrdom was later converted, as were Porphyrius, the captain of the army, and two hundred soldiers. Moreover, her words and wisdom were so convincing that she induced a group of fifty select philosophers to reject their pagan beliefs and embrace the faith of Christ. Subsequently they died for the faith by being cast into a great furnace. Countless examples similar to these can be found in the lives of the other martyrs.

Thus the marvels of grace that occurred in the lives of the saints manifest the divine goodness. There we see fulfilled and verified whatever we have said thus far about God's providence over His friends and the manner in which He treats them. Let us single out the lives of two women, one a sinner and the other innocent, one from ancient times and the other more recent: St. Mary Magdalen and St. Catherine of Siena.

What could be more remarkable than the favors and benefits that the Lord bestowed on the holy sinner of the Gospel after His resurrection? What greater marvel than that a woman should remain all alone in the mountains for thirty years, without eating or drinking during all this time; and that seven times a day she should be raised into the air by invisible hands to hear angelic canticles and melodies and then be restored again to her proper place? Who will not be moved with wonderment and admiration at such extraordinary events?

Many are the arguments in proof of the divine goodness and the greatest of all is that God became man for love of men and suffered death for them. Some, it is true, are moved more by one argument and others by another, according to their dispositions and devotion, but I confess that one of the arguments that has most moved me and has given me a great knowledge and appreciation of God's goodness and His love for pure souls is to see the wonders He worked in St. Catherine of Siena. Almost daily He showered favors and blessings upon her. Once He took the heart from her body and kept it for three days and then replaced it; at another time He espoused Himself with her in the presence of His blessed Mother and other saints. On one occasion when Catherine had drunk a most bitter potion while tending a sick woman, He appeared to her and let her drink a celestial fluid from the wound in His sacred side. Again, when she had divested herself of her tunic to give to a poor person, the Lord Himself gave her another one in which she never suffered from the heat in summer or the cold in winter. At other times He let her experience part of the sorrows and torments that He Himself had suffered in His sacred body and once He Himself recited the canonical hours with her.

And what can I say of her great revelations and the remarkable efficacy of her prayers; of the obstinate sinners whom she converted; of the length of time she passed without any other food save that of the Blessed Sacrament, as Pope Pius II testifies in the bull of her canonization? What of the ecstasies and raptures she experienced whenever she communicated, and to such an extent that once when a person pierced the sole of her foot with a needle she showed no more reaction than if she had been a marble statue? Who shall recount the numerous miracles performed during the three days that her corpse was on public view?

Whoever has eyes to see the wonders of all these marvels will surely understand how incomprehensible must be the love that our Lord has for pure souls, for thus He treats them and honors them, embraces and enriches them with gifts, purifies and sanctifies them, exalts them above the heavens, hears their prayers, converses with them intimately and imparts to them His secrets. Whoever considers these things will surely marvel at seeing the sovereign Majesty deal so familiarly with anything as lowly as man. Yet, on the other hand, he will cease to marvel when he realizes that one could expect no less from infinite and incomprehensible goodness, for as God is in Himself, so also must be the love that He has for good souls.

In the case of human love, when we see a person go to great extremes for another, we are wont to say that he is bewitched, that he has lost his reason, or some such thing, in order to describe to some extent the greatness of his passion. But since none of these things apply to infinite goodness and purity, we have no words to express the greatness of God's love and the marvelous favors and gifts that He bestows on His faithful friends. We content ourselves by saying that no less can be believed of infinite goodness save that He loves all good souls with an infinite love and that He treats them in conformity with such a love.

But if these marvels of grace so manifest Thy goodness to us, Lord, what must be said of the goods of glory? If Thou dost treat Thy friends thus in this vale of tears, how shalt Thou deal with them in paradise? If Thou dost delight and gladden them along the way, what joy wilt Thou give to them in the fatherland? If Thou dost console them during the time of captivity, what must be their consolation in that place of liberty? If they are so rewarded here when they do penance, what recompense will be theirs when they reap the fruits of their mortification? If they sleep and repose on Thy breast when they are armed for battle, what will it be like when they have put aside their arms and enjoy the triumphs of victory?

There Thou shalt show them Thy divine face; Thou shalt call each one by name; Thou shalt seat them at Thy table and give them to eat from Thy plate; Thou shalt become one thing with them and give them a share in all Thy goods, that is to say, of Thy glory, Thy beauty, Thy divinity, Thy eternity, Thy happiness. Thou shalt then be their all in all.

And when these souls find themselves forever secure and confirmed in grace, they shall open their mouths in Thy praise, saying with the Psalmist: "Praise the Lord, O Jerusalem; praise thy God, O Sion. Because He hath strengthened the bolts of thy gates, He hath blessed thy children within thee."[49] Then the greatness of Thy goodness will be clearly manifest and the celestial singers will chant without ceasing: Holy, holy, holy is the Lord God of hosts.

But if Thy goodness, Lord, is greatly manifested to us by the loving and friendly intimacy which Thou dost manifest to good souls in this life and the glory with which Thou dost crown them in the next, it is no less manifested by Thy abhorrence for wicked souls and the severity of the punishment that Thou hast prepared for them in eternity. Indeed, Thy inestimable love for the good springs from the same principle as does Thy abhorrence for the wicked, for it equally pertains to Thy infinite goodness to love and reward the good and to abhor and castigate the wicked. Therefore the great and terrible punishments which Thy prophets have predicted for the wicked, although they move our hearts to fear, also move us to love, for they give testimony not only of Thy justice, but also of Thy goodness. Thy very wrath and indignation against wickedness makes us see clearly how great is Thy goodness and how much Thou art to be loved.

But what shall I say? Not only Thy hatred of evil bespeaks Thy goodness but even the eternal punishment of hell which Thou hast prepared for the wicked. According to human judgment, the most terrifying thing about hell is that a temporal fault is punished with eternal pain and suffering. The truth of the matter is, however, that even then the fault is not sufficiently punished. But Thou, Lord, art an abyss of mercy and as Thou art liberal in rewarding, so also art Thou clement in

[49] Ps. 147:1, 2.

punishing, for Thy reward is greater than our merits and Thy punishments are less than our sins deserve.

But whence comes it that a punishment so terrible and so protracted as that of hell can be considered not only just but even too short and hardly enough for a temporal fault? The reason is that Thy goodness is so great that a sin committed against it is not fittingly punished even by eternal torment. So great is Thy goodness, Lord, that no punishment could ever suffice to atone for sins committed against Thee.

From all that has been said it would seem that nothing further can be added by way of a proof and testimony of God's goodness. Yet all this is as nothing when compared to the manifestation of divine goodness which is given to us in the incarnation of the Son of God. All other things that Thou hast communicated to us, Lord, are goods distinct from Thyself: the goods of nature and grace and glory. But within Thee is Thy being, which is Thine alone and cannot be communicated without making a god of him to whom it is communicated. For just as he who has the being of man is man, so He who has the being of God is a god.

But what can man say of all this, my God? Will he not be amazed and dumbfounded at this demonstration of Thy goodness? What more could possibly be done? What remains for Thee to bestow on man? What else could better manifest the nature of Thy infinite goodness than this supreme communication?

O Thou who art supremely good and worthy of being loved with infinite love! If I possessed an infinite number of hearts, I would have to love Thee with all of them; if I had an infinite number of tongues, I would have to sound Thy praise with all of them; and if I had an infinite number of lives, I would have to spend all of them in Thy service. Even if there were an infinite number of worlds, I would have to reject them all for Thy love. But since all this is impossible to me, Lord, give me the grace to love Thee as much as I can, so that by the strength of this love I may disdain every earthly love.

Thine is the supreme and immutable good which is not contained by place, is not changed by novelties, does not pass away with time, and has no need of help from anyone. It is sufficient unto itself; of itself it can do all things and in itself it finds all its delight. Thine is that supreme goodness which is not reached by the senses because it is spiritual and eternal, but it is known with the intellect and enjoyed with the will and experienced with the heart. It is sought by devotion, found by hope, embraced by charity, and will be possessed forever in glory.

CHAPTER 8 ✠
God's Love for Us

IF THE BENEFITS we have received from God prompt us to love our divine benefactor, how much more will our love be increased if we consider the greatness of His love for us, which is the cause of all His gifts to us? The greatness of this divine love is proved first of all by the many benefits we have previously enumerated, for since it is characteristic of love to wish well and to do good, it follows that He who has bestowed so many gifts must greatly love those for whom He has done so much. Therefore, in treating of the divine benefits and the goodness of God we have already demonstrated God's love for men, for goodness is the source from which love is born. At this point, however, we wish to treat in particular of three great works that prove God's love for us: creation, glorification, and redemption.

Beginning with creation, this act demonstrates in many ways the love that is contained in the divine heart. First, since man is the work of God's hands and is fashioned in His image and likeness and is, indeed, the noblest of all creatures in this visible world, how could God help but love what He has crowned with such dignity and excellence? This is one of the principal reasons which the prophet Isaias alleged in asking mercy of the Lord: "O Lord, Thou art our Father, and we are clay; and Thou art our Maker, and we are all the works of Thy hands."[50]

For this reason also David called upon God, saying: "Turn again, O God of hosts, look down from heaven, and see, and visit this vineyard; and perfect the same which Thy right hand hath planted: and upon the son of man whom Thou hast confirmed for Thyself."[51] And Job was amazed that God should permit the devil to torment so cruelly the work of His hands: "Thy hands have made me, and fashioned me wholly round about, and dost Thou thus cast me down headlong on a sudden? Remember, I beseech Thee, that Thou hast made me as the clay, and Thou wilt bring me into dust again. . . . Thou hast clothed me with skin and flesh; Thou hast put me together with bones and sinews; Thou hast granted me life and mercy, and Thy visitation hath preserved my spirit. Although

---

50 Is. 64:8.

51 Ps. 79:15–16.

Thou conceal these things in Thy heart, yet I know that Thou rememberest all things. If I have sinned and Thou hast spared me for an hour, why dost Thou not suffer me to be clean from my iniquity? And if I be wicked, woe unto me; and if just, I shall not lift up my head, being filled with affliction and misery."[52] Job says all these things on the supposition that God loves that which is the work of His hands.

But there is yet another consideration, filled with sweetness and tenderness: the fact that God so loved and esteemed man that He created this great and marvelous world for him. This truth is immediately evident, for it is clear that God did not create this visible world for the angels, who are pure spirits and have no need of corporal places nor material things. Much less did He create it for Himself, for He has no need of anything but Himself. In the beginning He was without any universe and as glorious and happy then as He is now. Finally, to say that this world was created for the animals would be a blasphemy, because the brute animals cannot know their Maker, they cannot give thanks for benefits received, nor do they merit that the most powerful and wise Creator should perform such a great work for them.

Whence it clearly follows that this entire universe was created only for the service, sustenance, and use of man and that it should be for him a mirror in which he can see the Creator, a book in which he can read and know the wisdom, omnipotence, providence, and goodness of God.

Does this not prove God's love and esteem for men? If it is a proof of a father's love for his child that he provides a house and land for him when he reaches his majority, how much love

---

[52] Job 10:8–15.

is manifested by the eternal Father in giving man the world as his palace and all the creatures of the world as his household, the sea and land to provide provisions for his table, and the stars in the heavens to serve as lamps to brighten the night?

Who does not see all this as a proof of the liberality and love of the Giver and who can contain his joy when he realizes the esteem which God has for man in bestowing such benefits upon him?

But the proof does not stop here; it goes even farther. God has provided not only for the well-being and sustenance of man, but also for his recreation and delight. In the former things God very generously provided for all the necessities of life, but in the latter, He has especially shown Himself to be a Father to the little children that He loves so tenderly, for fathers are accustomed to bestow on their little ones pleasant things for their delight and recreation.

Who could count the multitude of things that God has created for this purpose? What beautiful colors pleasing to the eye! What music of men and of birds so soothing to the ear! What perfume of flowers so delightful to the nose! What tastes and delicious savors to gratify the tongue! What numerous objects in which the eye can find delight and, in delighting, advance in a knowledge of the Creator! What picture is more beautiful than the starry heavens? What tapestry more lovely than the flowery fields or the rivers with their overhanging banks girded by forests? What colorings more perfect than those of rubies and emeralds? What silks more fine or brocades more resplendent than the varied colors of the flowers? If this were not so, the Savior would not have said, "Consider the lilies of the field, how they grow. . . . But I say to you, that not even Solomon in all his glory was arrayed as one of these."[53]

If, O Lord, the fact that Thou hast created this great and beautiful world with its variety of things is a strong argument of Thy love, how much more so that Thou hast created us for Thyself, to make us participate in Thee and in Thy happiness and glory? No Christian can have this right by any title of nature, for it is owing only to Thee, who art God. Through this grace Thou dost make us gods, so to speak, because Thou dost give us a share in Thy glory.

Apart from that highest grace of the union of human nature with the divine Word, what more couldst Thou give us? To what further honor could we ascend? Surely, Lord, just as there is no glory greater than Thine, so there is no greater dignity that we could receive but this. Even the seraphim, who see and delight in Thy beauty at much closer range, are not at greater advantage than ourselves, for although by nature they are incomparably greater than we, they are not so by reason of their state of happiness, because for the same end and glory for which they were created in heaven, we also were created on earth.

Here, Lord, Thou dost pour forth on us Thy treasures, for Thou didst create us for so lofty an end and so great a glory that no intellect, divine or human, could conceive of anything greater. Whence, if the heart and love are judged by the gifts, what must be the love that bestows such a gift on us, a gift which Thou in all Thy omnipotence could never surpass? O most liberal and benign Lord! O true Lover of men who hast created them for so lofty a good! Let the angels and the heavens

---

[53] Matt. 6:28.

and the earth proclaim Thy praise and may men spend all their lives in the love and service of Him who has manifested such great love.

It would seem that this gift could never be augmented, yet Thy infinite knowledge and Thy infinite goodness and love did find an addition. Thou didst set as the price of Thy house, whereby we can merit and buy it, the blood of Thy only-begotten Son. So great is this gift that just as the glory which is thereby given us cannot be greater, for it is God Himself, so neither can the price with which it is purchased. Both the one and the other are the very greatest and, therefore, neither the one nor the other can be more than it is. If gifts and benefits are true testimonies of love, what greater gift couldst Thou give us than this?

In giving us Christ, Thou dost give us all things, for in Him Thou dost give us father and mother, brother, master, advocate, king, priest, and sacrifice. He is our model, our doctrine, our justice, our wisdom, our sanctification, our redemption, our pardon from sin, our grace, our glory, our life and salvation, and all goods. What greater demonstration of love couldst Thou give us than this? Thy very own Son, who dwells in Thy bosom, the secretary of Thy heart, gave us this testimony of Thee when He said: "God so loved the world that He gave His only-begotten Son so that everyone who would believe in Him would not perish but would have life everlasting."

If this Son were given us only that we might know Him and love Him and serve Him, that would be a supreme mercy; but what exceeds all tenderness, Thou didst give Him to us for our use, so that we might use Him for barter and His precious blood might be our ransom. The Savior Himself manifested the greatness of this love when He said: "Greater love than this no man hath than that he lay down his life for his friends." Who will not conclude from this that Thou does love us dearly, since Thou hast lavished on us the most precious of all Thy divine treasures?

To all these proofs of divine love another powerful one can be added and it is so great that no human tongue could ever explain it: the institution of the Blessed Sacrament by which, the Lord ordained to remain in our company, to dwell in our souls, and to make us one with Himself. Since love is essentially the union of two hearts and souls in one, it is most proper that love should desire this union. Accordingly, what greater demonstration of love than that the Savior should have instituted a sacrament whereby He could join Himself to our soul and become one with us? What could be more proper to true and perfect love? His love is as great as the gift He has bestowed on us and in this Sacrament is contained the greatest of all gifts, which is God Himself. And since no other gift can be compared with this, so no other love can be compared to His.

Great as is the love of parents for their children, that love is not so great that parents will unhesitatingly admit into their presence a child who has married without permission or has committed some grave fault. But even if a man has committed all the offenses in the world, the love of the heavenly Father is such that if that man whole-heartedly turns to God, He will welcome and pardon him as a prodigal son. The prophet Isaias understood this when he said: "For Thou art our Father, and Abraham hath not known us, and Israel hath been ignorant of us: Thou, O Lord, art our Father, our Redeemer, from everlasting is Thy name."[54]

[54] Isa. 63:16.

Such a love, Lord, springs from Thy goodness, from which flow two mighty rivers of mercy and love; the one to cure our evils and the other to communicate to us Thy goods. And if the fount is infinite, what must be the river of love that springs from it? For that reason I am not dismayed nor do I lose confidence, though I know I am evil and unworthy of such love. The Lover is good; so good that He does not cast off sinners, but draws them to Himself and receives them and dines with them.

To all these arguments and proofs of Thy love, Lord, I add another, which is that Thou Thyself art love. A proof of this is found in the words of the Evangelist: "God is charity; and he that abideth in charity, abideth in God, and God in him."[55] O how sweet and marvelous to have such a God, who is all love and whose very nature is charity! If it is a thing of beauty and wonder to see the sun in all its splendor, what will it be to see such a God completely afire with love? And what can this love do but inflame and burn? Accordingly, I contemplate Thee, Lord, in the midst of this short sojourn as an infinite fire or as a burning sun that shoots its fiery rays across the heavens and inflames all things that it touches, because all things live and move in this love.

But if all these things clearly manifest to us the greatness of Thy love, and if love has such a power to arouse more love, why do I not love Thee, my God, with my whole heart? How can I resist the great force of Thy love? How can I be deaf and insensible to the voices of all creation that call me to this love? The cold, hard stone gives off sparks if it is struck repeatedly with a piece of steel. Will my heart be so obdurate that in spite of all the blows of all creation not even a spark of love will fly

[55] Cf. 1 John 4:16.

from it? If there is nothing else in the world more powerful for igniting fire, why does not the fire of Thy divine love inflame my heart?

If Thou, my God, art a fire of infinite love, why is not my heart inflamed when it is in Thy presence? What coldness is this that Thy fire cannot ignite it? O King of glory, do not permit such a monstrosity in the world that I should not be inflamed by that great fire. Inflame this cold heart, my Lord, this heart colder than snow and harder than ice, so that I may love Thee with all my strength as Thou dost command and dost deserve to be loved. Make this love burn always and for all eternity. Amen.

CHAPTER 9 ✠
The Grandeur of Divine Justice

THE FIRST THING that should move our hearts to a fear of the Lord is the consideration of His divine justice. This justice is so great that David said of it: "Who knoweth the power of Thy anger, and for Thy fear can number Thy wrath?"[56] How great this justice is can be understood only by Him who possesses it. Nevertheless, from the works of justice we can understand something of it. Considering, for example, the chastisements that God has inflicted on the world for sin, we can understand to some extent how just and fearful is He who inflicts such

[56] Ps. 89:11.

punishments. Consequently, the selfsame chastisements that declare how great is God's hatred of sin, serve also to manifest the rigor of His justice. By means of the one we abhor what God abhors and by the other we fear to commit any fault which He will punish so rigorously.

A second consideration which should greatly move our hearts to a fear of the Lord is the profundity of His judgments. So the Psalmist says: "Thy justice is as the mountains of God and Thy judgments are a great deep."[57] This is a much more moving consideration than that of God's justice, which serves principally to make evil men fear, for the consideration of the profundity of God's judgments is profitable both for the good and the evil alike. As the wise man says: "Who knows if the spirit of the children of Adam ascend upward, and if the spirit of the beasts descend downward?"[58] That is to say, who knows whether all the just will be saved or all the sinners condemned, for many times the just man falls from his justice and the sinner is converted by penance.

Since the attributes and properties of God are known through His works, it will be well to consider some of His judgments, especially those which we read in Sacred Scripture, in order to show with what good reason every man, no matter how just he may be, should fear God. Consider how fearful was the judgment of the two brothers, Esau and Jacob. Although they were children of the same parents and were born in the same parturition, God preferred Jacob to Esau, even before either of them had done anything good or evil.

Saul and David were chosen by God to be kings of their people but both sinned, and David more grievously than Saul.

---

57 Ps. 35:7.

58 Eccles. 3:21.

Nevertheless, God rejected Saul, who died by his own hand, but He pardoned David and perpetuated his kingdom and made him an ancestor of Jesus Christ.

Solomon also, a holy and wise king who did so many great works and wrote such wonderful things, fell into a foul sin; and Manasses, one of the cruelest and most sacrilegious kings of the world, became repentant after his captivity and was restored to his former place. What is even more astounding, though he had been the author of the sins of the people, Manasses was pardoned and freed, but his people were destroyed because of their sin.

Pharaoh and Nabuchodonosor were both kings who had held the Jewish people in captivity and tyrannized over them, but after being warned and punished by God, the one did penance and was converted and the other perished with all his people.

Two thieves suffered with Christ, each one enduring the same torment for his sins, but one was taken to glory and the other was left to his punishment. Yet both had committed the same sin. Judas was an apostle of Christ and Paul was a persecutor; yet the persecutor became an apostle and the apostle became a persecutor. The one hanged himself with a noose; the other was taken up to the third heaven.

The Jews were the chosen people, greatly gifted by God; the Gentiles were cursed and rejected. Yet by the just judgment of God the friends were cast out and the enemies were chosen. The Apostle himself marveled at this when he said: "What wonder is this that Israel, seeking justice, did not find what she sought and the Gentiles, who did not seek it, found it!"

But even more than all this, it is amazing to consider the fall of the first angel who, as some have said, was the most beautiful, the most wise, the most powerful, and the most celestial creature that God had created. Yet he fell headlong from the highest heaven into the deepest abyss and was changed from the greatest of the angels to the prince of the devils.

No less inscrutable is the mystery of predestination and reprobation. It is a surpassingly wondrous thing that God should choose some and not others and yet they are all His creatures. Another wonder is that, by reason of being born into a Christian or an infidel family, some receive the sacrament of Baptism and others do not, though neither the one nor the other is more deserving of it. Another strange thing is that while two souls may be in the state of sin, God may call one and not the other, so that one departs from his sin and the other remains in it, though both may be equally sinners and equally unworthy of this mercy. Another marvel is to consider the death of one in sin and his condemnation because of this, while to another, who could just as well have died in the same sinful state, God gives the grace of repentance and leads him to the state of grace.

In addition to this, it amazes one to see the countless nations beneath the heavens that live in darkness and ignorance even since the coming of Christ, to see how few are those who avail themselves of the grace of this mystery. One should not attempt to probe too deeply into these marvels; rather, they should arouse fear and astonishment in us and make us exclaim with the Apostle: "O the depth of the riches of the wisdom and of the knowledge of God! How incomprehensible are His judgments, and how unsearchable His ways!"[59]

Since all this is so, who will not fear? Who will not tremble? Who will think himself secure? This is what made the saints

[59] Rom. 11:33.

tremble most, as did Job and David, St. Paul, and all the others. For on this earth there was nothing to give them perfect security and assurance—neither the mercy of God, nor our redemption by Christ, nor divine providence, nor even a good life and the testimony of a good conscience. All these things were available to many good souls who fell in spite of everything. Then nothing remained to them but to humble themselves, to pray, and to live in constant fear, realizing that he who is in grace today may be a sinner tomorrow.

He who stands on the top of a lofty tower, although it is secure, experiences a tremor of fear when he looks down at the earth below. So also the just man, although he feels certain that he is in grace, experiences a holy fear when he considers the profundity of the judgments of God, who frequently permitted situations in which great saints have fallen from grace. And since the truly just man does not consider himself better than these, nor more humble nor more prudent, he fears that he also could fall as they did and be debased as they were.

Just as adoration is owing to Thee alone, O Lord, as the true God, so also toward Thee alone should one have the greatest fear and reverence. Thou Thyself didst testify to this: "And fear ye not them that kill the body, and are not able to kill the soul; but rather fear him that can destroy both soul and body in hell."[60] The Church teaches us the same thing when she says: "In the presence of nations have no fear, but adore and" fear the Lord in thy heart because His angel walks with thee to free thee."

Therefore, Lord, do my heart and soul fear Thee, for there is no less reason to fear Thee than there is to love Thee. As

[60] Matt. 10:28.

Thou art infinitely merciful, so also Thou art infinitely just; and as the works of Thy mercy are countless, so also are the works of Thy justice. Thou art to be feared, Lord, because of the greatness of Thy justice, the profundity of Thy judgments, the immensity of Thy grandeur, and also because of my countless sins and follies and, above all, my constant resistance to Thy holy inspirations.

I stand in fear and trembling before Thee, Lord, in whose presence the very pillars of the heavens and the earth tremble.[61] Who will not fear Thee, Lord, King of nations? Who will not tremble at the words which Thou didst speak through Thy prophet: "Will not you then fear Me, saith the Lord, and will you not repent at My presence? I have set the sand a bound for the sea, an everlasting ordinance, which it shall not pass over; and the waves thereof shall toss themselves, and shall not prevail; they shall swell and shall not pass over it."[62]

But if all the creatures of heaven and earth obey and fear Thee, what shall I do, I who am a vile sinner and but dust and ashes? If the angels tremble when they adore Thee and sing Thy praises, why should not my heart tremble within me when it performs this same office? Miserable that I am, why has my heart become so hardened that I do not shed copious tears when the servant speaks with his Master, the creature with his Creator, the man with his God, he who was made of clay with Him who made all things out of nothing?

I fear Thee, Lord, for the greatness of Thy judgments which Thou hast made from the beginning of the world until now. How great a judgment was the fall of the most beautiful of

---

61 Ps. 103:32: "He looketh upon the earth, and maketh it tremble; He toucheth the mountains, and they smoke."

62 Jer. 5:22.

all the angels! Great was Thy judgment whereby the whole human race fell through the sin of one man, and terrible was Thy punishment of the world through the deluge. Great was the judgment regarding the choice of Jacob and the rejection of Esau, the destruction of Judas and the calling of Paul, the rejection of the Jews and the election of the Gentiles. For all we know, such judgments are secretly passed on the children of men each day. Finally, we recall the fearful judgment whereby so many nations of the earth lie in the shadow of death and in the darkness of infidelity, bartering temporal goods for eternal torments.

I fear Thee, Lord, because of the greatness of these judgments and as yet I do not know whether I shall be one of those destroyed and rejected. If the just man is saved only with difficulty, then the sinner and the perverse one, how shall he fare? If the innocent Job quaked at the fury of Thy wrath as under the impact of violent waves, why should he not tremble also who is so far removed from Job's innocence? If the prophet Jeremias was sanctified within the womb of his mother and could find no corner in which to hide because he was filled with the fear of Thy wrath, what shall he do who came forth from his mother's womb in sin and afterward has added to it by so many other sins?

I fear Thee, Lord, because of the countless multitude of my evil deeds, with which I must appear before Thee in judgment when the burning fire will announce Thy coming and Thou shalt judge Thy people. There, before so many millions of people, all my evils will be made manifest; before so many choirs of angels, my sins will be published, not only the sins of word and deed but also the hidden sins of thought. There I shall have as many judges as there are those who have preceded me in good works; I shall have as many witnesses against me as there are those who have given me bad example. Yet, in spite of that future judgment, I have not put a restraint on my vices. Gluttony still debases me and lust pursues me; pride puffs me up and avarice straightens me; envy consumes me and calumny tears me asunder; ambition impels me and anger disturbs me; levity drains my energies and slothfulness oppresses me; sorrow depresses me and favoritism exalts me.

Here, Lord, Thou dost see the companions with whom I have lived from the day of my birth until now. These are the friends with whom I have conversed; these are the masters whom I have obeyed; these are the lords I have served. But enter not into judgment on Thy servant, for none of the living will be justified in Thy sight.[63] Whom shalt Thou find just, if Thou dost judge without pity? Casting myself at Thy feet with a humble and contrite spirit, I shall plead with the Psalmist: "O Lord, rebuke me not in Thy indignation, nor chastise me in Thy wrath. Have mercy on me, O Lord, for I am weak; heal me, O Lord, for my bones are troubled. And my soul is troubled exceedingly; but Thou, O Lord, how long? Turn to me, O Lord, and deliver my soul; O save me for Thy mercy's sake. For there is no one in death, that is mindful of Thee; and who shall confess to Thee in hell?"[64]

---

[63] Ps. 142:2.

[64] Ps. 6:1.

CHAPTER 10 ✠ *The Divine Omnipotence*

IN ORDER TO express how greatly God's excellence surpasses that of the lords of this earth, the Creed describes the heavenly Father as omnipotent. By a mere act of His will, God has made whatever exists in heaven and on earth, although this may seem impossible to human reason, since it far surpasses human understanding. Compared to God's power, the power of man and even that of the devils and angels is like a grain of sand compared to the whole earth or a drop of water compared to the ocean. The recognition of God's omnipotence is a great help in overcoming the many objections that human reason proposes to the more difficult articles of faith and it is at the same time a confirmation of the faith itself. Whatever arguments are placed before us by the devils, apostates, heretics, or pagans, we can destroy them all with this single weapon. As the angel said to Mary, nothing is impossible to God.[65] So also, David reminds us: "Whatsoever the Lord pleased, He hath done in heaven, in earth, in the sea and in all the deeps."[66] Although in the Creed omnipotence is attributed only to God the Father, it pertains no less to the Son and the Holy Ghost, for they have the same substance and power as the Father.

Now let us see in what way God manifests His omnipotence. He created heaven and earth from nothing but His word. He created the heavenly bodies, such as the sun, the moon, and the stars, with all their movements. He created the

65 Cf. Luke 1:37.

66 Cf. Ps. 134:6.

higher heaven, which is the seat of His majesty, as well as the celestial spirits, such as the angels, archangels, cherubim, seraphim, thrones, dominations, principalities and powers, and all the virtues and attributes they possess. He also created this beautiful world and all things in it: human beings and animals, the earth and mountains and valleys, the trees and plants, the meadows and fields, the rivers and canyons, and whatever else is in this visible world. Finally, He created all things visible and invisible, the light and the darkness, night and day. There is nothing in all of nature that He did not create.

We must note especially that God created all things good, as it is written in Genesis.[67] Therefore every good gift and perfect gift descends from Him alone, as St. James says.[68] God is not the author of evil, that is, of moral evil or sin; but He is the author of the evils of punishment, labor, and chastisements in this life. He made them all, as He tells us through the mouth of Isaias.[69] And since omnipotence belongs not only to the Father but in equal measure to the Son and Holy Ghost, we must understand that the creation of all things is common to the Son and Holy Ghost as well as to the Father. Not only the Father made heaven and earth, but also the Son and the Holy Ghost, according to the words of the Psalmist: "The heavens were established by the Word of the Lord and by the Spirit of His mouth was made all their power."[70]

In addition to this, for the same reason that we believe that God created all things, we must also believe that He Himself

---

67 Gen. 1:31: "And God saw all the things that He had made, and they were very good."

68 Cf. James 1:17.

69 Cf. Isa. 45:7.

70 Ps. 32:6.

governs and sustains them. For it is not compatible with the measureless love that He has for us, greater than that of a father, that His creatures should perish or be deprived of anything without His knowing it and permitting it. So the Lord said to His disciples: "Are not two sparrows sold for a farthing? And not one of them shall fall on the ground without your Father. But the very hairs of your head are all numbered. Fear not therefore; better are you than many sparrows."[71]

Concerning the same matter we read in St. John: "My Father worketh until now; and I work," that is, conserving that which We have created.[72] Therefore does the Psalmist say in all truth: "The Lord ruleth me, and I shall want nothing."[73] In another place he says: "The Lord is my light and my salvation, whom shall I fear? The Lord is the protector of my life, of whom shall I be afraid?"[74] Finally, the same inspired writer confesses: "The eyes of all hope in Thee, O Lord: and Thou givest them meat in due season. Thou openest Thy hand and fillest with blessing every living creature."[75] Whence, the apostle Paul concludes that one must place confidence solely in God, who gives to all whatever is needful.[76]

These two marvelous operations of God, the creation and government of all things, enable us to realize clearly His omnipotence in the work of creation, His goodness in calling it forth freely as an effect of His love, His wisdom in directing and sustaining it in such harmony, His liberality in doing all

---

[71] Matt. 10:29–31.
[72] John 5:17.
[73] Ps. 22:1.
[74] Ps. 26:1.
[75] Ps. 144:15–16.
[76] Cf. Heb. 10:35.

this for man's benefit, and the mercy of Him who, in spite of the many offenses we have committed against Him, has never on this account destroyed creation.

Chapter 11 ✠
God's Providence Over Men

All that has been said thus far substantiates the arguments given by the philosophers for the existence of a first cause, a first principle, and a first mover and governor of this entire universe, which we call God. It also enables us to realize the providence that the sovereign Lord exercises over all things, even as regards the instincts He has implanted in all animals for their conservation, procreation, and defense against enemies.

Philosophers of grave and serious judgment did not in any way doubt the fact of divine providence, but just as monstrous bodies are sometimes born into the world with an excess or a defect in some member, so also there are monstrous minds and intellects which propose beliefs that are against all reason and the common consent of the whole human race. Of such a type are those who, while admitting God's providence over brute animals, dared to say that divine providence does not extend to men. They were led to affirm this because of the disorder and confusion that they observed in human affairs. By failing to consider that animals are incapable of virtue or vice, they could not see that the Creator will exercise divine providence differently in regard to man. Against such erroneous opinions, true philosophers have armed themselves with weighty arguments to prove that the sovereign Lord also exercises providence over human affairs. We shall here mention a few of these arguments.

In the first place, what ears would not be scandalized on hearing that God has care of the beasts but not of men, since He has created the beasts and all other inferior things for the service of man? Who would say that a father has care over his slaves and servants but not over his own son? Since it pertains to prudence and good government to take greater care of better things and since man, a creature made in the image and likeness of God, is more noble beyond compare than all brute animals, how could it be true that God exerts His providence over lowly things and ignores men, whom He calls sons by reason of their likeness to Him? If He watches over brute animals, which do not recognize the benefits received and are unable to give thanks for them, with what greater reason should He watch over man, who can recognize and adore and praise God?

We know that love is the cause of the care which creatures have for their own and that the more they love their own, the greater is the care they manifest, as is evident in the watchfulness of animals over their young. Now if God has a greater love for man than He has for the brute animals (and this is evident from the advantages that man has over animals and the more excellent nature which God gave him), how is it possible that He would take care of the things that He loves less and not those things that He loves more? If a man plants and nurtures a tree, he is delighted when he sees it full grown and laden with fruit; but if any harm comes to it, he is grieved and he immediately cultivates and irrigates it. Now if a man has such solicitude for a little tree, how much more will God have for man whom He has fashioned?

Not only love but goodness also is the cause of providence. Thus we see that men of excellent and noteworthy goodness have a great respect for the common good and they desire and work for it even at great sacrifice to themselves. If this is characteristic of human goodness, how much more will it be so of the supreme and infinite goodness of God, especially since He knows that if man is well ordered, all the world that serves him will also be well ordered. On the contrary, if man is disordered, so also is the world, because it is then at the service of one who does not in turn serve the common Lord of all. Lastly, if all the perfections of creatures are found in God to an eminent degree and if providence over others is one of these perfections, who would dare deny that providence is also found in God, the author and sum-total of all perfections?

We see also that all intelligent causes have a special regard for the effects they produce: fathers for their children, kings for their subjects, and heads of families for their households. How much more, then, will the King of kings, the sovereign Father, and the Cause of all causes have a regard for man, the most noble effect that He has produced in this world?

Even more can be added. If God exercised no providence over human affairs, it would be because He is unable to do so, He does not desire to do so, or He does not know what takes place in this world. To say, however, that He does not know the happenings of the world is to deprive Him of wisdom; to say that He does know but does not wish to exercise providence, is to deprive Him of goodness, justice, charity, mercy, and, indeed, of all perfections and virtues, which is a horrible blasphemy; and to say that He is unable to exercise providence is a denial of His infinite power. He who was able to create this world, so vast, so beautiful, so well ordered, and filled with so many things for the use of human life, how is it possible that He would not be able to govern that which He has made? And if He created this world out of His own free choice and not through any necessity, if He did so out of pure goodness, which prompted Him to give being to things which had it not, why should He not also desire to conserve and govern that which He willed to create?

Finally, we see that all men, of whatever race or nation, when they find themselves in any difficult situation or danger, immediately and by an instinct of nature raise their eyes and hands to heaven, asking help from the Lord. Since this natural inclination is impressed on man by his Creator and since, as the philosophers say, there is nothing useless or without purpose in nature (for neither God nor nature perform futile acts), it follows that God has care over the affairs of men.

Moreover, in all nations, however barbarous and pagan, is found some kind of worship of God even though it is frequently false and erroneous. This veneration of a supreme being is not without any purpose, but is in view of some favor that is expected. For if they hoped to gain nothing, men would not honor a supreme being nor would they be concerned about His temples and sacrifices. Consequently, this is tantamount to an admission of divine providence and that God regards those who honor and venerate Him. Since this is a universal fact among all nations, such an inclination must be something innate, impressed on man's heart by the Author of nature. Just as He has infused into the hearts of children a natural inclination to reverence and respect their parents, so also He has infused the inclination to honor God, who in a far more excellent manner is the universal Father of all men. This was so patent to Aristotle that he said that just as we need not dispute whether snow is white, neither is it necessary to question whether parents and the gods should be honored; rather we should frown on one who denies that snow is white and chastise and punish one who would refuse due honor to parents and the gods.

These and similar arguments were sufficient proof of divine providence for the gravest philosophers, such as Plato, Socrates, and Seneca (who wrote an entire book on the subject). Thus, in a letter written to his friend Lucilius, Seneca says: "God is close to you; He is with you and within you, A sacred Spirit dwells in us who guards and notes our good deeds. He treats us in the same manner that we treat Him; and be assured that no man can be good without His help. For how could one despise the things of fortune without His help? He it is who gives us marvelous counsel. It is certain that God dwells in the souls of the good, although they may not know who this God is who dwells in them. Only God could fashion an excellent and moderate spirit that scorns all vile and lowly things and laughs at all that ordinary men desire or fear. So great an accomplishment could not be effected without His help. And yet the greater part of this divine Spirit is in the place whence He descended. As the rays of the sun reach the earth and yet remain in the sun whence they descend, so also the great and sacred Spirit, sent to the earth that we might know divine things, converses here with us but is still joined to the principle of which He is born."

In another letter Seneca says: "Marvel if you will that men should approach the gods, but a still greater marvel is it that God comes to men and, indeed, comes to dwell in them. For no soul is good without the help and presence of God." Such are the words of Seneca who, without having read the Gospel, admitted the necessity of grace, without even understanding what grace is, and taught the existence of divine providence. All the more reason, then, to be amazed at the blindness and foolishness of those who, though they have received the Scripture, have asserted that man, solely by force of his free will and without the help of grace, can perfectly observe all the commandments and merit the kingdom of heaven.

CHAPTER 12 ✠ *The Blessing of Predestination*

TO ALL THE divine benefits enumerated we must now add that of the divine election of those who from all eternity have been chosen for everlasting life. The Apostle gave thanks for this great blessing in his own name and in the name of the elect when he wrote to the Ephesians: "Blessed be the God and Father of our Lord Jesus Christ, who hath blessed us with spiritual blessings in heavenly places, in Christ; as He chose us in Him before the foundation of the world, that we should be holy and unspotted in His sight in charity, who hath predestinated us unto the adoption of children through Jesus Christ unto Himself, according to the purpose of His will."[77] Concerning this same blessing the Psalmist says: "Blessed is he whom Thou hast chosen and taken to Thee; he shall dwell in Thy courts."[78]

[77] Eph. 1:3–5.
[78] Ps. 64:5.

Truly, this can be called the blessing of blessings and the grace of graces. It is the grace of graces because it is given antecedent to all merit, through the infinite largess and goodness of God who, not wishing harm to anyone, gives sufficient grace to all for their salvation, extending His mercy to all as the generous and absolute Lord of His household. It is also the blessing of blessings, not only because it is the greatest of benefits, but because it is the cause of all others. Once a man has been elected for glory through predestination, the Lord provides him with all the other blessings and means that are required for its attainment. As God Himself says through the prophet: "Yea, I have loved thee with an everlasting love, therefore have I drawn thee."[79]

The Apostle expressed the same thought even more clearly when he said: "And whom He predestinated, them He also called; and whom He called, them He also justified; and whom He justified, them He also glorified."[80] The reason for this is that God disposes all things sweetly, and after He has chosen one for glory, He also bestows many other graces upon him, thus providing him with all that the first grace of predestination demands. Just as a father who wishes his son to be a priest or a man of letters begins in the boy's youth to interest him in the things of the Church or the practice of letters and directs all the steps of his life to this goal, so also the heavenly Father, after electing a soul for glory, to which the road of justice leads, always strives to guide the soul along that road until it reaches the desired end.

---

79 Jer. 31:3.

80 Rom. 8:30.

Those who recognize in themselves the signs of election should give thanks to God for this great and inestimable benefit. Granted that this secret is hidden from the eyes of men, nevertheless there are signs of election just as there are signs of justification. The principal sign of the latter is the amendment of one's life; the principal sign of the former is perseverance in a good life. He who has lived for many years in fear of the Lord and has been solicitous in avoiding every mortal sin, can hope, as the Apostle says, that God will preserve him until the end without sin and will finish what that man has begun.[81] Yet no one should for this reason consider himself secure, for we see that even the great and wise Solomon, after having lived well for such a long time, was deceived toward the end of his life. But these are exceptional cases, as the Apostle states and as Solomon himself admits: "It is a proverb: a young man according to his way, even when he is old he will not depart from it."[82]

From these and similar statements made by the saints one can humbly trust that through the infinite goodness of God he will be numbered among the elect. If one can rely on the mercy of God for salvation, so also he can hope that he will be among the number of the elect, for the one depends upon the other. Since this is so, how great is man's obligation to serve God in order to gain the great blessing of being inscribed in that book of which the Savior spoke to His disciples: "But yet rejoice not in this, that spirits are subject to you; but rejoice in this, that your names are written in heaven."[83] What a great blessing it is to be loved and chosen from all eternity, for as long, indeed, as God is God; to be placed in His loving heart

---

81 Cf. I Cor. 1:8.

82 Prov. 22:6.

83 Luke 10:20.

for ageless centuries; to be chosen as an adopted son of God when the Word was engendered the natural Son of God amidst the splendors of the saints who were even then present to the divine intellect!

Look closely, then, at all the circumstances of this election and you will see that each one of them is a great blessing and also a new obligation. See how worthy is He who has chosen you: God Himself, infinitely rich and happy, who needs nothing from you nor from any created thing. See also how unworthy is the one chosen, a miserable mortal creature, subject to all the poverty, weaknesses, and afflictions of this life, and deserving of eternal punishment in the next life because of his sins. See how lofty is this election, for you were chosen for an end so noble that there could be none greater: to be the son of God, the heir of His kingdom, and a participator in His glory.

See also how gratuitous is this election, for it precedes all merit and is effected only by the decree of the divine will, as the Apostle says: "Who hath predestinated us unto the adoption of children through Jesus Christ unto Himself, according to the purpose of His will, unto the praise of the glory of His grace."[84] And as the benefit is more gratuitous, man is more obliged to the Giver.

Consider also the antiquity of this election, for it did not begin with the world, but was before the world and is as ageless as God Himself. Therefore God, being eternal, has loved His chosen ones from all eternity; He keeps them before Him and looks upon them with a paternal and loving gaze.

Where will you find the time to consider such great mercies? What tongue could ever proclaim them? What heart could

[84] Eph. 1:5–6.

feel them? By what services could they ever be repaid? What amount of human love could ever correspond to the divine love of God? Who would wait until his old age to love Him who has loved from all eternity? Who would ever exchange this divine Friend for any other friend? If Scripture itself extols old friends, how much more praiseworthy is the Friend who is eternal? And if we should never exchange an old friend for a new, who would ever exchange the possession and tenderness of a Lover so ancient for all the friends in the world? And if, from time immemorial, possession of a thing gives a right over non-possession, what of Him who from all eternity possesses us under the title of this friendship and thus holds us as His own?

Accordingly, what goods in the world are worth exchanging for this divine good? What evils should we not gladly endure for His sake? What man would be so impious that if he could know by a special revelation from God that a certain beggar passing by were one of the elect and predestined, he would not kiss the very earth which that beggar trod? Would he not run after him and, throwing himself on his knees at the beggar's feet, beg a thousand blessings of him and say: "O blessed art thou! O fortunate art thou! Is it possible that thou art of that blessed number of the elect? Is it possible that thou shalt see God in His very beauty? That thou shalt be a companion and brother of all the elect? That thou shalt be near the choirs of angels? That thou shalt enjoy celestial music and shalt reign forever and ever? That thou shalt see the resplendent faces of Christ and His Blessed Mother? O blessed be the day on which thou wert born and even more blessed be the day on which thou shalt die, for on that day thou shalt live forever. Blessed be the bread which thou dost eat and the earth thou dost trod. Much more blessed be the works thou dost perform and the afflictions thou dost suffer, for these shall prepare the way for thy eternal rest. What sorrow could be so sad or what affliction so grave that it would not be dispelled by the pledge of this hope?"

Thus would we look upon a predestined soul if we were to know that he is such. From this you can see, Christian reader, the obligation that the chosen ones have to the Lord in return for so great a benefit, and no one should consider himself excluded as long as he is willing to do his part. Rather, each one should work, as St. Peter says, to make sure his election and calling by good works.[85] We know that he who acts thus will be saved and we also know that the divine favors and graces will never be lacking to anyone. On the certitude of these two truths, let us persevere in good works and we shall be counted among the glorious number of the elect.

CHAPTER 13 ✠

The Mystery of the Blessed Trinity

TO TREAT OF this mystery we should first ask permission of God to enter into His sanctuary and the light to see that which far surpasses all creation. We should, moreover, arouse in ourselves great reverence and sobriety, for this is a mystery to be adored rather than scrutinized. It is a dangerous thing

[85] See II Pet. 1:10.

to speak about God, says Cicero, even though we speak the truth, unless we speak with the reverence and fear that befit such great majesty.

The Apostle teaches the same thing when he says that we should not seek to know more than is fitting for us to know and even in this we should observe sobriety and prudence.[86] Solomon also warns of the danger of immoderation when he says: "As it is not good for a man to eat much honey, so he that is a searcher of majesty, shall be overwhelmed by glory."[87] For him who has refined the taste of his soul, there is nothing sweeter than to contemplate the infinite beauty of God, but he who attempts to pass beyond the boundaries of human knowledge and to scrutinize that which is incomprehensible, is blinded by the grandeur of the divine splendor, just as he blinds himself who tries to look directly at the full brilliance of the sun.

When God wished to speak to Moses on Mount Sinai,[88] He commanded him to mark certain boundaries beyond which the Jews were not to pass, under pain of death. So also, man should know how far he can go in the knowledge of God and not seek to probe farther. The boundary and limit of our knowledge are pointed out for us in the words of Ecclesiasticus: "Seek not the things that are too high for thee, and search not into things above thy ability; but the things that God hath commanded thee, think of them always, and in many of His works be not curious."[89]

---

86 Rom. 12:3.
87 Prov. 25:27.
88 Cf. Exod. 19:12–21.
89 Ecclus. 3:22.

St. John Chrysostom advises the same thing when he compares the temporal generation of Christ with His eternal generation: "If we are unable to understand the manner in which the human body is formed in the womb of the mother, how shall we understand how the Holy Ghost, by His power alone, formed the body of the Savior in the womb of the Blessed Virgin? With still greater reason, then, should they be ashamed and confused who have the temerity to probe into the eternal generation of the Son of God. For if our human minds cannot understand His temporal generation, what folly it would be to imagine that any human intellect could comprehend or any human language could describe that ineffable eternal generation! Be content, therefore, with the simplicity of faith and seek not to inquire into that which God wished to remain hidden. Such, brethren, is the discretion with which we must treat of this mystery."

But because we are obliged to believe the articles of faith explicitly and distinctly, and among them that of the Trinity is the principal one, it is fitting that we treat of this mystery, but with the necessary discretion and reverence. Leaving aside all subtleties and technical points, it seems best to treat of three things: first, the places in Sacred Scripture that refer to this mystery; secondly, the manner in which we should consider this mystery, lest we consider it in a manner unworthy of the divine majesty; and thirdly, the fact that unaided human reason cannot discover the existence of this mystery is no argument against it, for the mystery itself is ineffable and our human intellect is too weak to attain such heights.

As to the first, we should consider why it was necessary that the mystery of the Trinity be revealed more explicitly and clearly in the New Testament than in the Old. The principal reason is to be found in the mystery of the Incarnation, wherein we confess that the Son of God took on human flesh and was conceived in the womb of a virgin by the power of the Holy Ghost. This mystery could in no wise be grasped without the revelation of the mystery of the three divine Persons. But in the Old Testament there was not so great a need for the declaration of the mystery of the Trinity. Indeed, there was danger that the rude and illiterate people, not understanding the loftiness of the mystery, would believe that there was more than one God and thus be guilty of idolatry, to which the Jews were easily inclined.

The mystery of the Trinity is proclaimed in numerous passages of the New Testament. Thus, St. John says: "And there are three who give testimony in heaven: the Father, the Word, and the Holy Ghost. And these three are one."[90] Likewise, when the Savior commissioned His apostles to preach the gospel throughout the world, He said to them: "Going therefore, teach ye all nations; baptizing them in the name of the Father, and of the Son, and of the Holy Ghost."[91] We are commanded to believe all those things which the Savior told us about God, and since He has revealed to us the mystery of the Trinity, that is sufficient of itself to warrant our belief.

As to the manner in which we should conceive of the mystery of the Trinity, we should realize first of all that there are many things that we cannot understand about God. The reason for this is that we do not know God as He is in Himself, but only through His works. In observing the created universe, we can learn only those things about God that creation

---

90 See I John 5:7.

91 Matt. 28:19.

manifests; for example, the immensity of His wisdom in planning it, the greatness of His power in creating it, and the liberality of His goodness in providing for the necessities of all His creatures. But created things cannot exhaust or adequately declare God's greatness; through them we can know only as much as they are able to disclose to us. Similarly, if we were to be shown a perfectly fashioned work of art, we would thereby know something of the genius and artistry of him who made it, but we would be ignorant of his condition of life or the other talents and qualities he possessed, because this work of art tells us nothing about such things.

Now one of the things about God that we cannot discover for ourselves is the mystery of the Trinity: that in the one simple substance there is a distinction of three Persons—Father, Son, and Holy Ghost—and that although there are three Persons, there is only one God because they all possess the one and the same nature and essence. This is something proper to God alone, and in this way He differs from all other intellectual beings, such as angels and men. In the latter there is one nature and one person; in the one divine nature there are three Persons. The distinction of Persons in the unity of the divine essence cannot be learned through a consideration of created things. If we were to learn of this mystery, it was necessary that God reveal it to us in the new dispensation of His grace, and because He has done so, we have a clearer understanding of the mystery of the Incarnation as well.

The basis on which Catholic faith teaches that there are three divine Persons in the one divine nature is Sacred Scripture, which states that the Father is God, the Son is God, and the Holy Ghost is God, and yet there are not three gods, but only one God. That there should be three gods is, indeed, an absolute impossibility. For if there were three gods, there would have to be some difference among them. But this could not be unless there were in one of them some perfection not possessed by another. Then the one who lacked that perfection could not be God, for all men admit that God is a being so great and perfect that one could never imagine or conceive of any other being that is better or greater. Whence the conclusion follows that there are not many gods but only one God. Although the divine Persons are three in number and each one is God, the one and the same divinity is in all three.

Theologians, and especially Richard of Saint Victor, offer many arguments by which they seek to wed reason with faith. Our primary intention, however, is not to convince man's reason, but to humble him so that in his lowliness and weakness of intellect he will not presume to enter into the profundities of this mystery. Nevertheless, we shall state briefly one of the great reasons for believing in this mystery. To grasp the argument, one must recall a principle that we have stressed repeatedly: God is infinitely good. Now, if He is infinitely good, He must also be infinitely communicative, for according to the celebrated doctrine of Dionysius, the nature of goodness is to communicate itself to others. Wherever we find infinite goodness, we also find an infinite communication of goodness. But in God such a thing could not be unless He were to communicate His own nature and divinity. Whatever He has communicated to the angels and to all the creatures of this universe is a limited and finite good and does not correspond perfectly to His infinite goodness.

From this solid principle we conclude to the procession of the divine Persons. The eternal Father communicates to His beloved Son His nature and divinity, and the Father and the

Son communicate the same thing to the Holy Ghost. We thus avoid making God solitary and sterile, qualities that are totally foreign to Him, as He says through the prophet Isaias: "Shall not I that make others to bring forth children, Myself bring forth, saith the Lord? Shall I, that give generation to others, be barren, saith the Lord thy God?"[92]

But to return to a consideration of the mystery itself, when one hears the words, Father, Son, and generation, he must not understand by them anything material. It is important to remember that in the procession of the divine Persons there is nothing corporeal. God is a most pure spirit, without composition and without the admixture of any alien substance. There is nothing in God but God, and in His spirit there is nothing other than intellect and will. Consequently, whatever He has worked or yet works in this world is effected solely by the acts of His intellect and will. By His divine intellect He fashioned this great and beautiful universe; by His divine will He willed to create it and in that instant it was created.

The first Person of the Trinity is called Father because He engendered the Son from all eternity and in a manner that can be neither described nor understood. The Son was engendered from the substance of the Father, from Him alone and by Him alone, without help or association with any other being. In bringing forth His Son eternally, the Father does not give only a part of His substance to the Son, but He communicates it in its entirety. Nevertheless, He did not produce another God in the sense that now there are two gods. Neither is He who engenders prior in time to the one engendered; but just as both

92 Isa. 66:9.

are the one God, so the selfsame eternity is attributed to both the Father and the Son.

The Father likewise engenders all the faithful who believe in Him. Born of Adam in a miserable and wretched state, they are reborn of the eternal Father; not, however, of His substance, as was His only-begotten Son, but through the spiritual seed which is the word of truth; that is to say, through the gospel and the sacraments, by means of a living faith and the power of the Holy Ghost, as St. Peter and St. John declare.[93] Yet the sons of God are not reborn through their own merits, but through His great mercy, as St. Peter states: "Blessed be the God and Father of our Lord Jesus Christ, who according to His great mercy hath regenerated us unto a lively hope, by the resurrection of Jesus Christ from the dead."[94] Although He did not regenerate us out of His very substance, He has made us participants and sharers in His nature, that is, in His immortality and glory, and heirs of eternal life so that we may rejoice in Him as He rejoices in Himself.

The first type of generation, that of the Son, is proper to the first Person of the Trinity, whom we call Father by excellence; the second type of generation, which we call spiritual, is common to the Father, Son, and Holy Ghost. Thus the prophet Isaias, speaking of the Son of God, calls Him "the Father of the world to come"[95] and the Church calls the Holy Ghost the Father of the poor.

Since we believe that God effects all things by His intellect and will, we must also believe that in the procession of the divine Persons nothing other than the divine intellect and

93 See I Pet. 1:5; John 1:17; I John 3:1; II Pet. 1:4.

94 See I Pet. 1:3.

95 Isa. 9:6.

will intervenes. Thus the eternal Father, through His divine intellect, engenders and brings forth the Person of the Son, to whom He communicates His own nature and substance. Unlike the faithful, who are called and truly are sons of God, He is called the only-begotten Son of God. The former are reborn through the liberality and grace of God and through the merits of His only Son, Jesus Christ; but the latter is the natural Son of God, engendered by the Father from all eternity, consubstantial and co-eternal with the Father, splendor of His glory and living image of His substance, who sustains all things and governs them with the word of His power. The Father has made Him the heir of all things, Him through whom He made the world and in whom He is well pleased, as the apostles and evangelists teach us.[96]

The Son is also called the Word of the Father, His Image, and other names that designate some aspect of the divine generation. He is called Son to designate that He is of the substance of the Father and is therefore God as well as is the Father. He is called Word to designate that this generation, although it is substantial, is not material but spiritual, because it is by way of the intellect, as we have already stated. He is called Image and Figure of the substance of the Father because He represents all that there is in the Father and He possesses all that is contained in the Father. An image pressed in wax by a seal contains all that is contained in the seal itself, except that the image proceeds from the seal and not the seal from the image; so also, whatever is found in the Son is found in the Father, except that the Son proceeds from the Father and not the Father from the Son.

---

[96] See Heb. 1:2; Col. 1:15; John 1:3; Matt. 3:17.

The Father and the Son, loving each other infinitely by an act of the will, produce the Person of the Holy Ghost who is essentially love, according to the statement of St. John: "For God is charity."[97] If you ask why we call the third Person of the Trinity the Holy Spirit when each one of the Persons is a spirit, the answer is that we do not call Him the Holy Spirit for this reason. It is true that the three Persons are all spirits and that the divine nature is not something corporeal but spiritual, but the third Person of the Trinity is called the Holy Spirit by reason of the manner of His procession. The second Person of the Trinity is called the Son because He is engendered; the third Person is called the Holy Spirit because He is spirated.

Another reason, more evident and clear for those who are not well versed in theology, is because of the work that He effects in us, which is to breathe in us, that is, to give us spiritual life. For if in the spiritual order we live the life that God desires us to live, which is to live in His love and grace, it is effected through the breath and spirit of life that comes to us from the Holy Ghost.

In the mystery of the Trinity there are but two processions: one by way of the divine intellect, from which the Son proceeds, and the other by way of the divine will, from which the Holy Ghost proceeds. Thus we confess and adore three Persons and one nature which is common to the three. Here we can see the difference between the mystery of the Trinity and that of the Incarnation of the Son of God. In the latter, we find three substances joined in the one Person of Christ: body, soul, and the divine Word; in the former, we adore in the one substance the three divine Persons: Father, Son, and Holy

[97] See I John 4:8.

Ghost. In the Incarnation the substances are three in number and the Person is one; in the Trinity the substance is one and the Persons are three. But in both these mysteries shines forth the ineffability of that sovereign Majesty who far surpasses the capacity of any created intellect.

It is impossible to find in all creation anything that perfectly represents all the perfections of the Creator. Since the distance between Him and His creatures is infinite, no created thing could possibly manifest or contain in itself all that is to be found in Him. In spite of this, in order to assist our weak intellects, theologians make use of certain examples, however imperfect, to enlighten and clarify this mystery as much as possible. One of these examples is the functioning of man's intellect and will. Let us imagine a man such as Solomon, who far surpassed all other men in wisdom and of whom Scripture says: "And God gave to Solomon wisdom and understanding exceeding much, and largeness of heart as the sand that is on the sea shore."[98] Now this man sits down to reflect upon himself and all the gifts with which God has blessed him. Thus considering himself, he produces in his intellect an intelligible Solomon, that is to say, a concept or image of himself and his perfections. Then, seeing the perfections represented in this concept, his love is aroused for the object represented.

Three elements or steps can be enumerated in this activity: first, there is Solomon who knows his own perfection; second, the concept which he forms in his intellect concerning his perfection; third, the love that proceeds from this consideration. By a parallel we can enumerate the same elements in the hidden activity of the three divine Persons, although there

[98] Cf. III Kings 4:29.

are many differences between the one and the other, especially the fact that in man the intelligible concept and the love that follows are accidental modifications, while in God they are not accidental but substantial, and even God Himself.

Nor should one be astonished at what we say here, namely, that the eternal Father, in knowing Himself, engenders and produces the Son, for we experience something similar to this almost daily. If a person looks into a mirror, he sees there an image that perfectly represents his own figure and form. Why, then, should it be amazing that the sovereign Father, whose power and virtue are infinite, in gazing upon Himself should produce the perfect image of His Son? Here again, however, there is a difference: the image in a mirror is something accidental but the image of the Father is subsistent, as it must necessarily be. Moreover, if a person were continually looking in a mirror, he would continually produce the image of himself. So also, the heavenly Father, who is continually gazing at His own divine essence, is continually producing the Person of the Son.

It is something proper to God ever to be contemplating His infinite essence and beauty. Aristotle states that there is nothing proportionate or adequate to the divine intellect except the glory of His divinity and essence and that it would be beneath the dignity of that most high substance to abase Himself by contemplating anything other than Himself. Commenting on this statement, St. Thomas Aquinas remarks that God does not for that reason cease to understand and know all things outside Himself, for He sees them all in His own essence as in a spotless mirror.

Another example that theologians use in treating of the mystery of the Trinity is that of our soul and its faculties of memory, intellect, and will. By the memory, which is the storehouse of all knowledge, they exemplify the Father, "in whom are hid all the treasures of wisdom and knowledge";[99] by the intellect they signify the Son, who is engendered through the intellect of the Father; and by the will, which is the faculty by which we love, they symbolize the Holy Ghost, who proceeds from the conjoined will of the Father and the Son. But these three faculties of the soul are not three souls, but one soul.

Yet another common example used by theologians is that of the sun, the most excellent of all inanimate bodies. In the sun we find three elements: the sun itself, the light that proceeds from it, and the heat that is the result of the other two. Whence the Apostle calls the Son of God the brightness of the glory of the Father[100] and in the Book of Wisdom we read that the Son is "the brightness of eternal light, and the unspotted mirror of God's majesty, and the image of His goodness."[101] We should also note that just as the sun unceasingly produces light, and both the sun and the light together produce heat, so also the eternal Father is unceasingly producing the eternal light of His Son and the two together are producing the Holy Ghost. If the sun were eternal, eternal also would be the light that issues from it and the heat that comes forth from both. Since the Father is eternal, so also is the Son whom He produces and the Holy Ghost who proceeds from both of them. This happens in such a way that no one Person is before or after another but all three Persons embrace the same eternity. This example, like all others, falls short of the truth of the mystery because the light and heat of the sun are accidents and have no existence of

[99] Col. 2:3.
[100] Cf. Heb. 1:3.
[101] Wisd. 7:26.

themselves, whereas each of the divine Persons truly exists in one and the same nature.

Man's knowledge is so insignificant and the capabilities of his intellect are so limited that, as philosophers have stated, the most that we can know is equivalent to only a small part of what remains yet to be known. In other words, the extent to which the eye of the human understanding can penetrate is insignificant in comparison with that which remains to be seen. The reason for this is clear because our intellect, enclosed as it is in the prison of the body, can know only those things that somehow come in contact with the senses of the body or to which the senses themselves can somehow reach. Consequently, man cannot have a direct and immediate knowledge of spiritual things except by certain conjectures and deductions. Because of this, Aristotle says that in relation to the knowledge of the most lofty and clearest things of nature our human intellect is like an owl gazing into the sun. Therefore, whereas God, by reason of His perfection and infinity, is the most intelligible of all beings, He is actually the being that we least understand. Rightly did the philosopher say that just as there is nothing more visible than the sun and yet nothing less able to be looked upon, because of its splendor, so also there is nothing more intelligible in itself than God and nothing less comprehensible, because of the loftiness of His being.

This is verified by an account given by Cicero in one of his treatises on the nature of the gods. The king of Sicily asked a philosopher named Simonides what God is and the philosopher requested a day in which to prepare his answer. When the day had passed and the king asked for the response, the philosopher begged for two days more, and each time thereafter when the king sought an answer, the philosopher doubled the space of time desired. Marveling at this, the king asked the philosopher why he acted thus and the philosopher answered that each time he thought about God he found the knowledge of God more difficult to acquire.

The reason for this difficulty is, as we have already stated, that our intellect can know only those things that somehow enter through the portals of our bodily senses. Hence, we can know only those things that enter our souls by means of some kind of bodily image or representation. But God, as God, has no body; He is a pure spirit. And since no corporeal image can represent His essence, He cannot be understood as He is essentially.

For the same reason we cannot have immediate knowledge of an angel, which is also a spirit and has no image that could represent it to our intellects. Even more, up to this time no philosopher has ever been able to comprehend the essence of the soul by which we live. Although we experience its effects in us, we cannot comprehend its essence and substance because it, too, is spiritual. Now, if this spiritual substance which we possess within ourselves, our own souls, cannot be known directly by us, what folly to think that by any means we can comprehend the nature of that spiritual substance which is God and not to realize that this is something which our poor reason can never attain?

But why should we speak of attaining to a knowledge of God, when we cannot even know perfectly the majority of the works of His hands? So Solomon tells us: "I understood that man can find no reason of all those works of God that are done under the sun; and the more he shall labor to seek, so much the less shall he find; yea, though the wise man shall say that he knoweth it, he shall not be able to find it."[102] And if such palpable and ordinary things cannot be understood by us, how can we presume to know their Creator?

But why should we mention the works of God, when we are scarcely able to understand the works and deeds of men? If you were to show a piece of silk to a person who had never before seen such material and were to ask him how such a beautiful work could be done by little worms, what would he say? Or if you were to show him a piece of glass and ask how such a thing could be made from sand and by blowing, how could he answer you if he had never heard of glass-ovens? Or, finally, if you were to ask the wisest of men how the bees make their honey and wax and honeycombs, what would he say? How, then, can any man who knows not the secrets of so tiny an insect, rise above all the heavens and comprehend the lofty and sovereign God who dwells there? "Hardly do we guess aright at things that are upon earth, and with labor do we find the things that are before us. But the things that are in heaven, who shall search out?"[103]

All that has been said up to this point humbles our intellects and prevents us from saying that there is nothing that we cannot understand, since there are so many lesser things that we handle almost daily and yet we do not understand them. We now wish to declare that the very reason that the infidels give for not believing in this mystery is one of the principal reasons why they should believe in it. What is more logical than to consider very profoundly that which is ineffable and to attribute to it the most excellent and noble being that our

---

[102] Eccles. 8:17.

[103] Wisd. 9:16.

minds can imagine? And when we have actually attributed to God the most excellent perfections we can conceive, we should then realize that there yet remains an infinity of perfections that we cannot in any way understand or imagine. He would be a little God indeed if He could be grasped and comprehended by our lowly intellects; in fact, He would not then be God at all, because He would not be infinite, for that which is infinite cannot be comprehended by us. Hence, the fact that our intellects cannot understand this mystery is an indication and proof that it must be of God who, being infinite, is incomprehensible.

We have treated this mystery extensively because one of the principal benefits in considering the question of the Trinity is to humble man and make him realize the paltriness of his knowledge. Then, perhaps, he will not try to look too closely into the sun with his weak and bleary eyes, that is, he will not try to scrutinize this mystery with his limited intellect. We are not commanded to understand the mystery, but to believe it.

To conclude our discussion of the Trinity, it is fitting that we speak of the various works that are attributed to each of the divine Persons. To the Father is attributed creation and power, not because power and creation are not common to the entire Trinity, but because the Person of the Father is not produced by either of the others but is the principle in the production of the other two.

The work of our redemption is also common to the entire Trinity, because it was with the counsel and will of all three Persons that the Son came into the world, was made man, died for us, atoned for our sins, and was the sacrifice through which the entire Trinity was satisfied and received us again into its love and grace. But because only the Son was incarnate and only He was sacrificed and is the meritorious cause of this pardon and grace, our redemption and salvation are attributed to Him in a special manner.

The fact that we know and believe the things that the Son did for us and all the things that He taught and commanded, and that we possess the love, purity, and goodness that we ought to possess, is not a question of our own strength and power, but we must attribute it all to God and especially to the Holy Ghost. To Him, of all the divine Persons, is attributed goodness and love, and from these sources springs His desire to make us good and to sanctify us. Thus we say that our redemption is the common work of the entire Trinity, but since the Son died for us, Christ is our Redeemer, Mediator, Sacrifice, and the source of our merit. Likewise, because the Spirit illumines us to know all this and gives us the power to thank and serve God, we say that our spiritual life and all our good depend on the gifts that come to us from the Holy Ghost.

BOOK TWO

The Marvels of Creation

Chapter 14 ✠

Creation of the World

What has been said up to this point is based on that which Sacred Scripture tells us of the immensity and greatness of our Creator. We shall now continue the same subject by considering the works which He has made in the universe, because they also give clear testimony of the greatness of God.

Before we consider the visible works of God, we should point out one of the many differences between the Creator and His creatures. All created things have limits and boundaries to which their natures and powers extend. Consequently, they have a limited or finite being and limited powers, knowledge, and faculties which flow from that being. This limitation is according to the measure that the Creator willed to impart to His creatures, giving more to some and less to others.

But since God Himself was not created by any superior being, neither is there any being that can put limits or boundaries to His essence, power, knowledge, goodness, happiness, or any of His other perfections and attributes. And since there are no limits or restrictions of any kind in God, He is infinite in every respect. Therefore, His being is infinite as also are His beauty, His glory, His riches, His mercy, His justice, and all His attributes. He is on that account incomprehensible and ineffable and no creature that has been made or could be made will ever comprehend Him; God alone can perfectly know and comprehend Himself.

We have an appropriate example of this in the kings of this world. They distribute the duties and offices in their kingdom to various persons, as it pleases them, limiting the jurisdiction and power given to each one lest it be prejudicial to others. But the king who thus restricts this delegated power, possesses in himself the supreme and universal authority throughout his entire kingdom, so that he acknowledges no one superior to himself. Consequently, there is in the kingdom no jurisdiction or power, however great, that is not surpassed by that of the king. Such jurisdiction and power is called infinite or absolute, in the sense that it is not restricted to any limit or boundary within its own area of jurisdiction.

Comparing the relationship between the Creator and His creatures with that of a king and his subalternates, we can readily grasp the notion of God's infinity. True, the example fails in this respect, that the authority of the king is infinite only in a relative sense, while that of the Creator is absolute and infinite in every sense.

The same truth can be demonstrated in another way. According to philosophers and theologians, God is so great a being that it is not only impossible that there actually exist a being greater than He, but one could not even imagine a greater being. Since a being that possesses infinite perfections is much greater than one that possesses finite and limited perfections, if the perfections of God were in any way limited, we would be able to imagine other perfections greater than His. But this is impossible, for we have already stated that our concept of God is that of a being so great that we could not even imagine one that is greater.

Before we enter in this sanctuary wherein we are to consider such great things, let us take as our theme and starting point the words of the angel who represented the person of God. When asked his name by the father of Samson, he replied: "Why askest thou my name, which is wonderful?"[104] This is a word well suited to the greatness of God and all His works, for there is nothing however small which, if well considered, will not cause hearts to marvel at the Creator, saying to us in His name: "Why askest thou my name, which is wonderful?"

That cannot be considered true eloquence, says Cicero, which does not arouse wonder and admiration in the listeners. But if merely human genius, aided by study and diligence, is able to construct so perfect and polished an oration that it causes admiration in all who hear it, how should one react to the works fashioned by infinite Wisdom, in comparison with which the wisdom of the cherubim is pure ignorance? Surely, if one is not filled with admiration and wonder in the contemplation of the works of the Creator, it is because one does not understand them, for their majesty and brilliance are sufficient to dazzle the human mind.

Before commencing our consideration of the works of creation, we must observe that although it is true, as St. Augustine says and as we read in Ecclesiasticus, that God created the entire universe and all things in it simultaneously, nevertheless Moses prudently divides the works of creation into six days. God created all things out of love of Himself, that is to say, as a manifestation of the greatness of His perfections, but our intellects cannot easily encompass so immense a world and all the things that are in it. Rather, we would be overwhelmed if we tried to consider all these marvelous things at the same time. For that reason, the inspired writer divided this work

[104] Judg. 13:18.

into many parts. Even then, each work of the six days is of itself so great and significant that it must again be divided into many parts in order to be considered perfectly and adequately.

We must also note that creation in its proper sense does not mean to make one thing from another (this is called generation), but to make something from nothing. Such a power is so proper to God that it cannot be communicated to any creature, however perfect. Observing the changes that are effected in natural things, we see that the greater the distance from one extreme to the other, the greater the power required to cause such a change. But the distance between non-being and being is infinite; consequently, an infinite power is required for the work of creation. This power is found in God alone, who "calleth those things that are not, as those that are."[105]

We shall first treat of the world and its principal parts, namely, the heavens and the elements. Then we shall treat in particular of all living bodies: plants, animals, and man, who was created on the sixth and last day. And since the Christian reader will derive greater profit from this doctrine if he knows the full purpose to which it is directed, let him know that my intention is not only to declare that there is a God who is Creator and Lord of all things, but much more to demonstrate the divine providence that shines forth through all creatures, as well as the other perfections that accompany it, especially the divine goodness, wisdom, and omnipotence, for these are, as Isaias says, the three fingers on which God has poised the bulk of the earth.[106]

Of the three last-named perfections, which in God are all one, divine goodness desires to do well to His creatures, divine

---

[105] Rom. 4:17.

[106] Isa. 40:12.

wisdom plans and ordains how this is to be done, and divine omnipotence executes and effects what His goodness desires and His wisdom ordains. These three perfections are, so to speak, the component parts of divine providence, by which God, with a pious and fatherly concern, furnishes a wide variety of things that are necessary for His creatures. It is my intention to demonstrate how these four divine perfections and countless others shine forth in all the things of this world, the great as well as the small.

The fruitfulness and value of such a consideration can be understood from the words of David: "Blessed are they that search His testimonies; that seek Him with their whole heart."[107] And they will be no less blessed who search God's works; not only those of grace, but also those of nature, because they all spring from the same source. Uncreated Wisdom promises: "They that explain Me shall have life everlasting."[108] That is what we are seeking to do here: to reveal the plan of divine Wisdom as it is manifested in all created things.

A great aid in acquiring oratorical skill is to observe the plan and technique that a great orator employs in his speeches. St. Augustine considered it extremely helpful that he himself had done so in regard to certain passages in St. Paul.[109] How much better a study it is to observe the admirable plan of divine wisdom in the structure and government of the created universe. And if it is written of the Queen of Saba that "she had no longer any spirit in her"[110] when she saw all the wisdom of Solomon and the house that he had built, how much more

---

[107] Ps. 118:2.

[108] Ecclus. 24:31.

[109] Cf. St. Augustine, *De doctrina christiana*, lib. IV.

[110] See III Kings 10:5.

will the devout soul be humbled when, gazing upon the works of incomprehensible wisdom, he seeks to comprehend the art and prudence with which they have been made?

CHAPTER 15 ✠ The Splendor of the Firmament

THE PURPOSE OF the following considerations is to see how the divine perfections are reflected in the created works of God, so that our hearts may be moved to love the goodness of God and our minds may be aroused to a holy fear and reverence for such great majesty. May we likewise be inspired with hope in His paternal care and providence and with greater admiration for the mighty power and wisdom that shine forth through the works of His hands.

We accept as a fundamental proposition that when, through His infinite goodness, the most gracious and sovereign Lord determined to create man and place him in this world, so that by knowing and loving and obeying his Creator he might merit the happiness of the world to come, He likewise determined to provide man with all the things necessary for his sustenance and preservation. Consequently, God created the visible world and all things in it for the use and necessities of human life.

In any workshop two things are required: the material from which things are made and the worker who makes the things. In the great workshop of the universe these two requirements have been amply provided for by the Creator. The material from which new things are made is the variety of elements, and the agents that generate new things from the elements are the heavenly bodies, such as the planets and stars. Granted that God is the First Cause and moves every other cause, these heavenly bodies are among the principal instruments that God uses for the government of the world. So dependent is the world on these planets that the ancient philosophers used to teach that if their movement were to stop, all other motion would cease.

Since the heavenly bodies are among the principal agents of the First Mover, God has ennobled them and made them excel over all other bodies. They are seemingly incorruptible, so that even after the thousands of years since they were created, they appear to continue in the same entirety and beauty that they possessed from the beginning. Time, the destroyer of all things, seems not to have impaired any of them.

God also endowed them with brilliant light, not only for the ornament of the universe, but also for the benefit of human life, as the Psalmist says: "Praise ye the Lord of lords . . . who made the great lights, . . . the sun to rule the day . . . the moon and the stars to rule the night."[111] He gave them such constancy in their movements that they seem never to have varied from the orderly motion that He placed in them from the beginning. As a result, all those whose function it is to rule and govern others, either in the Church or in nations, can learn from the planets how well regulated and constant they must be in their lives so that there will be no disorder in the lives of those under their care. But if the light that is supposed to illumine the darkness

[111] Ps. 135:3–9, *passim*.

of others is obscured, then how great will be the darkness! And if one blind man leads another, what is to be expected but that both shall fall?

The magnificence of the heavenly bodies is such that it causes admiration in anyone who considers it. Indeed, it would seem incredible, were it not that we know that nothing is impossible to Him who created them. And the beauty of the firmament, who can describe it? How pleasant it is, in the serenity of a midsummer's night, to see the full moon in all its brightness, surpassing in clarity the light of all the stars! And when there is no moon, what is more enchanting and more indicative of the omnipotence and beauty of God than the vast heavens sprinkled with a variety of stars, so numerous that no one can count them except Him who made them? But the custom of seeing these things so often robs us of admiration for their beauty and of the incentive to praise the divine Artist who has thus beautified the mighty vault of the heavens.

If a child were born in a prison and lived there until he reached the age of manhood, without ever seeing anything outside the prison walls; if, in addition, he had become a man of intelligence and learning, then the first time he left the prison and saw the starry sky on a tranquil night, certainly he could not help but be astonished at such great beauty. Nor could he help but exclaim: "Who could have adorned such great heavens with so many precious jewels and with diamonds so brilliant? Who could have created such a great number of lamps to give light to the world? Who could have filled the meadow of the skies with such a variety of flowers? Who, but some most beautiful and omnipotent Creator?"

A pagan philosopher once said: "To look at the heavens is to become a philosopher." In other words, when one contemplates the great variety and beauty of the firmament, he recognizes the wisdom and power of its Author. So the Psalmist exclaims: "O Lord our Lord, how admirable is Thy name in the whole earth! For Thy magnificence is elevated above the heavens. . . . For I will behold Thy heavens, the works of Thy fingers; the moon and the stars which Thou hast founded."[112]

If the beauty of the planets is admirable, no less remarkable is the influence they exert on the things of the earth. This is especially true of the sun. For example, when it is farthest removed from the earth, as during the autumn and winter, the trees and bushes lose their foliage and become sterile and almost dead. Then in the spring, when it is closer to the earth, the fields are again dressed in green, the trees are covered with buds and leaves, and the vines and bushes bring forth new shoots, as if impatient to manifest the beauty that they contain hidden within themselves. So many marvelous qualities are to be found in the sun that when the ancient philosopher Anaxagoras was asked why he was born, he answered that it was to see the sun.

But although the sun is so remarkable a planet, few persons marvel at the powers and virtues which the Creator has given it, because, as Seneca says, the custom of seeing things that always operate in the same manner makes them cease to appear admirable, however great they may be. No one marvels at things as long as they follow their regular course, but when they depart from it, all are amazed and ask what the change could signify. Men marvel at new things rather than at great things. However, St. Augustine says that wise men marvel more at great things than at new and unusual things, because

---

[112] Ps. 8:2–4.

they have eyes to see the dignity and excellence of the former arid to evaluate them properly.

One of the greatest and most universal effects of the sun is that it gives light and brilliance to all the other planets and stars that are scattered throughout the firmament. And since these lesser planets exert their influence on the world by means of the light that they receive from the sun, it follows that, after God, the sun is the first cause of all generation, corruption, change, and alteration which take place in the world. The sun also draws the vapors of the oceans on high and when they reach the regions where the air is very cool, they condense and are turned into rain which irrigates the land, thus producing the fruits and grains by which men and animals are nourished. In this sense we can say that the sun gives us bread, wine, meat, fruits, and almost everything else that is necessary for life.

It is also the sun that causes the four seasons of the year, as its distance from the earth is lessened and increased. Divine providence regulates these seasons both for the health of our bodies and for the production of the fruits of the earth by which we are sustained, and so equally is the time divided among them that none of them prevails over the other. Just as masters who have servants and families are accustomed to allot a certain sum each year for their maintenance, so also the Lord, whose family is the entire world, provides for the maintenance of each of the members of His great house and family by means of the four seasons. Thus the divine Ruler sustains and governs this world, increasing His family each year and providing food and nourishment for it. Who, then, seeing the order of divine providence, would not exclaim with the Psalmist: "How great are Thy works, O Lord; Thou hast made all things in wisdom; the earth is filled with Thy riches."[113]

---

[113] Ps. 103:24.

By its presence or absence the sun also divides time into day and night, to the happiness and welfare of the earth's inhabitants. The day is of greater benefit for the duties and tasks of human life, while the night is more beneficial to the plants of the earth, for after the long warm days, plants are refreshed by the coolness and dew of the night hours. At night also men and animals, fatigued with the labors of the day, take their rest. The night is likewise the time most suitable for man to refresh his soul with spiritual things, for then he is freed from the cares and business of the day. Then he can meditate in silence on the goodness of God, singing His praises, as David says: "In the daytime the Lord hath commanded His mercy and a canticle to Him in the night. With me is prayer to the God of my life. I will say to God: Thou art my support."[114] To this practice of prayer David especially invites those who live in the house of the Lord, saying: "Behold, now bless ye the Lord, all ye servants of the Lord who stand in the house of the Lord, in the courts of the house of our God. In the night lift up your hands to the holy places, and bless ye the Lord."[115] Jeremias calls men to the same duty with these words: "Rise up at midnight, and pour forth your heart as water before God," and the prophet Isaias lifted up his soul to God and exclaimed: "My soul hath desired Thee in the night; yea, and with my spirit within me, in the morning early I will watch to Thee."[116]

Therefore, in the calm, silent night, arouse your heart to humble devotion, fixing your eyes on the beauty of the moon or the splendor of the stars which proclaim the beauty and glory of their Creator. Indeed, the brightness of the stars presages the beauty of the glorified bodies which will be ours on

---

[114] Ps. 41:9–10.

[115] Ps. 133:1–2.

[116] Isa. 26:9.

the day of resurrection. "There are bodies celestial, and bodies terrestrial, but one is the glory of the celestial and another of the terrestrial. One is the glory of the sun, another the glory of the moon, and another the glory of the stars. For star differeth from star in glory. So also is the resurrection of the dead. It is sown in corruption, it shall rise in incorruption. It is sown in dishonor, it shall rise in glory. It is sown in weakness, it shall rise in power."[117]

In addition to all these things, the sun enlightens everything that God has created in the heavens and on the earth, so that nothing is hidden from it. And as the sun is the most visible of all corporeal things and the one least able to be gazed upon because of its great brilliance and the weakness of our vision, so also God is the most intelligible of all beings and yet He is the one least comprehended because of the loftiness of His essence and the lowliness of our understanding. Likewise, of all bodily creatures, the sun is the most communicative of light and heat, so that if one closes the door to keep out the sun, it enters through the chinks of the door. What better symbol of the infinite goodness of God, who liberally communicates His riches to all creatures, making them, as St. Dionysius says, as much like unto Himself as their natures permit and even seeking those who flee from Him!

From the resplendent brilliance of the sun the stars receive their brightness and efficacy, just as from the plenitude and abundance of the grace of Christ, the Savior, all just souls receive light and power to perform good works. Moreover, as the presence of the sun is the cause of light and its absence results in darkness, so also the presence of Christ in souls

[117] See I Cor. 15:40–43.

enlightens and teaches them, shows them the way to heaven, and points out the obstacles that must be avoided. But when He is absent from souls, they remain in darkness and obscurity; as a result, they stumble and fall into a thousand occasions of sin, without knowing what they do or realizing what a great danger it is to their salvation when they live thus.

In so many ways does the sun manifest the perfections of God. What sight more delightful and beautiful could be offered to our eyes than that of the sun in its morning rising? With the clarity of its splendor it dispels the darkness and sheds its light on all things, gladdening the heavens, the earth, and the sea. We can compare its beauty to that of a bridegroom and its strength to that of a giant.

But now let us leave the consideration of the sun to speak briefly of its vicar, the moon. To this planet the Creator has committed the task of providing light in the absence of the sun, otherwise the world would be left in total darkness. In addition to many other characteristics, the moon has great power over the waters of the ocean. As the magnet draws iron filings to itself, so the Creator gave to the moon the power of attracting to itself the waters of the ocean, thus causing the ebb and flow of the tides. The moon holds the reins, so to speak, whereby it controls the ocean.

In addition to its power over the ocean, the moon also influences the bodies of men and animals. Thus, we notice the alterations that the moon causes in the human body, especially in the sick, according as the moon is full or in crescent. What we should especially notice is the remarkable power that the Creator has given to this planet, in spite of the fact that it is so distant from the earth and has no light of itself, but receives it from the sun.

Lastly, consider the stars. The number and power and effects of the stars, who can describe them except the Lord, of whom David said that He alone can number the stars and call each one by name?[118] Thus does the Psalmist reveal the complete dependence of the stars on their Creator, who caused the things which are not as if they were, giving existence to those things which have it not.[119]

Of this dependence and obedience the prophet Baruch says: "And the stars have given light in their watches, and rejoiced; they were called, and they said: Here we are. And with cheerfulness they have shined forth to Him that made them."[120] In saying that God calls each one by name, the prophet means that He alone knows the properties and nature of the stars and that He has given them their names accordingly. No human tongue can speak of these things, for they are reserved to divine wisdom. Among the many uses and benefits of the stars, they serve as guides for those who traverse the seas. Since there are no markings in the waters by which the sailor can direct his navigation, he raises his eyes to the heavens and finds his guidance in the stars, especially in the north star, which never changes but serves as a stable and certain guide of the seaways.

---

118 Ps. 146:4.

119 Rom. 4:17.

120 Bar. 3:34–35.

Chapter 16 ✠

Benefits of Air and Rain

In treating of each of the elements, we shall begin with a consideration of the air, the benefits of which are numerous. First of all, it is because of the air that men and animals are able to breathe. Moreover, the coolness of the air refreshes them and tempers the heat of their bodies. It is also the medium through which the light of the sun reaches them, at the same time that it diffuses the light rays so that the heat of the sun is beneficial rather than harmful.

The air also performs an important function in the production of rain. The heat of the sun causes vapors to rise from the waters of the earth and when these vapors reach the upper regions where the air is cold, they condense into drops of water and fall from the skies as rain. We witness a similar phenomenon in distilleries or perfumeries, where the intense heat of the fire drives the moisture from the herbs or flowers and the vapor ascends to a cooler area, condenses into liquid, and then drips into the vessel prepared for it. This is another example of the manner in which art imitates nature.

It is likewise a cause of admiration to see how the Creator has ordained that the rains should fall from above. If all the wise men of the world were to discuss in what way the earth should be irrigated, they could not discover any method more convenient and efficacious than this one. The water falls from the heavens as if it were run through the small holes of a sieve, and thus it is equally distributed in all parts of the ground. It penetrates into the earth itself to give nourishment to plants at their roots, while externally it refreshes the leaves and fruits of the trees.

This is one of God's marvels to which Job refers when he says: "He bindeth up the waters in His clouds, so that they break not out and fall down together."[121] So also Moses writes in praise of the Promised Land: "For the land which thou goest to possess, is not like the land of Egypt, from whence thou camest out, where, when the seed is sown, waters are brought in to water it, after the manner of gardens. But it is a land of hills and plains, expecting rain from heaven. And the Lord thy God dost always visit it, and His eyes are on it from the beginning of the year unto the end thereof. If then you obey my commandments, which I command you this day, that you love the Lord your God, and serve Him with all your heart, and with all your soul, He will give to your land the early rain and the latter rain, that you may gather in your corn, and your wine, and your oil, and your day out of the fields to feed your cattle, and that you may eat and be filled."[122] The Psalmist likewise sings the praise of this blessing when he says: "Who covereth the heaven with clouds, and prepareth rain for the earth."[123] Again, Job says that God not only irrigates the seeded and tilled lands but even the deserted places and the uncharted paths, so that they produce green and fresh foliage.

But who could ever explain and sufficiently extol the many blessings that come to us because of rain? Whoever considers it attentively will see that everything necessary for human life is somehow provided by the Creator through this medium. It is because of the rain that we have bread, wine, oil, fruits,

[121] Job 26:8.

[122] Deut. 11:10–15.

[123] Ps. 146:8.

vegetables, medicinal herbs, and pasture for the animals that provide our meat as well as the wool and leather for our clothing and shoes. The Psalmist was aware of this when he said that God "maketh grass to grow on the mountains, and herbs for the service of men."[124] He also states that man gives food to animals because the animals, in turn, perform many services for man. So numerous are the benefits that we receive from the rain that one of the ancient Greek philosophers, Thales by name, maintained that water is the material from which all things are made.

So great and universal are the blessings of rain that the Creator Himself holds the keys to it and reserves to Himself its distribution. He uses it to give sustenance to His faithful servants and chastisement to the rebellious, by depriving them of this benefit. Thus it is written in the book of Job that God so judges and punishes His people[125] and in the Book of Leviticus we read how God will provide for His faithful ones: "If you walk in My precepts, and keep My commandments, and do them, I will give you rain in due seasons. And the ground shall bring forth its increase, and the trees shall be filled with fruit."[126] But for those who despise His laws and condemn His judgments, God promises that He will visit them with poverty and a burning heat that will destroy their lives. They shall sow their seed in vain; the ground will not bring forth its increase nor the trees yield their fruit.[127]

Not only sins but also ingratitude for such great blessings can be the cause of losing them, as we learn through the words

[124] Ps. 146:8.

[125] Job 36:31.

[126] Lev. 26:3–4.

[127] Lev. 26:14 ff.

of Jeremias: "They have not said in their heart: Let us fear the Lord our God, who giveth us the early and the latter rain in due season; who preserveth for us the fullness of the yearly harvest."[128] Surely it is a great cause of sorrow that there are so few who acknowledge this great blessing from the Creator and who give thanks to Him and serve Him because of it, especially since He gives us so many other things through the bountiful rain that we could not subsist without it. We should think of these things when we see the rain falling from the heavens and understand that the Lord sends us these things. Otherwise we imitate the irrational animals, who receive pasture and sustenance from God but neither acknowledge the Giver nor give thanks to Him, for they lack reason.

The wind is another blessing from divine providence and the Psalmist acknowledged it as such when he stated: "He bringeth forth winds out of His stores."[129] First of all, the winds carry the clouds and the waters that are in them wherever the Creator wishes those rains to be sent.[130] So we see that it rains in Spain when the wind is from the southwest, coming in from the sea and bringing the rain clouds from that direction. On the other hand, in Africa the rains come with the north wind, which likewise passes over the sea and brings that continent the rain-filled clouds which are the waterbuckets of God.

And what would happen to navigation and ocean commerce between islands and nations if there were no winds and the air were always calm? The winds enable the navigators to travel to the very ends of the earth, so that they can collect the products that are plentiful in one place but scarce in another and bring

---

[128] Jer. 5:24.

[129] Ps. 134:7.

[130] Job 37:6.

back the things that others have in abundance but which we lack. Thus all things are made common and all nations receive a sufficiency. The whole world becomes a common market place. What is more, these same winds have carried the missionaries to all parts of the world and the gospel message that they brought is the best kind of merchandise that could be transported from one place to another.

The winds also serve another purpose, as Seneca points out, for they purify the air and remove from it any corruption or harmful substance with which it may be contaminated. We need but recall the great pestilence in the city of Lisbon in 1570, which was ended when an unusually cold and strong wind carried away the germ-laden air and caused the sea water to overflow into the wells and fountains along the coastline.

The winds also help the farmer to winnow the corn and to remove dust and straw from the grain. And when he is oppressed by the withering heat of summer, a fresh breeze lessens the force of the heat and refreshes him. From these examples Christian souls can learn how to refer all things to God and how to be edified by God's works. Let them also consider how great must be the torment of the eternal flames where the damned are burning in the never-ending fire and can never hope for any kind of alleviation or refreshment.

CHAPTER 17 ✠

The Grandeur of the Sea

WE NOW COME to a consideration of the second element, water, which at the beginning of creation covered the entire earth, as the air covered all the water. But since no one could have inhabited the earth under such conditions, the Creator, who made the earth for the service of man and made man for Himself, commanded that the waters be gathered together to form seas and oceans and thus uncover the earth as our dwelling place.

There are many aspects of the oceans that are worthy of consideration, such as their grandeur, fruitfulness, and depths, their shores and ports, their risings and fallings, and, finally, the great benefits that they bring us. All these qualities preach a silent sermon of praise to Him who created them. So the Psalmist praised God for the grandeur of the oceans when he said: "How great are Thy works, O Lord! Thou hast made all things in wisdom; the earth is filled with Thy riches. So is this great sea, which stretcheth wide its arms."[131]

The Creator ordained these things so that all nations might enjoy the benefits of the various bodies of water which serve to bring nations closer together by means of navigation and serve also as a source of nourishment for men by supplying a great variety of fish and other sea food. Consequently, the Creator willed that the ocean should have many bays and gulfs so that the fish would seek shelter there and thus be more easily caught. Moreover, in all the seas and oceans there are ports

[131] Ps. 103:24–25.

and harbors where ships can rest secure from tempests and storms and the violence of the winds.

The omnipotence and providence of the Creator are likewise manifested in the multitude of islands that are distributed throughout the oceans and seas. St. Ambrose compares them to little jewels that adorn the great bodies of water. God in His providence has fashioned them as a stopping-place where sailors can renew their strength, find refreshment, and take refuge in time of storm. The omnipotence of God shines forth in the conservation of these little islands, especially when the towering waves would almost seem to cover them over or the angry seas would threaten to wash them away. It is a marvel of which God spoke through the mouth of Job: "Who shut up the sea with doors, when it broke forth as issuing out of the womb; when I made a cloud the garment thereof, and wrapped it in a mist as in swaddling bands? I set My bounds around it, and made it bars and doors; and I said: Hitherto thou shalt come, and shalt go no further, and here thou shalt break thy swelling waves."[132]

All the elements have a tendency to seek their natural positions or places and the natural place for water, as we have seen, is to cover the entire earth. But God, by His word alone, has removed it from its natural place and has gathered it together into oceans and seas. Thus it has remained for many thousands of years and the waters have not surpassed the limits which He assigned to them. God uses this obedience of insensate creation as an argument to confound the disobedience and irreverence of men. So He says through Jeremias: "Will not you then fear Me . . . and will you not repent at My presence? I

---

[132] Job 38:8–11.

have set the sand a bound for the sea, an everlasting ordinance, which it shall not pass over; and the waves thereof shall toss themselves, and shall not prevail; they shall swell, and shall not pass over it."[133]

Who would not be moved to adore the omnipotence and providence of the Creator who is able to establish and maintain what He wishes? He has placed a limitation and restraint on the waters of the world so that they will not cover the entire earth. Although the waves of the ocean beat furiously against the sand and shore, they never dare to pass beyond the assigned limits. Beating against the shores and boundaries of the earth, the waters of the ocean see the law of the Creator written there and they turn back, much like a runaway horse feels the pull of the reins and bridle and stops and turns around, although he does not want to do so.

The sea both divides the lands and nations and promotes friendship and concord among those same nations. The Creator desires that nations should be friendly with each other. Consequently, He did not give each nation all that is necessary for life, because the dependence of one nation on another prompts them to be friendly to each other. But the highways and roads that cross the continents are often difficult to travel and it is impossible to transport every kind of merchandise over the roads of the earth. Therefore, the Creator provided this new path on which ships both great and small could navigate and one ship can carry a cargo that would require the use of many beasts of burden. Thus the ocean is like a great fair or market place where all the nations of the world exchange goods and each receives the things necessary to itself.

---

[133] Jer. 5:22.

We should note also that the ocean serves as a symbol of the meekness of God as well as His anger and indignation. What is more meek and tranquil than the ocean when it is calm and no winds blow, or when a soft and gentle breeze sends the rippling waves to the shore, where with regular succession they break silently and return to the ocean? This is a symbol of the meekness and gentleness of God toward the good and the just. But when the sea is buffetted by violent winds and lifts its terrifying waves high into the sky, revealing the dark chasms of its depth; when it lashes with fierce strength against the sides of ships, raising them on high and suddenly dropping them with a jolt, so that the men who are at the mercy of the sea are placed in mortal fear and trembling for their lives, we have a symbol of the divine wrath and of the magnitude of divine power that is able to stir up such tempests and appease them when He wills.

The Psalmist speaks to us of this when he says: "O Lord God of hosts, who is like to Thee? Thou art mighty, O Lord, and Thy truth is round about Thee. Thou rulest the power of the sea, and appeasest the motion of the waves thereof. . . . Thine are the heavens, and thine is the earth; the world and the fullness thereof Thou hast founded; the north and the sea Thou hast created."[134]

There is yet another benefit of the ocean which is so great that the pen hesitates to treat of it. For what words could describe the wide variety of fish that are found in the sea? What great wisdom has fashioned them, not only in such a multitude of species, but in so many different shapes and sizes? Some are small and others are of incredible size, and between

---

[134] Ps. 88:9–12.

the two extremes is infinite variety. The same God created the whale and the frog but He did not labor more in the making of one or the other.

With a pair of scissors a child can cut many different figures or designs out of cloth or paper because the cloth or paper are perfectly submissive to the designs and wishes of the child. Yet, the child does no more than fashion a figure or shape, without adding anything further to the cloth or paper. But the Creator not only gives form and figure to the things He fashions, He gives them life and sense and movement. He gives them the power to seek nourishment, defensive measures for their preservation, and a fruitful means for the conservation of the species.

Who can count the eggs of the shad or the codfish or any other fish? Yet each egg is capable of producing another fish as large as the one from which the egg originally came. Like a tender mother, the ocean receives these eggs and protects and nurtures them until they evolve into fish. And since divine providence has created fish for the sustenance of men, but the fishermen cannot see the fish in the waters as the hunter sees the game on the land or in the air, God disposed that the number of fish should be so great that some could usually be caught wherever the net would be let down. The number and variety of animals and birds is almost countless, but greater still is the number of fish in the sea.

How pleasing are the works of the Lord, and all are made with consummate wisdom. Consider, finally, the sweetness and taste of the various kinds of fish and sea foods. St. Ambrose exclaims that these delicacies were created before man himself and that man's temptation already existed before man was created. But the Creator did not intend these things as temptations for man; they were created for his sustenance. God treats us as His beloved children and He intends the tastiness of these foods to lead us to love and praise the Lord who provided them. But many men are so slothful and self-centered that although all the creatures of the world invite us to praise the Giver of all gifts, these men are so occupied with pampering their appetites that it never occurs to them to give thanks to God or to acknowledge that these things have been given to us without any merits on our part.

Chapter 18 ✠ *The Beauty and Fertility of the Earth*

We now come to the consideration of the earth, our common mother, from which man's body originally came and by which we are nourished. Of all the elements, the earth is the lowest and least active, yet it is more serviceable and profitable to us than any other. So the Psalmist states: "The heaven of heaven is the Lord's, but the earth He has given to the children of men."[135] In obedience to the command of God, the earth receives us as a benign mother when we are born, sustains us after we are born, and at the end of our life again receives us into her lap and faithfully guards our bodies until the day of resurrection.

[135] Ps. 113:16.

The earth is also more gentle and favorable to us than the other elements. The oceans and rivers sometimes cause tidal waves and floods that do considerable damage to men and their property. The air is sometimes whipped into tornadoes, hurricanes, or windstorms that damage the crops and destroy the work of the poor laborers. But the earth is the faithful servant of man. What fruits it produces! What beautiful colors it presents! And who could describe the riches of the earth, especially when we consider the variety of metals that were taken from it for five thousand years before the coming of Christ and have been mined since that time and will be extracted until the end of time. As the poet Ovid says, men will ultimately arrive at the very gates of hell in their pursuit of the gold and silver and precious stones that are hidden in the bowels of the earth.

Still more noteworthy are the fountains and rivers that irrigate and refresh the earth. As the Creator has placed veins and arteries throughout the human body to sustain and refresh it, so also He has provided a network of rivers to refresh and irrigate the great body of the earth. But in many parts of the earth there is a deficiency of springs and rivers, and for that reason divine providence has ordained that the whole earth should be saturated with water, so that by digging wells men can supply for the lack of springs or rivers.

Again, who will not be filled with wonder when considering the origin and source from which these rivers and springs proceed? In many lands far removed from the sea we discover wide ribbons of water cutting across the plains or gushing springs racing down the mountain sides. What is the source of this water? How is it that the water flows at all times of the year, both in winter and summer, and never runs dry even after thousands of years? The Psalmist praises God because He brings forth winds out of His stores,[136] but how much more He should be praised for having deposited in the earth such great supplies of water.

This should prompt us to give glory to God for so great a benefit and to marvel at His providence and power. One would have to be very stupid indeed not to see this. A story is told about an uneducated negro who was crossing the river between Córdoba and Castro del Río. After gazing at the rushing water, he turned to his master and said: "Flowing, flowing, and never filled up; flowing, flowing, and never ending; a great thing is God." This illiterate negro confounds us and reminds us to praise God for this blessing. Even more pointedly did the angel of the Apocalypse invite men to praise God when he flew down from heaven, crying out to the people of the earth: "Fear the Lord, and give Him honor, because the hour of His judgment is come, and adore ye Him, that made heaven and earth, the sea, and the fountains of waters."[137]

Since we are treating of the earth, it is fitting that we should say something of its fertility and the fruits it produces. This brings us to a consideration of living things, for the heavens, the stars, and the other elements which we have previously discussed do not have life. Since things that possess life are more perfect than those which do not, they are a greater manifestation of the wisdom and providence of the Creator, and the more perfect the life, the more clearly do they reflect their Maker. God, as they say, is not penny-wise and pound-foolish. The more perfect a thing is, the greater is His care and

---

136 Ps. 134:7.

137 Apoc. 14:7.

providence over it and the more clearly does He manifest His wisdom through it.

To God alone we owe the great blessings of the fruits of the earth. By His word alone He created the plants and trees of the earth, as we read: "Let the earth bring forth the green herb, and such as may seed, and the fruit tree yielding fruit after its kind, which may have seed in itself upon the earth."[138] Once spoken, the command was effected and the earth was clothed in verdure and adorned with many flowers and plants and trees.

Who can describe the beauty of the fields? What can our words convey of such splendor? But we have the testimony of Scripture, where the holy patriarch compares the blessing and grace of the saints with the sweet aroma of a fertile field: "Behold the smell of my son is as the smell of a plentiful field, which the Lord hath blessed."[139]

Who can portray the beauty of the purple violets, the white lilies, the blood-red rose? What artist could reproduce on his canvas a summer's meadow with its flowers of various hues, some yellow, some red, and others a mixture of many colors? Indeed, one cannot say what pleases him most, the color of the flower, the delicacy of its shape, or the sweet odor that comes from it. The eyes feast on the beautiful spectacle while the perfume of the flowers delights the sense of smell. Such is the grace and beauty which the Creator applies to Himself when He says: "The beauty of the fields is in Me."

Gaze upon the lily and note its dazzling whiteness. See how the slender stem rises gracefully and terminates in a chalice of

[138] Gen. 1:11.
[139] Gen. 27:27.

lovely petals that protect and enclose grains of gold so that no harm may come to them. What human artist could ever make anything like it? The Savior Himself praised the lilies of the field when He said that not even Solomon in all his glory was dressed as richly as one of these flowers.

Even more amazing is the fact that the seeds scattered on the earth do not bring forth fruit unless they first die. St. Ambrose waxed eloquent on this point when he described the way in which a grain of wheat grows, using this as an example of how one can seek and find God in all things. He describes how the earth receives the grain of wheat and, like a mother, gathers the seed to her womb. Gradually the seed is changed into a sprout and ultimately becomes full-grown. When it reaches maturity, it produces a sheath or head that contains little pods wherein new seeds are formed. Thus, the cold cannot damage the seeds nor can the sun burn them with its intense heat; the wind will not blow them away nor will water damage them. The sheath also protects the grains of wheat from the birds, not only by reason of the pods that contain the seeds, but also by means of little pointed whiskers or strands that protrude from the sheath. And because the slender stem could not of itself bear the weight of the sheath of wheat, it is strengthened by a covering of leaves with which it is adorned and by the knots or knuckles that are distributed at intervals along the stem. This is not true of oats, however, for this grain does not need such protection. We see from this that the divine Creator does not fail us in those things that are necessary but neither does He make things that are useless.

The earth also produces many kinds of vegetables for our sustenance. Some are kept dry and can be used at any time during the entire year; others we eat as soon as they are ripe.

Some grow under the ground and others above it, and of those that grow above the ground, some reproduce seeds within themselves, to be used for future planting. We read that the children of Israel yearned for such vegetables while crossing the desert. Here again we have evidence of divine providence, which not only provides fresh fruit in the summertime for the refreshment of the body, but also made vegetables that are to be eaten in due season. Not content with providing us with the flesh of so many animals, fish, and birds, and with a variety of fruits and abundant grains, He also gave us many kinds of vegetables so that no type of nourishment would be lacking to us. But how badly man uses these gifts! Even while he enjoys them, he does not think to raise his eyes to see the hand from which these gifts and benefits flow, not only to the good, but even to sinners.

From what has been said, it will be understood that the naked pagans of Africa are not the only barbarians, but there are many civilized barbarians dressed in the costliest garments. If a traveler were to stop at the home of a wealthy citizen and if the rich man, without any obligation, were to receive the stranger as a guest and treat him with every possible kindness; if he were to seat his guest at a table laden with the choicest foods that he had in the house; if, after eating, the traveler should depart without bidding his host farewell or thanking him for his hospitality and generosity, what would we think of such a person? We would say that he was more of a barbarian than the most inhuman savage.

What, then, is the status of so many wealthy and powerful men who sit every day at a table laden with the countless gifts that God has provided, not for Himself nor for the angels, but for the sustenance and well-being of man, and yet they neither thank Him who, without any obligation on His part, has so generously provided for man, nor do they even advert to the liberality of God? Every day they see the proof of God's blessings but they never give a thought to His generous and magnificent providence. Who will deny that men such as these, who live in complete forgetfulness of God, are worse than barbarians? They are like the rich man in the Gospel who dined every day in great splendor, but gave not a thought to God or to the poor beggar who sat at his gate.

The provision and abundance of the things on this earth are a clear manifestation of the providence of God, who is a Father to His family. But what shall we say of the variety of beautiful flowers, which do not serve for man's sustenance but for his delight? What other reason is there for the carnations, marigolds, lilies, irises, violets, and numerous other flowers that fill the gardens and cover the hills and fields and meadows? Consider their various colors, the beauty and artistry with which they are fashioned, the order and harmony of the leaves with which they are embellished, and the delightful scents which many of them emit. Of what service are all these things, except to give man something on which he can feast his eyes? Even more, they give joy to the soul when, in contemplating the flowers, a man can recognize the beauty of God and the great care that He has shown for us in showering us with gifts.

God is not content merely with providing us with the necessities of life; He has created things for our recreation and delight. Not only did He desire that we should gaze upon the splendor of the stars on a serene night, but He desired also that we should enjoy the sight of the multicolored flowers against the fertile valleys and green plains, like another heaven splashed with flowery stars. Such beauty serves a double purpose: on the one hand, it delights us with its loveliness and splendor; on the other hand, it arouses us to the praise of the Creator who made all these things, not for Himself or for the angels or for brute animals, but for the honest pleasure of men.

Let us take any one flower from among the great variety and ask: Since God does nothing without a purpose, why did He create this most beautiful and sweet-smelling flower? It is not, surely, for the sustenance of man nor for medicinal use or any other utility. Then, what other purpose can this flower have but to delight our vision with its beauty and our sense of smell with its sweet aroma? Consider also how many different kinds of flowers God created for the same purpose and how many other things He has made for the delight of the other senses. Consider the brilliance of jewels and precious stones which dazzle the eye, the music of the birds which pleases the ear, the various perfumes and herbs which captivate our sense of smell, and the infinity of savors which satisfy our sense of taste.

All these things declare to us the sweetness and benignity of the sovereign Lord who had such a regard for men that He not only created a variety of foods and other things necessary for man's sustenance, but He took special care to create many different things for man's honest recreation. So liberally did God provide for man that none of the bodily senses lacks its proper object in which it can find delight. What greater proof of our Father's love for us than the gratuitous blessings He has bestowed on us?

Not content with this, God also created a variety of trees, such as the laurel, the myrtle, the cypress, the cedars, the poplar, and the ivy which adorns the walls of gardens and serves them as cover of protection. Some trees bear fruit and others are sterile; some give nourishment to men, others to beasts;

some never lose their leaves, others change each year; some serve only for shade and adornment; others serve various purposes. Among the fruit-bearing trees, some give fruit for consumption in the summer; others give fruit that can be kept for the wintertime. Here again we see a manifestation of God's liberality and providence in creating trees of various kinds so that there would be both a sufficiency and a variety of fruits.

Consider the variety of plums and apples and grapes. Not only that, but consider how even on the one tree, the fruit does not ripen all at once, but gradually. Thus, we see that on the fig tree some fruit ripens while the rest is yet green and in this way the one tree provides a supply of fruit over a longer period. But the wisdom of divine providence is still more evident in the summer fruits. In the heat and dryness of the summer, men naturally seek the refreshment of cool and juicy fruits which the Creator has provided at that season. Nor does the fact that many men get sick on fruit militate against God's providence, for this is not the fault of the fruit but of the intemperate man who uses God's gifts badly. In like manner, it is not the fault of the wine that many use it immoderately, but it is the fault of the one who partakes of it.

No less does divine wisdom manifest itself in the structure of the trees themselves. If a man wishes to build a house, he first prepares the foundations on which the house will be supported. So also in fashioning trees, God has decreed that before the tree raises its branches into the air, it should be firmly rooted in the earth, and these roots will be in proportion to the height and breadth of the tree. The higher the tree, the deeper its roots. Once the young tree is firmly rooted, the trunk gradually thickens until it resembles a column or pillar of a building and can support the canopy of the branches with their leaves and blossoms and, later, the mature fruit. Seneca observes that in spite of the great diversity of trees and shrubs and plants, no one leaf is exactly like any other but there is always a difference in size, shape, color, or some other detail. He made the same observation in regard to the diversity of human faces, noting that there is scarcely one man who looks like another.

No less remarkable is the manner in which trees are nourished and maintained. The little hairlike strands that protrude from the roots absorb moisture from the earth and then the heat of the sun draws this moisture upward through the trunk of the tree and through all its branches. The bark of the tree serves as a protective covering over the pores of the tree through which the moisture passes. The leaves are equipped with veins similar to those in the human body. A large vein divides the leaf into two equal parts and the smaller subsidiary veins which branch off from it carry nourishment to all parts of the leaf. I once observed this in the leaves of a pear tree which had been so eaten by worms that the whole network of minute veins was exposed.

Not only is the tree sustained and nourished, but it also grows to a great size because of its vegetative soul. Animals possess the powers of the vegetative soul as well as those of a sensitive soul; consequently they are not only occupied with the sustenance and growth of the body, but even more so with functions of the external senses. Plants, however, lack a sensitive soul and therefore their powers are concentrated on nourishment and growth. So also we see that men who are more given to study or contemplation have more flaccid bodies because they exercise their intellectual faculties rather than their bodily members.

And who could fail to observe the beauty of the trees when they are laden with ripe fruit? What, for example, is more pleasing to the sight than an apple tree when its branches are weighted down with apples of different shades of color that send forth a delightful odor? Again, how beautiful is the grapevine with its copious green leaves, among which are half-concealed the large clusters of grapes of various shapes and colors? They are like so many jewels suspended from the branches of the vine.

Nor did providence fail to take precautions to safeguard the ripe fruits. The trees have leaves not only for beauty and shade but also to protect the fruit from the heat of the sun, which would otherwise wither the fruit. And if the fruit is especially tender, as are figs or grapes, the leaves are larger, in order to afford greater protection. However, the leaves do not cover the trees and vines like a solid blanket, but little openings are provided here and there so that the warm winds and snatches of sunlight can touch the ripening fruits.

God's providence is even more evident when we consider the manner in which the fruits of the tree are protected from greater dangers. The fruit of the tall pines, which grow in windy places or on mountain sides, would never ripen had God not fashioned the pine comb wherein each seed is placed in its own compartment and so well protected that all the fury of the winds cannot dislodge it. So also the chestnut trees, the fruit of which becomes the food of the poor when they have no bread, are found in mountainous places and subject to the violence and coldness of the winds. Therefore, the chestnut is covered with a prickly husk and with two inner tunics, one very hard and the other soft. Thus the chestnuts are protected against damage from the heat of the sun and the force of the winds. Moreover, since some trees bear a fruit that is large and heavy, such as the citrus fruits, the Creator provided that the branches of such trees should be strong and thick so that they could more easily support the weight of the fruit. And thus we see that in no created thing has divine providence been wanting or wasteful.

Let us, finally, consider the beauty of the pomegranate. How well it manifests the artistry of the Creator! First, the Creator has covered this fruit on the outside with a tunic that is made to its measure and completely encircles it to protect it from the violence of the sun and wind. The outside of this tunic or skin is hard and durable, but its inside is soft and downy so that it will not injure the tender fruit contained within. The seeds of the fruit are distributed into sections and each section is divided by a membrane more delicate than silk. Further, if any one of these quarters or sections should become spoiled, the membrane preserves the neighboring sections so that they are not contaminated. In much the same way, God divided the lobes of our brain and surrounded each with a membrane so that harm done to one section would not affect the others. Each seed of the pomegranate contains within itself a white bony substance so that its soft exterior will be better preserved and at its base it has a little stem, as thin as a thread, through which the seed receives its nourishment, in much the same way as the embryo in the womb of its mother is nourished through the umbilical cord. The seeds rest upon a white, soft substance similar to that of the inside of the skin that covers the entire fruit. Lastly, a royal crown adorns the top of the pomegranate, as if the Creator wished to designate it as the queen of all fruits. From the color of its seeds, which are as beautiful as coral, to its delicious taste and health-giving qualities, there is no fruit to compare with the pomegranate.

But why is it that men, who are so astute at philosophizing about human affairs, do not see the wise and loving providence that has created so beneficial and beautiful a fruit? The bride in the Canticle of Canticles understands this much better, for she invites the bridegroom to go forth to the vineyards to see if the flowers be ready to bring forth fruits and if the pomegranates flourish.[140] And since we have mentioned the vineyard, let us consider that although the vine is a small tree, its fruit is not at all insignificant. It supplies grapes for the whole year and the wine that strengthens and gladdens the heart of man. It also provides vinegar, must, and raisins. Therefore it is fitting that the Savior should compare Himself to the vine when He says: "I am the vine; you, the branches. . . . As the branch cannot bear fruit of itself, unless it abide in the vine, so neither can you, unless you abide in Me."[141]

Since the vine is small and cannot grow to great heights, it has been provided with tendrils that attach themselves to the branches of trees and climb to the height of the tree itself. Here we have a symbol of our redemption, for in the same way we, who are so base and lowly in comparison with the angels, ascend on high by clinging to that cedar of Lebanon which is Christ, our Redeemer. By uniting ourselves to Him with the bonds of love we shall rise with Him and ascend to heaven with Him. St. Gregory says that since we were unable to grasp the divine greatness, God abased Himself in coming down to earth in order to lift us up and carry us on His shoulders. For

[140] Cant. 7:12.

[141] John 15:4–5.

by the mystery of the Incarnation human nature was ennobled and exalted above the angels.

We have mentioned that some trees are sterile and purely forest trees, and yet God has created them out of regard for our needs. For men need not only sustenance by way of food, but they also need houses and dwellings as a protection against the inclemency of the weather, and God has created trees suitable for this purpose. He ordained that fruit trees should usually be low and that their branches should extend outward like long arms so that the fruit could be more easily gathered. But the pine, the oak, the poplar, and other trees that were made to supply wood for building are tall and straight. Lastly, many different kinds of trees provide food for the animals that eat of their leaves and bark, supply fuel for the fire that is so necessary to men, and serve as a source of medicinal elements that are beneficial to human health.

In closing our consideration of this matter, we must not neglect to recognize the great care that divine providence has shown for the conservation of the various species of plants. First, He provided that an abundance of seeds should be produced by each plant so that seeds would never be lacking from which a plant could be reproduced; and secondly, He endowed each seed with such power that from the smallest seed a shrub or tree is reproduced. We see proof of both of these things in the mustard seed to which the Savior referred in the Gospel parable. Each tree produces millions of seeds and each seed is capable of producing another tree that will again produce millions of seeds. A melon seed produces a vine of melons and each new melon contains numerous seeds that can again produce new melons. Or think of the seeds of an orange and and how many other oranges and seeds they can produce.

How, then, can there ever be lacking a sufficiency of fruits and plants, when there is so much material from which they can be reproduced? How well God has provided for us! And when you have considered God's generosity in these things, consider also how copious was the redemption that He sent to us through the incarnation of His Son. If He was liberal in providing for the preservation of plants, how much more liberal and merciful has He been in restoring and sanctifying the human race? The Apostle realized this when he said that the riches of grace which the Son of God brought down to earth are incomprehensible.[142] And Christ Himself said: "I am come that they may have life, and may have it more abundantly."[143]

Chapter 19 ✠

Variety and Perfections of Animals

The animals possess another and more perfect grade of life than that of the plants which we have been considering, for they are capable of sensation and movement. And since the animals are more perfect than the plants, they give greater evidence of the divine providence of the Creator who necessarily exerts greater care over things that are more perfect.

There are books written by famous authors who so marveled at the structure of the bodies of animals and their powers

---

[142] Eph. 2:7.

[143] John 10:10.

of self preservation, that they were prompted to make detailed studies of the nature and characteristics of animals. Alexander the Great, for example, even in the midst of great military enterprises which were sufficient to occupy his full time, was so anxious to know about the nature and properties of animals that he commanded hunters, fishermen, mountaineers, and shepherds of Greece and Asia to give Aristotle a complete account of all that they knew so that he could write his famous books on the animal world.

But how much more is gained by the religious man when he considers these matters, for he is thereby raised above all creation and arrives at a knowledge of the sovereign Maker, in which knowledge is contained a good part of our happiness. So Jeremias says: "Let not the wise man glory in his wisdom, and let not the strong man glory in his strength, and let not the rich man glory in his riches; but let him that glorieth glory in this, that he understandeth and knoweth Me, for I am the Lord that exercise mercy, and judgment, and justice in the earth."[144]

It is to such knowledge that this chapter is dedicated. If the treatment seems longer than a philosopher would desire, do not censure me for it, because I do not write of these things as a philosopher but as a theologian, directing all things to a better knowledge of the Creator. Moreover, I write of these matters because the subject itself is so interesting and manifests the wisdom and providence of God in a singular manner. The reader will find some facts so amazing that he will be reminded of Pliny's statement that the works of nature are so majestic that they sometimes surpass human faith and credulity.

[144] Jer. 9:23.

God supplies for the lack of reasoning power in animals by implanting in them certain natural inclinations and instincts, so that in many things animals act as if they possessed perfect reasoning power. If one remembers this fact, he will not consider incredible some of the things we shall narrate. In creating the animals God gave them whatever was necessary for their conservation. So St. Thomas Aquinas states that animals are like instruments in the hands of God who, as their first and principal cause, moves them in accordance with their natures through the natural inclinations and instincts which He implanted in them when He created them.[145] Moreover, God did not merely provide for the needs of the animals themselves; He also manifests His glory through them, and this is more evident as the marvels He performs are greater and more numerous. Therefore, no one should consider any of these matters incredible, for God is the efficient cause who makes all these things possible and they are all the more credible as they give greater testimony of His glory, which is the final cause of all creation, both visible and invisible.

It will also help our credulity if we recall the statement of Aristotle, namely, that the works of animals are very similar to the works of men. What men do for their conservation, the animals likewise do for theirs. To select one example from many others, consider the art with which the swallow builds her nest. Just as the mason, when he wishes to cover a wall with adobe, mixes straw with the clay to give the adobe the necessary consistency, so the swallow does the same thing in the building of her nest. And in all those things required for

---

[145] *Summa theol.*, Ia IIae, q. 1, a.2.

the care of her young ones, the swallow acts the same as any being that possesses an intellect.

The Creator gave man an intellect so that out of the infinite number of things required for his conservation, he could discover or invent whatever is necessary for his well-being. But it was not necessary that God preserve the life of animals in the same way, for although they lack the power of reasoning, He has implanted in them those natural inclinations and instincts by which they can do all that they would do if they had an intellect and sometimes they do things much more perfectly than man. Working through instinct, they have greater certitude, more infallibility, more regularity than men do in performing the acts that pertain to their own conservation. Moreover, animals are so adept at recognizing those things that are beneficial or medicinal and in sensing the changes in the temperature and weather that men frequently have to learn these things from the animals. God has here manifested the greatness of His power and wisdom and providence, for although the species of animals are innumerable, in none of them, however small, did he omit or overlook a single detail.

To begin with a consideration of the characteristics common to all animals, the first thing that comes to our attention is the fact that God in His infinite goodness has created animals for the service of man and has provided the animals themselves with all that is necessary for their own conservation and well-being. Thus, animals have the power to nourish themselves, defend themselves, cure themselves of sickness, and procreate their offspring.

For the preservation and nourishment of animals, God has created a variety of foods proportionate to the different kinds of animals. Some live on flesh, others on blood, some on herbs, others on grain, and still others on insects of the earth or air. And since there is an infinite variety of animals, both great and small, God has provided such a variety of nourishment that there is no animal, however small, that lacks food for its sustenance. So the Psalmist says that God has provided food for all flesh[146] and gives beasts their food.[147]

This is especially evident in the case of those birds which do not feed on plants. During the month of May, when there is as yet no wheat, no barley, no flax, and no other grain in the fields, we see so many swallows in Spain that every church and house and farm is swarming with them. What serves as food for the mouths of so many parents and young ones at a time when there is no grain on which they can feed? Only the Lord who provides for them knows what they eat. Christ Himself uses this example to arouse our confidence in the heavenly Father when He says: "Behold the birds of the air, for they neither sow, nor do they reap, nor gather into barns; and your heavenly Father feedeth them. Are not you of much more value than they?"[148]

To ensure that animals would have sufficient nourishment, the Creator gave them all the faculties, powers, and senses they need to find their food. He gave them eyes so that they could seek out their food and the power of movement, by means of feet, wings, or fins, so that they could approach their food. Moreover, many animals have their bodies inclined earthward, in order to be closer to the source of their food. And since there are many animals that feed upon the weaker species, the Creator fashioned their bodies in such a way that

---

146 Ps. 135:25.

147 Ps. 146:9.

148 Matt. 6:26.

they could defend themselves against the strength and violence of those fiercer animals, lest they be killed and eaten. Consequently, some are swift of foot, some have the speed of wings, some have a hard defensive shell, such as oysters and clams, or strong arms for attack, such as lobsters and crabs, while others have the astuteness to hide in their burrows or to take refuge in flocks and herds and thus be assisted by many against the attacks of a few.

And since animals, like men, are subject to sickness, God gave them a natural instinct for curing themselves and seeking remedies against disease. They also possess instinctive knowledge of the danger that may come to them from other animals that are their enemies. So the sheep flees from the wolf but does not flee from the mastiff, which is very similar to the wolf. God also gave the animals the faculty of anticipating changes in the weather that would prove harmful to them, so that they can prepare themselves against the changes of seasons. Thus, the birds move from place to place, spending the winters in the south where it is warm and then returning to the north in the summer. Animals also have a sense of providing for the future by way of storing up food in the summer so that they will have nourishment during the winter.

We have already observed how God has provided for the preservation of plants by ordaining that they should produce many seeds so that material would never be lacking from which new plants could spring. In like manner He has taken care of the conservation of the species of animals. At certain times of the year animals are vehemently inclined to satisfy their instinct for the preservation of the species. Both Plato and Cicero marveled greatly at the infallible regularity with which divine providence intervened for the conservation of the animal species. However, although the inclination for the procreation of young ones is extremely vehement in animals at certain times in the year, when this period is passed, the animals return to their former tranquillity and repose. Then the male and female animals can again associate and live together in all honesty and temperance. The temperance of animals outside the season of procreation is a proof of the effects of original sin in man, because many men are extremely lax in observing the law of temperance.

How solicitous are the animals in the nourishment and defense of their offspring! Consider the care which birds have for their young. God seems to have given birds the greatest love for their young ones because they have the greatest difficulty in caring for them. Birds must remain light in weight if they are to fly, and therefore the Creator did not equip them with organs for producing milk nor weigh them down with the milk like other animals. As a result, it is necessary for birds to share with their young the food that they have gathered at the cost of much effort. And since birds have greater difficulty in finding food and feeding their young, the Creator gave them a stronger parental love, for love can do all things and conquer all things, and to the one who loves it is considered no hardship at all but rather a delight. Sacrifice is easy for one who loves. So St. Bernard tells us: "Let us love Christ, my brothers, and then everything difficult will become easy."

It is also remarkable to observe the facility which birds have for building their nests. As a rule they are made after the fashion of little baskets which easily accommodate the number of their young. Inside the nest they place soft grass or downy feathers so that the tender little fledglings will not be wounded by the roughness of the nest. What more could the parent birds do even if they had the use of reason? And in order that the little ones will not dirty the nest with their excrement, they are placed at the edge of the nest to purge themselves and later the parent bird cleans the nest with its beak, a masterly organ which serves not only to build the nest but also to keep it clean.

Some birds and other animals are much hunted but are too weak to defend themselves well. Consequently, divine providence has given them a remarkable fertility so that the species would be preserved, as we see in the case of doves and rabbits, which bring forth their young almost every month, and the partridges, which sometimes lay as many as twenty eggs. Moreover, all animals have either defensive or offensive weapons. Some have horns, some have claws, and others have teeth. The animals that are not strongly armed have the astuteness and speed to protect themselves from the violence of the strong; for example, the hare and the deer which, for their size, are the fastest and lightest of animals. The animals instinctively know how to make the best use of their various weapons, as we see in the case of the calf, which tries to attack or wound with that part of the body where its horns will later be developed.

Moreover, animals know by instinct the force of the more powerful and harmful animals. Thus, the little birds tremble at the sight of a hawk. Animals also know which food is healthful for them and which will do them harm and they will eat from the one but never touch the other, however hungry they may be. The Creator has taught them those things which men could never know except by study or experiment. But the Creator also knew that since the animals lack the power of reasoning, they would be unable to seek and find clothing for the body and covering for the feet. Consequently, He provided all animals with these things as soon as they were born and sometimes even before birth; some with feathers, some with hides and skin, others with wool, some with scales, others with shells. Some animals change their clothes every year but others keep the same covering all their lives, and it never gets old or torn. Lastly, although the animals do not have the power of speech, they are able to manifest their anger, courage, meekness, hunger, and pain by various sounds. Thus, the fledgling birds make known their hunger by peeping and in this way they beg their parents for food.

In addition to all that we have said, there is another fact that greatly manifests the goodness, tenderness, and magnificence of the Creator. Not content with having given the animals the means whereby to preserve themselves and procreate their species, He also gave them every kind of happiness and delight which they are capable of enjoying. The Psalmist speaks of this when he says: "The eyes of all hope in Thee, O Lord, and Thou givest them meat in due season. Thou openest Thy hand, and fillest with blessing every living creature."[149] These words signify that every animal enjoys a happiness proportionate to its nature.

Let us take some examples. When we hear the singing of the swallow, the nightingale, or the canary, we should realize that if such music is delightful to our ears, it is no less pleasing to the bird that is singing. We notice, moreover, that the bird does not sing when it is sad or when the weather is dismal and dreary. When we see young calves briskly scamper from one place to another, or young sheep withdraw some distance from the flock in order to romp with one another, we know that this is a sign of their happiness and contentment. And when we see

[149] Ps. 144:15–16.

kittens or puppies playfully fight one another, rolling over and over and biting each other without doing any injury, is this not a sign of their happiness and joy? The same thing is true of the schools of fish as they swim to and fro or the flocks of birds as they fly after each other in circles, singing with delight.

From all this we can see what the great Dionysius meant when he said that God made all things like unto Himself, so far as their natures and capacities would permit. Just as God is happiness and joy, so also He desired that all creatures should enjoy happiness in due measure. Therefore He did not rest content with giving animals the means for self preservation; He also wanted them to imitate Himself in happiness and contentment.

What a great testimony this is to the goodness and liberality of God. O immense goodness of God! O ineffable tenderness! That Thou, Lord, shouldst have acted thus toward rational creatures, who are able to recognize Thy blessings and give thanks to Thee, would not be unduly strange. But to do so for creatures that can neither know Thee nor praise Thee nor thank Thee for Thy gifts and blessings, this declares to us the greatness of Thy nobility and royalty, Thy goodness and liberality toward Thy creatures. Out of Thy gratuitous love Thou hast given them every blessing, without expecting any return or thanks. Here we are given to understand what Thou must have reserved both in this life and in the life to come for those who serve and love Thee, since Thou hast been so generous to insensible creatures that know Thee not.

The earth, air, and sea are filled with all Thy marvels, Lord, so that the Psalmist exclaims: "O Lord our Lord, how admirable is Thy name in the whole earth! For Thy magnificence is elevated above the heavens. . . . I will behold Thy heavens, the works of Thy fingers; the moon and the stars which Thou has founded. What is man that Thou art mindful of him, or the son of man that Thou visitest him? Thou hast made him a little less than the angels; Thou hast crowned him with glory and honor and hast set him over the works of Thy hands. Thou hast subjected all things under his feet, all sheep and oxen, moreover the beasts also of the fields, the birds of the air and the fishes of the sea. . . . O Lord our Lord, how admirable is Thy name in the whole earth!"[150]

Chapter 20 ✠

God's Care of the Animal Kingdom

So numerous are the creatures through which the divine Majesty manifests Himself to man and so varied are the ways in which His wisdom and providence shine forth, that the divine attributes are reflected not only in the larger animals but even in the small and lowly. So St. Jerome states that we marvel at the Creator not only in the making of the heavens and the earth, of the sun and the oceans, of such animals as elephants, camels, horses, bears, and lions, but also in the creation of such tiny insects as ants, mosquitoes, flies, and many others whose bodies we know better than their names. No less in these little insects than in the large animals do we venerate the wisdom and power of Him who made them.

[150] Ps. 8.

God's artistry in making these little things seemed more admirable to St. Augustine than the creation of greater things. "I am more amazed," he says, "at the lightness of the insects that fly than the greatness of the beasts that walk and I marvel more at the work of the ants than at that of the camels." Aristotle also states in his treatise on the animals that there is no animal so lowly and insignificant that we cannot find in it some cause for admiration.

Pliny gives an example of this when he speaks of the mosquito, which was more a cause of wonder to him than was the elephant. In large animals, he says, there is an abundance of material for various parts and organs, but in these little insects which are almost nothing, what harmony of parts, what great concentration of power, and what perfection is to be found. Consider the various senses of the mosquito: the eyes, the taste, the sense of smell, and that fearful stinger which is so large in proportion to the rest of the body. Then consider the delicacy of the wings and the length of the legs. Men marvel at the bodies of elephants, which are strong enough to pull down towers and castles, but the truth of the matter is that in no creature is nature more perfect and compact than in these little insects.

Hugh of St. Victor observes that many things are admirable and for different reasons; some, because they are great, and others, because they are small. Thus we marvel at giants among men, at whales among fish, at the ostrich among birds, and at the elephant among animals. Of the smaller creatures, we marvel at those that have the smallest bodies: the tiny moth, the mosquito, the ant, and other creatures of this kind. Consider, for example, whether you should marvel more at the teeth of the wild boar or those of the moth, the wings of an eagle or those of the mosquito, the head of a horse or that of a grasshopper, the legs of an elephant or those of a tortoise. In the former animals you are amazed at their size; in the latter, at their smallness; and we find nothing in the larger animals that is not duplicated in the smaller ones.

Let us now consider one of the smallest of all animals, which is the ant. After the wounds and loss that came to man because of original sin, the principal remedy that remained to him was a hope in divine mercy, as David signifies when he says: "In peace in the selfsame will I sleep, and I will rest, for Thou, O Lord, singularly hast settled me in hope."[151] We have many motives for strengthening this virtue, but we cannot treat all of them here. Yet I do not think I am wrong in saying that this virtue is greatly animated by a consideration of the remarkable faculties and powers that the Creator has given to a creature as insignificant and lowly as the ant.

Consider, first of all, that the majority of animals are concerned only with the present and pay little heed to the past or the future, as Cicero remarks. But this little creature is very much concerned with what is to come, for it provides in the summer for the coming of winter. It would please God if men would imitate the ants in this regard by storing up a provision of good works in this life in order to have happiness in the next. Thus, Solomon[152] warns us to perform good works in earnest, for in the next life there will be no opportunity for work and merit. But if men do not imitate the foresight of the ants, they will fulfill the prophecy uttered by the same Solomon: "He that gathereth in the harvest, is a wise son; but he

151 Ps. 4:9–10.

152 Eccles. 9:10.

that snorteth in the summer, is the son of confusion."[153] So also the five foolish virgins were confounded because they did not trim their lamps and fill them with oil, as we read in the Gospel.[154]

Consider also that without any tools or materials the ants build a storehouse or granary beneath the earth where they can preserve their food supply. The passages leading to the storeroom are not made in a straight line, but with many twists and curves, so that if an enemy insect enters the portals, it cannot easily find the ants or rob the storehouse. And with the same mouth with which they make their homes, they carry out the sand and dirt to place it in a heap outside the entrance.

When they go to the fields to gather wheat or grain, the larger ants climb up the stalk, break off the seeds, and throw them down to the smaller ants who, without any instrument except their mouths, strip off the husks or shell. When the grain is cleaned and stripped, they carry it to the storehouse, walking backwards and dragging the grain with their mouths. Pliny observes in this regard that in comparison with the size of their bodies, ants have more strength than any other creature. It would be almost impossible to find a man who could walk around for a whole day, carrying another man on his shoulders, but an ant can carry a grain of wheat that weighs more than four ants and he can stay at this task not only for a whole day, but all night, too.

And what prevents the grains of wheat from sprouting when they are placed under the ground, especially when it rains? What measures would man take to prevent this, granted that

[153] Prov. 10:5.

[154] Matt. 25:1–13.

the grain must be kept in the same place for some time? For my part, I admit that I would not know what to do; but the ant knows, for it has been taught by another Master. It sterilizes the grain of wheat by eating away that part where the sprout would normally appear. But what protects the grain from humidity, which is the mother of plant corruption? How is it that the grains do not putrefy when kept in the damp earth? The ants have a remedy for this also, for on sunny days they carry their deposit into the sunshine and when it is dried out, they put it back in storage. In this way food can be preserved for the whole year.

Not only do the ants store small items of food, but if the things are large, they break them into little pieces so that they can drag or carry them. Another remarkable thing is that when they are scurrying from place to place in search of food and carrying their burdens to and fro, they pay no attention to each other. But on certain days, known only to themselves, they gather together into family reunions and will not admit other ants to the gathering. They are very partial to sweet things and have such an acute sense of smell that even if the sweets are well hidden or placed at a great height, they will search for it and find it.

Here again we see with what great confidence man should seek from God the remedy for all his needs. Let him place his trust in God and say to Him: "Thou, O Lord, who hast given so many remarkable powers to the insignificant ant for the conservation of its life, how couldst Thou ever be unmindful of man whom Thou hast created in Thy image and likeness, destined for a share in Thy glory, and redeemed with the precious blood of Thy Son? If Thou hast such great care of little things, how much greater must be Thy care of man? What does it matter whether an ant lives or dies? How much more important it is that man should live, to whom Thou hast given life through Thy blood?"

Let man rid himself completely of his sins, for they are, as Isaias says,[155] a wall that divides man from God. Let him be assured that God will have a greater care for him than He does for the ant, because man is a far more noble creature than the ant. God is not, as the saying goes, one who gathers ashes and scatters wheat. Whatever He does for the ant is not for the ant itself, but to make known to man His wisdom and providence and by this example to arouse man's confidence in Him. So also the Gospel reminds us of His care of the birds, which neither sow nor reap, in order to arouse our confidence in God.

We can also take a lesson from the spider, which is of no use to human life but nevertheless has received no few powers from the Creator for the preservation of its own life. Spiders are nourished on the blood of flies and other insects and in order to catch their prey they weave webs that have threads more delicate than those of the finest fabrics. For this purpose they need no foreign substance, but draw the threads from their own stomachs. The web serves to conceal the small holes or chinks where the spider lies in wait like a highwayman to leap out and attack its victim. When a fly innocently lands on the web and gets entangled in it, the spider approaches quickly and binds the fly on all sides. When this has been done, it leaps upon the fly and kills it.

Other spiders make their webs in the air, attaching the threads to the branches of trees or bushes. They then proceed to weave a perfectly meshed net, similar to that of a fisherman.

[155] Isa. 59:2.

Then they await the arrival of their game, poised at the center of the web where all the threads meet and where they can feel the movement of any thread on which the fly lands. For if the spider were to stand on a single strand at some distance from the center, it would not feel the movement of the web.

Other spiders make their nests just beneath the surface of the earth and line it with a texture of interwoven threads, so that if the earth should crumble, it will not fill up their house. They then make a large stopper or cover to fill the mouth or entrance to their nest. Taking a piece of dirt, they cover it with many threads, so that it fits perfectly into the mouth of the nest and can scarcely be distinguished from the surrounding earth. What is still more admirable is that the threads that are woven around the pellet of earth are then connected with the other threads and webs that adorn the whole nest, thus making a hinge for the cover of the nest. Who could have taught this insect how to seal its house and even attach a door to it, unless it was He who created the spider?

The reader may accuse me of discussing very insignificant things, whereas I began to treat of the creation of the universe. But Aristotle states in his treatise on animals that the smallest creatures manifest more of a similarity to intelligent activity than do other animals. Consequently, the more lowly and insignificant the animals, the better they manifest to us the omnipotence and wisdom of the Creator who has placed such extraordinary powers in such tiny bodies. Likewise, they better manifest the largess of divine providence which does not fail even the little and insignificant creatures in those things necessary for their preservation. How much greater will be His care and provision for larger creatures if He is so solicitous about things that are small.

God is so admirable in His creatures that if we were able to contemplate the structure of the body of each one of them and the faculties that they have for their preservation and provision, we would never cease to marvel at the immense majesty and wisdom that formed them. The truth of this statement is readily seen in the animals which we have already considered, but there are two other small creatures that to my mind are more remarkable than any of the rest: the silkworm and the bee.

Is it not a thing of great wonder that a creature as small as a silkworm can spin threads so delicate and beautiful that all the art and ingenuity of the human mind have never been able to duplicate them? Is it not a marvel that the Creator has given this little worm the power to manufacture the material for the elegant robes with which nobles, grand ladies, kings, and emperors are clothed? There is no land so uncivilized or so far distant that its kings and rulers do not strive to obtain the material that is made by these little worms.

Silkworms are produced from tiny eggs that are hatched in the sun or by the body heat of the parent. Within the short space of three days the eggs are hatched. From the beginning the little worms have all the faculties required for their existence. St. Basil made use of this fact to teach us about the general resurrection, for He who can give life to such a small egg in so short a time, can also give life to the dust and bones of our bodies, wherever they may be.

The new-born worms have voracious appetites and the noise they make while their little teeth bite and chew their food is like the patter of raindrops on the roof. After eating for several days they go to sleep, while the food is gradually changed into their bodies, which rapidly increase in size. This procedure takes place three times, after which the worms are grown to full size and they cease eating. They then find a suitable branch and begin to spin their threads. When they have made a network of threads on a branch, they proceed to build their cocoon in the center of it. Weaving threads very closely and tightly, they construct a wall as strong and firm as if it were made of parchment. And as men whitewash the walls of a building so that they will be smooth and beautiful, so the silkworm paints the inside of the cocoon with its snout and makes it watertight.

This is a particular manifestation of God's providence, for if it were otherwise, the work of the silkworm would be of no profit to man. When the cocoon is thrust into boiling water, the outer silken threads are easily disentangled and separated from one another. At the same time, however, the boiling water kills the worm inside the cocoon and this is the reward it gets for its labors. Nevertheless, those worms that are to be used for the procreation of the species do not suffer this fate. Not desiring to be imprisoned in their own house, they make a small opening in the cocoon with their mouths and at the proper time they come forth as a kind of butterfly. The male and female remain together for four days and then the male dies. After depositing her eggs, the female also dies.

It is evident from this that the silkworms were created by divine providence only for that one function and after they have finished their task they die at the appointed time. The Creator has made these little creatures simply and solely for the benefit of mankind. Once their work is completed their life comes to an end. It is as if the little silkworm would say to man: "I was not born for myself nor do I live for myself, but for you; therefore, when I have finished my service, I leave you."

Thus, God has provided us with clothing made not only from the wool of sheep and the furs of other animals, but from fine and delicate silks. The threads of the cocoon are finer than hair but they can be woven into durable cloth. A little worm that is hatched in a few days and lives only for a few months is used by God to effect a work so delicate and precious that all the genius of man cannot duplicate it.

What shall we say now of the bees? They provide us with delicious and salutary honey which is used to sweeten foods or serves as a remedy for certain illnesses. They also give us the wax from which we make the candles to be used in churches, processions, and funerals, as well as for light and ornament on the tables of nobility. Yet all these benefits come from an insect that is little larger than a fly.

But if we are amazed at the benefits that come to us from the bees, we should be even more astonished at the order and unity they observe in their work and manner of life. Anyone who has studied or observed bees knows that they live in well-ordered colonies under the rule of a queen and with nobility and officials who perform special duties, that they have arms for attack and punishments for those who do not do what they ought, and that each one receives what is due to him by way of merit.

The life of the bees may be compared to that of a religious community of strict observance. First of all, the bees have their prelate or superior whom they obey. They live together without any private possessions, but all things are had in common. Offices and duties are assigned to each one and punishments and penances are meted out to the guilty. All of them eat together at the same time and at night there is a signal for silence which is strictly observed. Again in the morning they have another signal for rising and those laborers are punished who do not start work promptly. They have watchmen who stand on duty to guard the hive and see that the drones do not eat the honey. Porters are assigned to the entrance of the hive so that no one can come in and steal the honey. Lastly, they have lay brothers to carry food and water and perform other menial tasks.

All these things were arranged by the sovereign Artist with such harmony that they cause great admiration in all who contemplate them. It is written of the Queen of Saba that when she saw the splendor and order of the house of Solomon, she was overwhelmed to find everything so well arranged by the talent and intelligence of so great a king. However, it is not to be wondered at that a man so far superior to others in wisdom should do things worthy of admiration. But that such little creatures as the bees should manifest so well-ordered a life and should do things so wisely, that is truly something to awaken our admiration. But the fact that we see these things around us every day lessens our admiration.

I shall now repeat what Pliny and others have written on this subject, wherein there is nothing that will not serve for wonder and will not give further testimony of the wisdom and providence of God who made all these things. The interpretation and application of these marvels I leave to the devotion and prudence of the reader, for if I were to comment on each detail, the discussion would be too lengthy. I should like only to remind the reader that man is created in the image and likeness of God because of his immortal soul, which is illumined with the light of reason. As a result, man is able not only to know divine things, but also to establish and govern nations, with all their necessary offices and functions. But the reader should realize that while man does all these things through the light of reason with which he has been endowed, God's smallest creatures perform many of the same functions much better than does man himself, although they lack the use of reason. This applies to many of the things we shall now describe, and we should remember that God did all this to manifest His greatness and providence, so that knowing these things, we would honor and reverence Him.

I shall begin our consideration with a fact that we already know, namely, that the bees have a queen whom they obey and follow wherever she goes. And as the rulers of nations have royal insignia, such as the crown and scepter and other such things by which they are distinguished from their subjects, so the Creator has distinguished the queen bee by giving it a larger and more beautiful body than the others. Hence, where men have fashioned the royal insignia by art and design, nature herself has marked out the queen of the bees.

Into each swarm of bees are born three or four queens, so that if one should die or come to harm there will always be a queen. But the bees seem to know that they must not have more than one ruler and therefore they kill all but one of the queens. However much they may regret doing this, the love of peace overcomes sorrow, for they know that such a procedure is necessary if they are to avoid war and a divided house.

Aristotle states that since it is bad to have a multitude of leaders, the republic of this universe has but one ruler, God. The bees never learned this from Aristotle, but they realize the danger that comes from having many princes and rulers and for that reason they select one queen and kill the others.

Once the queen has been chosen, the bees begin to construct and furnish their home. First, they cover the walls of the beehive with a waxlike substance made from very bitter plants, for they know that the honey which they are to make is very much sought after by other animals and if they cover the hive with this offensive substance, the intruders will be disappointed at the first bitter taste and will desist from further harm. For the same reason, two or three columns of wax nearest the entrance are left empty so that the thief will not find any honey to satisfy his taste.

They then proceed to make little individual houses or cells within the hive. They first construct a grand and magnificent home for the queen bee, in conformity with her royal dignity, and they encircle it with a kind of fence for greater safety and security. Then they make their own homes—the cells of the honey comb where they lay their eggs, provide for their young, and deposit their honey. Each little cell is exactly the same, having six sides, and is perfectly proportioned, although the bees have no rule or plane or any instruments other than their mouths and legs to fashion the cells. One knows not which to marvel at more: the perfection of the work or the way in which it is effected. The bees also make houses for their servants, the drones, but they are somewhat smaller in size.

Once the house is constructed, the bees proceed to make preparations for their labor, and the first thing they do is to assign tasks to various members of the hive. The oldest bees, who are jubilarians retired from labor, accompany the queen bee so that she will be more honored and have greater authority. Those next in age, who are more experienced with the work, are assigned to the making of honey. The younger bees go forth into the fields to gather the material from which the honey and the wax are to be made.

These carrier bees cover the fleshy part of the thighs (which is rough so that the bees will not lose their load in flight) with the nectar from the flowers; then they use their mouths to load their front legs with more nectar and return to the hive with four loads of material. When they reach the hive, other bees are assigned to unload the nectar that has been brought from the fields and meadows. A third group of bees then brings the material to those who are engaged in making wax, placing the load at the bottom of the honeycomb. Other bees are at the hand of the wax-makers to supply the material as it is needed, while another group is engaged in polishing and smoothing out the walls of the cells that have already been made. Some bees are assigned to bring food and others carry water to those who are working inside the hive. They carry the water either in their mouths or on the tiny hairs of their body so that, returning to the hive all damp with moisture, they can quench the thirst of the laborers.

Over all this presides the queen bee, who walks through her domains to examine the works of her subjects and to encourage them by her royal presence, but she herself never applies herself to the work. She was not born to serve, but to be served, as befits a queen. In her company are the older bees that make up her cortege.

If the bees must move to another locality, they do not take a step without their queen. In the process of moving, they all surround her so that she is well concealed and all try to be as close to her as possible and to perform all manner of services for her. If the queen is old and cannot fly easily, they carry her. Wherever the queen bee rests, there all her followers rest. If she should leave them or be separated from them, they seek her out with the greatest diligence and bring her back to her subjects. Whether or not the queen bee has a stinger, she surely has no use for one, since it is beneath her royal dignity to execute or to inflict punishment personally. The philosophers state that kings should grant benefits directly but should inflict punishment only through others, for nothing more befits the royal state than clemency and nothing makes a king more lovable or his office more secure. This is one of the reasons why bees are so loyal to their queen. If she dies, they all surround her to keep vigil and they will neither eat nor drink. If they are not taken from her, they will die with her. Such is their love and loyalty for their queen.

The creator did not neglect to provide the bee with some kind of defense. Indeed, in proportion to the size of its body, there is no weapon more powerful than that of the bee: the stinger with which it can kill or wound those that try to harm it. Since the honey they provide is a treasure desired by so many other creatures, there is good reason why the bees should have the means to protect that treasure. For this reason they keep vigil at the door of the hive so that nothing can harm the hive or the bees without being resisted as strongly as possible.

The bees do not go out to the meadows at all times of the year, but only when the flowers are in bloom, although all types of flowers serve for their purpose. In the time of snow and frost the bees stay in their house and busy themselves through the winter months with tasks within the hives. Moreover, they do not go farther than sixty paces from the hive without sending their scouts ahead to look over the land and to report what type of pasture is there. Sometimes one swarm of bees will fight against another over a meadow or, if there is a lack of nourishment, they will try to rob the food from others. The captains sally forth with their armies in the attempt to rob from other bees and many die in the fierce battle that ensues.

So strong is the force of necessity that it ignores all the laws of humanity and justice.

All that we have said up to this point gives evidence of the way in which the bees imitate the prudence and actions of men. And if we are amazed that such little creatures should so closely imitate men, how much more should we be amazed that they seem to know some of the things that men do not know. Thus, the bees know when there will be storms and rain even before they happen. At such times they do not go afar to gather nectar, but remain buzzing around the entrance to the hive. And when the caretaker of the bees sees this, he warns other men that there will be a change in weather.

But what causes the greatest astonishment in this matter of the bees is the production of honey, to which all their other talents are ordained. We know how many instruments and how much care are required for the making of jams and preserves: the fire, the cooking of the fruits, the vessels needed for this work, and an individual who knows how to perform this function. But I ask you, what instruments does this little creature have? And yet, without any instruments or fire or cooking, it makes a sweet preserve from the nectar abstracted from flowers.

Who taught this little creature such an alchemy whereby it can transform one substance into another? Let all the makers of preserves join together with all their instruments and art and knowledge and let them try to change flowers into honey. Not only has man been unable to effect such a transformation, but neither does he know how this change is effected. Yet foolish men will spend their time in scrutinizing the myteries of the heavens and miss the significance of those things that happen every day before their very eyes.

It is also amazing to think that from the load that the bees carry back to the hive, part is used for making honey and another part for wax. How can they, from one and the same material, make substances that are so different? And if the flowers provide two different substances, who taught the bees how to distinguish one from the other? Who taught them to use the one part for honey and the other for wax?

It now remains for us to give thanks to God, who has provided the bees with the faculties whereby the fruit of their work is beneficial not only to them but to us. But men are such that even while they enjoy these fruits they do not give thanks to God nor do they see the grandeur of God's power and wisdom that is manifested here.

O God, how wonderful and admirable Thou art in all Thy works, both of nature and of grace! Yet, this should not cause us astonishment, for both the one and the other have Thee as their Author. They are both the children of the same Father, and for that reason do they have so many points of similarity. In the order of grace we see that sometimes Thou dost select the weakest instruments to do wonderful things. With twelve fishermen Thou didst convert the world; with the strength of a single woman Thou didst crush the power of the Assyrians; with the footmen of the princes of Israel Thou didst vanquish the Syrian army; with a stone and a sling Thou didst enable a shepherd boy to conquer a heavily-armed giant; and with the jawbone of an ass Thou didst give Samson the power to kill no less than a thousand Philistines. This same disposition of things that Thou dost observe in the order of grace, Thou dost also observe in the things of nature, for Thou dost ordain that these two lowly creatures should provide kings and nobles with the costliest vestments and the sweetest of foods. Indeed, the more lowly and insignificant the creatures and the more excellent their works, so much the more do they manifest to us the greatness of Thy glory.

CHAPTER 21 ✠
Wonders of the Human Body

HAVING CONSIDERED THE universe and its principal parts, it is fitting that we treat next of the microcosm or little universe which is man, for a meditation on man leads to as profound an appreciation of God as does a meditation on the entire universe. But first we should recall that the beginning and basis of all our blessings is a knowledge and appreciation of God. And however numerous the truths we may learn about God, the one which is of utmost importance for our salvation and which gives us the greatest consolation is that of His divine providence. We have already pointed out in a previous meditation that this attribute includes and embraces three others, namely, God's goodness, wisdom, and omnipotence.

All that we have said up to this point concerning the created universe gives clear testimony of divine providence and the three divine attributes that are intimately connected with it. The same will be seen when we consider man. The reason why man is called a microcosm or little universe is because everything found in the greater universe is also found in some way in man. Man possesses being, as do all the natural elements; life, as do plants; sensation, as do the animals; and understanding and free will, as do the angels. For that reason St. Gregory calls man "every creature" because in man the nature and properties of all created things are to be found.

God created man on the sixth day, after He had created all other things, for He wished to make man a compendium or *summa* of all that He had previously made. Much the same thing is done by those who, at the termination of a detailed account, place a summary or schema of that which has been treated previously in many pages. For that reason we can more quickly and more easily see in man the traces of the divine perfections than if we were to scan the vast reaches of creation, which would take a long time. So also, map makers are wont to make charts and maps wherein they indicate the principal parts and nations of the world so that in a brief glance one can obtain a comprehensive view of the entire earth.

Of all the wonders and works of God, let us consider the power that He has placed in the seeds of plants. In the tiny seed of an orange, for example, He placed the power to become an orange tree, and in the kernel of the acorn, the potentiality of becoming a mighty oak. But these things are very insignificant when compared with the power that He has placed in the material used for the formation of a human body. From the seed of a plant come the roots, trunk, and branches of the tree or shrub, with their leaves and fruit; but from the substance used in the conception of a human being come a variety of members of the human body: bones, veins, arteries, nerves, and numerous organs. The various parts of the human body are so well adapted to the ends of human life that if a man observes all the particular uses and functions and providential benefits which they impart, he will be amazed at the wisdom and providence of the Creator who could produce such a variety of effects from such a simple substance.

There is nothing about the human body that does not cry out continually: "Who but God could have done this?" Who but God could have fashioned the womb of a woman as a fleshly house for the unborn child? Everything about the human body proclaims that it is a work fashioned by infinite wisdom. Thus, it is said that there are more than three hundred bones in the human body, so that on each side of the body there are approximately one hundred and fifty bones. Moreover, each bone has ten properties: a certain shape, position, connection with others, hardness, blandness, and so forth. Consequently, if we multiply these properties and attribute them to each of the one hundred and fifty bones, there are fifteen hundred properties in the bones of each side of the human body.

Three marvelous characteristics are worthy of special consideration regarding the bones of the human body. The first is the connection and interlacing of the various bones with each other, so that one fits perfectly into another. The second is the likeness between the bones on each side of the body, both as to size and the ten properties. Consequently, as the bones of the hand grow, the matching bones on the other side of the body likewise grow, so that there is no disproportion in the size of the two hands. The same thing is true of the ribs and the bones of the arms, legs, and feet.

The third marvel, which is more astonishing than the other two, is the shape and properties of each bone in the human body; how each is fashioned to serve the office for which it was made. We can demonstrate this marvel by means of the things of art, which imitate nature, for artificial things are better known to us. Thus, we see that the carpenter uses a saw, an adz, a plane, a level, and other such tools. We see also how well proportioned and how well built these instruments are to fulfill their office. We find this same quality to an even higher degree of perfection in the three hundred bones of the human body. They are so well proportioned and suited to the functions for which they were made that all the intelligence of men and angels could not improve upon their perfection.

But the marvel does not stop here. What we have said of the proportion and likeness of the bones on each side of the body is also true of the muscles and ligaments that surround the bones, and the nerves and veins and arteries of each side of the body. All these things are instruments necessary for the preservation of our life and are very well suited to the functions for which they were made, so that neither a ring for a finger nor a sword for its sheath are so well fitted as are the parts of the human body. What could better demonstrate the wisdom of the divine Artist than all these organs and instruments which He made with such perfection for the fulfillment of their functions?

From all that we have said, it should be evident how ridiculous is the opinion which states that our bodies were made by chance. Things that are made by chance rarely turn out well and at most they turn out perfectly in only a few instances. But a body composed of innumerable parts and organs, so perfectly constructed that it surpasses all created intelligence, could not have come about by chance; it must be the work of a supreme intelligence. Would it not be the height of foolishness to say that on removing a mass of metal from a furnace, one could expect to find a perfectly fashioned watch, with all its wheels and parts in perfect balance? How much more foolish it is to state that the human body was fashioned by chance in the womb of the mother, when the bones and sinews and other parts of our body are much more numerous and more complicated than the parts of any watch?

For that reason, students of anatomy rightly maintain that this study is a certain and secure guide to lead us to a knowledge of the Creator and of His perfections or attributes as manifested in His creatures. Hence, the human body is sometimes called a book of God, because in every part of the body, however small, one can read and observe the supreme artistry and wisdom of God. Although art and the created universe may help us to arrive at this knowledge, this happens only now and then or when we come upon something rare and extraordinary. But in this microcosm which is man there is no vein or artery or bone, nothing so small that it does not proclaim the excellence and artistry of Him who made it.

What shall I say of the major parts and organs of the human body? What marvelous things the anatomists say of the human eye, the skeleton, and the remarkable network of the nervous system and brain! What a wonderful thing is the human hand, which has produced a vast artificial world wherein is to be found almost as much variety as in the world created directly by God! Consequently, I consider them fortunate indeed who dedicate themselves to the study of the structure of the human body, for if they but raise their minds to God and see the human body as the work of His hands, they will time and again be overwhelmed by the marvels and wonders that He has made.

David says in the Psalms that those who go down to the sea in ships see there the works of the Lord and His wonders in the deep.[156] I say that this is no less true of those who

[156] Ps. 106:23–24.

enter into themselves and contemplate what the Creator has effected in the human body, for they will see there how God has provided man with all the instruments and organs necessary for the preservation of life and so perfectly that nothing is superfluous or lacking.

Nor is it any less a cause of admiration when we consider how these various organs and faculties are situated in the body. It is impossible to imagine another body more beautiful or better designed for the purposes for which it was created. The ancients said of the eloquence of Plato that if a wise man were to take away a single word from one of his discourses and supplant it with another, even after long consideration and thought, he would rob it of some of its elegance. We could say the same thing, although the comparison is a humble one, when we compare the things of human intelligence with those of the divine intellect. If all the wise men of the world, desiring to refashion the smallest part or member of the human body, were to form it in another manner or put it in a different location in the body, they would not only destroy its use and function, but they would also destroy the grace and harmony of the human body as a whole. Consequently, when Galenus disputed against Epicurus, who had denied divine providence and stated that the human body had been made by chance and without any plan or counsel, he said that he would give Epicurus a hundred years to change the shape of the human body, the position of its various organs and parts, or to construct it in another manner. Then Epicurus would learn that it is impossible to improve upon it or to fashion it in a better way than it has already been made.

Realizing that the human intellect is incapable of comprehending the excellence and artistry of the divine mind,

Solomon stated that just as man does not know the paths of the winds or how the human body is fashioned in the womb of the mother, so also it does not fathom the works of the Creator who has made all things. David states that all things past and future are present to God and that darkness and night are as light to Him. Then, speaking of the human body, he says: "For Thou hast possessed my reins; Thou hast protected me from my mother's womb. I will praise Thee, for Thou art fearfully magnified; wonderful are Thy works and my soul knoweth right well. My bone is not hidden from Thee, which Thou hast made in secret; and my substance in the lower parts of the earth. Thy eyes did see my imperfect being, and in Thy book all shall be written. Days shall be formed, and no one in them. But to me Thy friends, O God, are made exceedingly honorable. Their principality is made exceedingly strengthened. I will number them, and they shall be multiplied above the sand."[157]

In these words the prophet declares the wonderful wisdom of God which shines forth in a singular manner in the construction of the human body. We should especially note the phrase, "Thou art fearfully magnified," because the word "fearfully" would seem more properly to denote God's justice than His wisdom. But after considering the profundity of God's wisdom, which is so clearly and variously manifested in this work, and the greatness of the divine power which could make such a variety and perfection of members and organs from a simple substance, the Psalmist was so amazed and overawed by the majesty and greatness of God that he deliberately used the word "fearfully." It is similar to the reaction experienced by

[157] Ps. 138:13–18.

a man who stands on a high cliff and looks down into a chasm; he feels that he is gradually losing his balance and fears that he will fall, although he may be standing in a secure and safe place. So also, David was filled with fear when, considering the wondrous work that is the human body, he realized the grandeur of the Creator who fashioned it.

Yet, it is not surprising that a prophet, filled with the spirit of God, should marvel at this work of God and be moved to praise and honor Him for it. But it is surprising that we should find the same reaction in a pagan philosopher. Galenus, the prince of doctors, wrote eighteen books on the human body, and when he saw how the power and greatness of God is manifested therein, he said that his writings were a hymn of praise and thanksgiving composed to the honor and glory of God. It is not an honor, he says, in which we offer incense to Him or sacrifice a hundred cattle; it is an honor in which, through the knowledge of this wonderful work of His hands, we acknowledge the supreme wisdom which fashioned such things, the power which executed such things, and the goodness which deigned so liberally to provide creatures with all that was necessary for their maintenance. All this was admitted by Galenus who, through a study of the human body, attained a high grade of theological appreciation for this work of God. The same idea was expressed by the prophet Osee: "For I desired mercy, and not sacrifice, and the knowledge of God more than holocausts."[158]

Let us now consider another marvel which is no less wonderful than the foregoing. The philosophers teach that our soul comes to us from outside ourselves and is not educed

[158] Os. 6:6.

from the matter of which our body is formed, as are the souls of brute animals. The human soul is a spiritual substance, like that of the angels; consequently, it could not proceed from any material or body because there is no proportion between these two things. Having said this much, many of the philosophers tell us no more about the human soul. But what the philosophers fail to tell us, we learn from the Christian religion which reveals to us that God by His own power creates the human soul and infuses it into the body which has been conceived in the womb of the mother.

Let us consider this point for a brief space. Let us first cast our eyes over the entire created universe, considering the various continents of Asia, Europe, Africa, and the New World, and all the islands in the various oceans and the many lands wherein the savages and barbarians dwell. Let us consider the vast number of women who are pregnant or who are yet to carry in their wombs the bodies of children as yet unborn. Then we shall realize that day and night God is creating human souls and infusing them into bodies. This will continue until the end of time and in all parts of the world, as it has been going on since the foundation of the world until now.

All these creations and infusions of human souls are effected directly by God and not through the instrumentality of the heavens or the ministration of angels. Yet God does not on that account lose any of the peace and tranquillity that are His nor is it a source of anxiety or solicitude to Him. What must be the wisdom of such a God who at the proper moment and in all parts of the world is continually infusing souls in the matter disposed by the parents in the womb of the mother? What must be His careful and delicate concern and solicitude? And what must be the power of a God who creates such beautiful spiritual souls out of no pre-existing material, and yet in each soul the image of God shines forth in a spiritual manner? This is something that overwhelms our minds with wonder and declares to us how great a distance there is between the beatific substance of God and human understanding.

Chapter 22 ✠
Man's Lower Faculties

Before we begin to treat of the vegetative powers of the human soul, it will be helpful to recall some general notions that will enable us to understand these powers. The human soul possesses three types of powers or faculties. The first are the vegetative powers, and their primary functions are nourishment and growth; the second are called sensitive powers, to which we attribute the properties of sensation and movement; and the third are intellectual or rational powers, which distinguish men from brute creation and make them like unto the angels.

These three types of powers or faculties were given to the human soul by the Creator. This is a great marvel, for although the human soul is a simple substance, it is of such a nature that it possesses powers that are common to angels, animals, and plants and, consequently, it exercises functions that are characteristic of these widely divergent beings. Hence, man has the power of intellection, as do the angels, but he also eats and reproduces himself as do the brute animals. As a result of these diverse powers, some philosophers have denied the unity of the soul and taught that the three powers were actually three distinct souls. Some philosophers have even attempted to locate the vegetative soul in the liver, the sensitive soul in the heart, and the rational or intellectual soul in the brain. Only the last-named, according to Plato, was essentially human, because he did not think that anything as lowly as a material body could be considered an essential part of man. For him, the body was a house wherein the soul dwells or a candlestick on which is placed the lighted candle of the soul. Following the division we have already made, we shall treat first of the qualities of the vegetative soul, which we possess in common with plants; then we shall treat of the other two types of soul: the sensitive and the rational.

It is a fact known to all that nourishment is necessary for the maintenance of life. The reason for this is the natural heat of our bodies, which is the cause both of our death and of our life. When it is excessively intense, it can consume the flesh and substance of a man, as we see in the case of those sick with fever or those who diet—if they do not eat, they become thin and haggard. The flame of a lamp will gradually consume the oil that feeds the fire, and if we wish to keep the lamp burning, we must replenish the fuel from time to time. The same thing happens in the human body, for the natural heat of the body gradually consumes the moisture and tissues of the body, so that they must be restored from time to time by the food that we eat. But since that which is restored is not as perfect as that which has been lost, the body one day reaches a point where it begins to lose its vigor and power and ultimately life itself begins to wane, unless some disease or violence sets in to take life away before this stage has been reached.

Moreover, since the entire body and all its parts need nourishment and repair, it is necessary that throughout the body there be some system of channels or pathways whereby nourishment and energy are carried to the parts where they are needed. For that reason the Creator equipped the human body with veins and arteries. A similar phenomenon can be seen in the leaf of a tree, especially in larger leaves, where we see a network of veins, some large and others as fine as a hair, by which the leaf is nourished and preserved.

The Creator has also endowed the vegetative soul with three powers that are necessary for its maintenance: attraction, conversion, and expulsion. Each member of the body draws from the veins whatever is necessary for its nutrition and converts this into its own substance, and if there is anything superfluous, it is expelled. But the most amazing of these three powers is the power of attraction. The blood that circulates through the veins contains certain elements or humors that are beneficial to certain parts of the body. Each organ and member of the body selects from the blood whatever is suitable to its nature but does not touch the rest.

If a magnet is surrounded by various metals, it will draw only the iron and leave the rest. A similar power is found in the various organs of the body so that they select from the blood only that which is most suitable. We see the same thing verified in the selection of food by animals. If you were to set out a piece of meat, some grains of wheat, and some green leaves, a sheep would eat the greens, a dog would eat the meat, and a hen would eat the grain. He who gave the animals an instinctive knowledge of their proper food, also gave to the members and organs of the human body the power to abstract from the blood whatever nourishment they need.

The human body also manifests a remarkable harmony, of which St. Paul often spoke. All the members of the body complement and serve each other at the same time that they perform their functions for the common good of the whole body, which is its preservation. Thus, the inferior members and organs serve the superior members and organs and these, in turn, make use of and govern the functions of the lesser faculties. Moreover, God does not wish anything to be lost or useless; for that reason He has so fashioned the human body that whatever is excessive or superfluous in one part may be of service in another part, as we see in the case of the bile, which is distilled by the liver and is then used for the nourishment of the spleen.

In addition to what has been said, we should observe, as Aristotle states, that the Author of nature fashions the proper instrument for each office or function. In the house of a moderately rich man there are no more than one or two servants to do all the work of the house. But in the palace of a king there are a great number of offices and officials, each one deputed to a certain duty. Applying this example to the case at hand, there has never been any royal house or palace in the whole world that possessed as many servants as does the royal house of our body, which was fashioned by God as a dwelling place for our soul. However numerous and varied the offices and functions of the body, there is no member or organ that has more than one function, and if any appears to have more than one duty, it is by reason of the diversity of parts that are in it. This is evident not only from the five external senses but even more so from the internal members of the body, such as the stomach, the intestines, the liver, the heart, and so forth. Not only does this manifest the marvelous order of divine providence, but it also serves to give instruction and knowledge in the field of medicine. For if doctors understand the nature and functions of the various parts of the body and their intimate relationship and interdependence, they can learn how to apply medicines and treatments for regaining or preserving the health of the body.

Our consideration of the nature and functions of the human body should demonstrate how smoothly divine providence arranges and disposes all things, proceeding from causes to effects and disposing those causes in proportion to the excellence of the effects to be produced. The more noble the form that He desires to introduce, the more perfectly He disposes the matter in which that form is to be received, for there must be no disproportion between cause and effect and matter and form. Applying this principle to spiritual matters, we can understand that it is necessary for us to dispose ourselves properly for any given degree of grace. Accordingly, the penitent sinner who desires to reap the fruit and benefit of a good confession will make a good examination of conscience, will be filled with sorrow and repentance for his past sins, and will have a firm purpose of amendment. Likewise, to receive the fruits of the Holy Eucharist, one will strive not only to be free from sin but also to have actual devotion, rejecting all thoughts and distractions that may lessen that devotion. Indeed, for any grace or spiritual gift one must make the proper preparations and be properly disposed to receive them.

Accordingly, he who desires to enjoy the sweetness and consolation of the Holy Ghost must rid himself of all the tastes and consolations of the world, as David did, when he said: "My soul refused to be comforted; I remembered God and was delighted."[159] Likewise, he who would aspire to the perfection of the love of God must detach himself from the disordered love of worldly things. If he would seek to be so united with God as to be one spirit with Him, which is to become a spiritual and divine man, he must mortify whatever is earthly and carnal in him and may prove an impediment to the divine. If he desires to be like unto God, who is his one and highest good, he must withdraw from things of the world, even from those things that are not in themselves evil, for although they be good in themselves, they may easily demand too much of his attention and smother his spirit of devotion.

Further, if in his pursuit of spiritual things a man desires to give himself to the contemplative life and wishes also to have a mind that is tranquil and free of other considerations when he thinks about God, he must be, as the saints advise, deaf, blind, and mute to the things of the world. If he acts otherwise, he cannot help but be molested by worldly thoughts and distractions. Finally, he who desires to find God should realize that he must truly seek Him, and he who wishes to attain the greatest gifts must conform his work and efforts to the dignity of those gifts, just as one who desires to be learned must be diligent in study.

Solomon teaches us this truth when he tells us that if we wish to possess true wisdom we should seek it as arduously as men work for money and as zealously as men dig for treasures in the earth.[160] Moses also states that we shall find God if we seek Him with our whole heart and with all the energy of our being.[161] This is the ordinary manner in which our Lord

---

[159] Ps. 76:4.

[160] Prov. 2:4.

[161] Deut. 4:29.

communicates His gifts and graces to His creatures: He first disposes them and prepares them to receive such gifts. It is true, however, that God is not restricted by the laws according to which He normally and commonly operates, for without any previous disposition or preparation and as a sign of His liberality and magnificence, He sometimes bestows unexpected gifts, as we see in the conversion of St. Paul and the vocations of St. Peter, St. James, and St. John, who were called to the dignity of apostles as they mended their nets.

CHAPTER 23 ✠
The Life of the Senses

AT THE BEGINNING of our treatment of the structure of the human body we stated that philosophers teach that there are three types of soul: vegetative, as possessed by the plants; sensitive, as possessed by animals; and rational or intellectual, as possessed by man. The human soul, although one and simple, possesses the characteristics and properties of the three different kinds of soul. Consequently, the one and the same soul is the principle of the operations of man's lower faculties and organs, of his sensations and movements, and also of the operations of his intellect and will.

We have already treated of the vegetative activities of the human soul, which we possess in common with plant life; we now proceed to a consideration of our sensitive life, which we share with the animals. Divine wisdom shines forth even more resplendently in this higher activity of the soul because the sensitive operations are more noble than those of the vegetative level.

It should be noted that since all our knowledge comes to us through the external senses, which are concerned with material things, and since we cannot see or touch or taste spiritual things, many men either do not believe in the existence of spiritual realities or do not understand the power and virtue that they possess. Such was the case with the Sadducees, of whom mention is made in the Acts of the Apostles. They were so dull intellectually that they did not believe in angels or spiritual beings. There are also other men today who, although they accept the existence of such beings on faith, cannot understand how such things can exist without bodies. For that reason they do not appreciate or understand the dignity, excellency, and power of their own souls, for they imagine the soul as some sort of airy substance. I should like to take such men by the hand and lead them little by little to a realization of the dignity and power of spiritual beings so that they would arrive at a better understanding of the nature and power of their own spiritual souls.

According to the teaching of the ancient philosophers, all corporeal beings are composed of four elements, although this may not be immediately evident because of the mixture and blending of these elements in the various bodies. The lowest and most material of the four elements is that of earth. Next in dignity is the element of water, which makes the earth fertile, for by its nature the earth is sterile and dry. More perfect than water is the element of air, by which we live and breathe, and which brings the waters from the ocean to rain upon the land, as we have previously explained. The fourth element, which is the most subtle and powerful, is that of fire.

Since all corporeal beings are composed of these four elements, it should be noted that so far as a body has less of earth in it, it is more excellent and more powerful in its operations. Of itself, the earth has no power to do anything; it receives whatever the other three elements may produce in it. The other three elements are therefore superior because they are more active and less material. We see that this same principle also applies to other things. The heavier liquids we reject as being more earthy and we select the lighter ones for drinking purposes. The cloudy and heavier wines are of inferior quality, while the lighter and more delicate wines are more excellent. Bread that is made of white flour is more delicate and is served at the tables of the wealthy, while that which is made from coarse flour is for the servants and the poor.

From the examples given it should be evident that the more gross and earthly a thing is, the less power and efficacy it possesses; the more immaterial and spiritual the substance, the more noble and powerful it is. In this way we can understand something of the dignity of our human soul, which is a purely spiritual substance, as are the angels. And since the human soul is a spiritual substance, we should not be surprised to see the variety of offices and functions that it performs. What God works in the greater universe or macrocosm, our human soul effects in this smaller universe or microcosm.

We have said that the sensitive soul is not only the principle of local movement but also of sensation; consequently, it is necessary to speak of man's external and internal senses. The external senses are five in number and they are united, so to speak, in an internal sense which is called the common sense. The nerves that proceed from the brain to the end organs of the various external senses give sensibility to these receptors. Likewise, the species and images of things perceived by the outer senses are carried to the brain along the same nerve track. The common sense then enables us to perceive the various images and sensations as a pattern or unity. This, as the philosophers claim, is the beginning of our knowledge, for there is nothing in the intellect which was not first presented in some way to the senses.

A second internal sense, the imagination, receives the sense images and preserves them faithfully. Like the common sense, it is also located in the brain. Another power or internal sense is called the estimative power or instinct in animals, but in men it is called the cogitative power. This faculty is the most spiritual of all the internal senses and enables us to perceive things that have neither form nor body. Thus, a sheep perceives an enemy in the wolf but sees the dog as a friend. Although such concepts have no material counterpart, the Creator provides both men and animals with an instinctive power for discerning between those things that are useful for their conservation and those that are dangerous and harmful.

The fourth internal sense, also localized in the brain, is the power of memory. This faculty enables us to recall past events as past, and if the memory is strong, it is a great help in acquiring the virtue of prudence, which relies to a great extent on the recollection of past experiences. Memory is also the mother of eloquence and for that reason the masters of eloquence assign memory to the fifth place in their work of forming orators. It helps us in all the arts and sciences by enabling us to remember rules and precepts without which, as they say, reading books or attending lectures would be like pouring water into a sieve. Lastly, memory makes us grateful to God by recalling the many favors received from Him.

David was right in confessing that God is admirable in all His works, however small. But let us leave the consideration of the internal senses to consider the external senses, beginning with the structure of the human eye. Professors and students in such matters confess that the human eye is the most delicate and remarkable organ that God has fashioned in the human body and that it is no less beneficial than it is marvelous. What is more pitiful than a man without sight? The saintly Tobias, who so patiently endured the loss of his eyesight, was greeted by the angel with the hope that God would give joy to him. And Tobias answered: "What manner of joy shall be to me, who sit in darkness and see not the light of heaven?"[162]

Our admiration is aroused first of all by the species and images that are required in order that we may see external objects. All visible things have color and, consequently, they are able to produce images and likenesses of themselves, which the philosophers call species and which represent things as they really are. The necessity for such species, as the philosophers state, arises from the fact that in order to produce a certain effect, a cause must be in contact, substantially or virtually, with the thing on which it is to act. But the various external objects that we wish to see are at some distance from the eye. Consequently, it is necessary that the objects of vision in some way be brought into contact with the human eye. To effect this, the Creator has provided that the images or species of external objects should be conveyed to the eye through the medium of light waves in the air.

The human eye then receives these impressions as in a kind of mirror, and since the eye is not transparent, the light waves

[162] Tob. 5:12.

cannot pass through. As a result, the eye faithfully represents whatever is placed before it. Thus, the eye can see mountains, valleys, fields, trees, entire armies, and anything else that is in front of it; and if thousands of eyes were fixed on the same object, all would reflect that same object. This is true not only of the things in the immediate vicinity, but also of things in the heavens. For we could not see the stars which are so far removed from us if their likeness were not impressed on our eyes to serve as a medium of vision.

I shall pass over the more complicated details of the human eye but I cannot neglect to say something of the structure of this organ. The eyeball is made up of three layers or tunics. The first is an opaque and tough layer which gives form to the eyeball and covers it entirely, except for a small area in front where the layer is transparent and crystalline. The second layer or tunic is reddish brown in color and contains a network of blood vessels. It terminates at the iris of the eye, which serves as a colored diaphragm and regulates the amount of light that enters the eye. The third and deepest layer is the retina and it contains the nerve endings for actual vision. Passing through these various layers, the representations of external objects are ultimately carried along the nerve track to the common sense, which is located in the brain. Consequently, we can say that the whole visible creation enters our soul through the portals of the eyes. That is the reason why Aristotle states that the sense of sight is so precious: man, as a rational animal, naturally desires to know things, and it is the sense of sight that reveals to him the infinite variety of things in the visible universe.

More excellent still is the fact that through vision we can see the marvels of the works of God whereby our soul is raised to a knowledge of Him. So David says: "I will behold Thy heavens, O Lord, the works of Thy fingers; the moon and the stars which Thou hast founded."[163] This saintly king used the sense of sight in a much better manner than do those who use it to offend God, making an instrument of sin that which has been given for God's praise and glory, and thus making war on the Giver with the very gift He gave them. What a remarkable gift is that of sight! If you were to lose your sight, what would you do? Where would you go to find a remedy? And what thanks you would give to one who could restore your sight! Men know very well that their gift of sight is from God and that He conserves it, but they do not give even a thought of gratitude to Him for it.

Let us now proceed to the sense of hearing, which is also a noble sense and no less helpful in acquiring wisdom. We have an example of this in Didymus, who was born blind but nevertheless became a great theologian. The inner ear is connected by a nerve tract to the brain and the common sense, which is the ultimate terminus of sensations. Separating the inner and outer ear is a delicate membrane like the covering of a drum, and as the vibrations of air move this membrane, sound is transmitted to the inner ear and ultimately to the brain. But if this drum or membrane should be punctured or broken through injury, hearing is destroyed. For that reason the Creator has provided the outer ear to protect this membrane, just as He has supplied the eyelid to protect the eye.

The sense of smell is also connected with the common sense and the brain by means of a nerve track. The nerve endings terminate in the soft and delicate mucuous membrane of the nostrils where the particles of external objects come into

---

[163] Ps. 8:4.

contact with the membrane and cause a sensation. To protect the sense of smell, the Creator has provided the nose, which also serves to beautify the face. Here again we see the infinite wisdom of God who knew how to join in the structure of our senses and members two qualities that are united only with great difficulty: utility and beauty.

From here we proceed to consider the sense of taste, whereby we can enjoy the various savors of food. The sensation of taste is caused by the fact that the tongue is humid, filled with pores, and of itself lacks any kind of savor. The tongue is filled with pores so that the particles of food may come in contact with the nerve endings or taste buds that receive the sensation. The tongue is humid so that the food may be saturated with saliva; otherwise the nerve endings in the pores of the tongue would not come in contact with the food and there would be no sensation. It is no less necessary that the tongue have no taste of its own, just as the ear of itself is void of sound, otherwise the tongue could not distinguish between various tastes. For if the tongue had its own savor, it would experience this taste and no other, as happens in the case of the sick or feverish to whom all things taste bitter or insipid because of the phlegmatic condition of the patient.

The last external sense is that of touch, whereby we receive sensations of the qualities of bodies, such as cold and heat, humidity and dryness, solidity, resistance, and pressure, as well as roughness, smoothness, and softness. This sense is not localized in any specific organ but it extends over the entire body, so that men and animals can be aware of what is helpful or harmful and may flee the one and seek the other.

To conclude this subject, I should like to summarize what Cicero says concerning the utility and beauty of the external senses and various parts of the human body. He treats of these matters in order to prove that all these things have been fashioned by a supreme wisdom and providence for the utility and benefit of human life. Cicero begins his account by stating that divine providence raised up men from the earth and made them to walk and stand upright, so that by looking at the heavens they could come to a knowledge of God. For men are not made to be permanent dwellers and inhabitants of this earth, but to be contemplators of heavenly and sovereign things, and this is given to no other animal but man.

Divine providence has marvelously fashioned the external senses which serve as the interpreters and messengers of external things and has localized them in the head of man as in a lofty tower. Since the eyes serve as watchtowers of the body, they have been placed in the highest part, so that they may better exercise their office. The ears were fashioned for the perception of sound and for that reason they also have been fittingly placed at the upper part of man's body. For a similar reason, the sense of smell is located in the head, because vapors naturally tend upward and carry with them the particles of odor. Moreover, the sense of smell was wisely placed near the mouth, because the odor of things that we eat and drink plays an important role in judging whether a thing is good or bad. The sense of taste must differentiate between various things by which we are nourished and for that reason it is rightly located in the mouth, through which pass the things that we eat and drink. Lastly, the sense of touch is rightly extended throughout the whole body so that we may be aware of wounds and blows, cold and heat, or anything that may do us harm.

Since wise men usually give more protection to things that are precious than to those that are base or common, the divine

Artist has placed greater safeguards around the eyes than around the other senses, for the eyes are much more valuable and more highly esteemed. He first covered them with very delicate layers of skin which are transparent at the front so that we may see through them, but He also made them of a tough and durable matter so that they would stand much use. He has fashioned the eyes so that they could be easily moved from side to side, in order that a man may quickly turn away from anything harmful or easily cast his glance on that which he desires to see. The pupil of the eye is relatively small, to give sharpness of vision and to lessen the danger of harm to vision. The lids of the eye are soft and flexible so that they will not irritate the eye itself, but at the same time they can be opened and closed with the greatest ease to prevent anything harmful from entering the eye. The eyelids are furnished with lashes, which are like little brushes, so that when the eyes are opened they can catch whatever shall fall upon them. Moreover, the eyes are set more deeply into the head and above them are the eyebrows, which also serve as a protection, as when they prevent perspiration from the forehead from running into the eyes. Beneath the eyes the fleshy cheeks likewise serve as a protection and form the valley in which the eyes are set. Finally, the nose protrudes from between the eyes and thus serves as a fence or wall to protect them.

Unlike the eyes, the ears are always open, because we have need of hearing even while we are alseep, so that we can be awakened by a sound. The canal of the ear has many twists and turns, for if it were short and straight, something harmful could easily enter in. But if an insect or anything noxious should enter into the canal of the ear, it is caught in the natural wax that serves as a snare. The outer ear or pinna protects the auditory canal and also helps to convey sounds to the inner ear. The flesh around the entrance of the outer ear is hard and trumpet-shaped so that the sound waves will more easily be received and even magnified when necessary.

The nose also is always open, in order to fulfill its proper function, and it has two narrow entrances so that harmful objects from outside cannot easily enter it. It is also supplied with a mucuous substance and discharge so that dust and other particles can easily be expelled. On the other hand, the sense of taste is very carefully enclosed within the mouth, so that it can the better perform its office and also be protected.

These observations from the writings of Cicero manifest to us the supreme wisdom and counsel with which God has fashioned and safeguarded all the external senses. He has not neglected a single detail, however small. How much more solicitude, then, must He exert over the great things in creation if He is so particular about the lesser things?

Chapter 24 ✣ *The Passions*

Having treated of the internal and external senses, which are proper to the sensitive life of the human soul and serve to give man a knowledge of material things, we now turn to a consideration of the affective part of the sensitive soul, where the passions and emotions are located. Since they enable man to desire and seek beneficial things and to flee harmful things, they are necessary for our conservation.

Among the passions are two principal ones that are, so to speak, the root and foundation of all the others: love for particular goods that are beneficial to us and hatred of those things that are harmful to us. Thus, the animal seeks what is good and convenient for its conservation and avoids the evil that would work for its destruction. Without these two basic passions, the animal would be like a bird without wings, for it would not then be able to seek its good or to avoid the opposite. For that reason, the Stoics rightly stated that these two passions are like a tutor which divine providence has provided for man, for just as the tutor strives to obtain all that is good for the child and to forestall whatever is harmful, so these two passions perform the same service for man as long as they are properly controlled.

Moreover, all the other passions spring from the two basic passions of love and hatred. When the good that we love is absent, desire springs forth; and when the good is actually possessed, we experience joy. On the other hand, from the hatred of an absent evil springs aversion or flight; but when the evil is present to us, we experience sorrow. These six passions, love, desire, joy, hate, aversion, and sorrow, are called by the philosophers the concupiscible appetites, because their function is to seek and desire sensible goods.

However, if the good to which we are drawn by love is difficult but possible to obtain, the desire we have for it is accompanied by the hope of attaining it, for men readily hope for the things that they desire. But if the difficulties or obstacles to the desired good are so great as to be insuperable, then they kill our hope, and the contrary passion of despair is aroused. At other times, if our desire for a good is very intense and we judge that we can successfully extricate ourselves from a dangerous situation, courage is aroused to face the threatening evil. But if the difficulties and obstacles are so great as to be insuperable in the face of danger or evil, the passion of fear is aroused. This passion serves as a protection for the animal, so that it will not attempt to do that which it cannot, but will seek another remedy, such as flight or hiding. But if, in addition to this, one finds himself completely impeded from the attainment of what he desires or if he loses the good that he once possessed, he then bristles with anger, which is the avenger of the hurts and disappointments that we suffer.

These five irascible passions are also necessary for the conservation of life. If we possessed appetites merely for the things that are suitable for our preservation, but had no courage or valor for overcoming the difficulties that often accompany them, we would never attain many of them and we would, therefore, lack many things that are necessary for life. But the divine Governor, who has been deficient in nothing, took care to provide us with the five passions of hope, despair, courage, fear, and anger. Each in its own way helps us overcome the difficulties that beset us or warns us to fear danger and not to hope for victory when it is impossible.

We find here an application that is very profitable for the spiritual life. From what has been said of the various passions and their function in human life, those who have ardent desires for perfection will understand that good desires are not enough to obtain the virtues that they seek. Desires must be accompanied by great courage and fortitude in overcoming the difficulties that inevitably beset the good Christian in his pursuit of virtue. Consequently, if no valor or effort is expended in the acquisition and increase of virtue, a man will remain sterile and without fruit, in spite of all his good desires. For that reason it is said that hell is paved with good intentions but paradise is filled with good works. However, when the desire for virtue is intense, it is usually accompanied by valor and courage.

Returning to our consideration of the passions, we must note here that the passions not only serve for the preservation of human life and of the human species, but they also assist greatly in the practice of certain virtues. Thus, anger is the instigator of vindictive justice, which has as its function the punishment of the criminal. Because of the anger and indignation felt toward such persons, judges are moved to punish them. So Aristotle has wisely said that anger is good for a soldier, but not for a captain.

Likewise, from the desire for those things we judge to be good, two affections spring and, if well regulated, they are of great help in acquiring virtue and avoiding vice: love of honor and a sense of shame. Since noble men and rulers generally have a high regard for honor, the divine Governor has made virtue honorable, so that men would esteem virtue. It is as if He had sweetened virtue and placed honor as a bait to make men seek it, although it would not be true virtue if sought only for this reason. Such was the basis of the heroic deeds of the Romans, who attempted heroic feats in the name of honor. For the same reason, Scipio and the other Roman captains did not accept the beautiful maidens that were presented to them, but returned them to the husbands or fathers.

As the love of honor attracts the heart to virtue, so also does the sense of shame withdraw men from vice, because of the disgrace and dishonor that follow in its wake. A sense of shame has been especially imprinted by God in the hearts of women, to serve as a bulwark of chastity. It is fitting that the most wise Creator should provide greater protection for that which is more precious and more ardently desired. Therefore, in addition to the virginal seal, He has given women this natural sense of shame, which acts as a rein upon the vice of impurity. Confirmation of this truth can be found in the writings of Plutarch. He states that in a certain city in Greece such a heavy mood of melancholy prevailed among the citizens that each day many maidens committed suicide and no one could find a remedy for the evil. Finally a wise man, taking heed of woman's natural sense of shame, ordered that an edict be published whereby any woman who committed suicide should be buried naked and in view of all the people. So great was the dread of such a punishment that what could not be cured by any other remedy was effected through a woman's natural sense of shame, and the plague of suicides was ended.

We should also advert that the passions are of themselves neither virtuous nor vicious, but are natural inclinations which may be good or evil according to the use we make of them. When the passions, which are in the inferior part of the soul, follow the dictates of the superior part, where the intellect and will are located, they can be used well and for the purposes for which they were given to us. But when they follow a rule other than reason, as when they are moved by the imagination or the apprehension of sensible things, they lose their way, because they follow a blind leader.

The hierarchy of our spiritual kingdom is so arranged that the will is like a king that commands all the members and faculties of man, and the intellect is the faithful counselor of the will. It makes known to the will the dignity and excellence of spiritual things so that the will can love them, and it points out the ugliness of sin and vice so that the will can abhor them. The will has as its servants the bodily organs, which are moved in conformity with the command of the will and without any resistance. They obey as they are commanded. But there are also in this kingdom, as in all kingdoms, fawns or parasites that advise the king to do things that are improper. Such is the role of the passions when they attach themselves to sensible and delightful goods and seek to draw the king to the same sensate things, although the intellect objects and warns the king that such goods are dangerous. And when the passions are strong enough to blind the intellect and pervert the will, they take the reins of government into their own hands. We have an example of this in a person suffering from intense thirst. He knows how much damage drinking will do to him, but the desire for water is so intense that it carries the will with it and the man drinks his fill.

At the risk of departing somewhat from the subject at hand, I would like to observe that the evil effects of original sin are most in evidence in our passions and appetites. As long as Adam and Eve were in the state of innocence, all their appetites were under control, well regulated, and obedient to reason. But once the gift of original justice had been lost by sin, the passions were let loose to rebel against reason. As a consequence, the world and the devil wage a relentless war against us through the passions.

By reason of the appetites and passions our flesh is naturally inclined and attracted to the things that are in conformity with its nature. The enemy takes advantage of this by arousing the passions and putting them in disorder so that they will exceed the limits and control of reason. Thus Job says of the devil that he fans the flames by his breathing, that is, he blows on the flames of our passions so that they pass beyond the limits of temperance.

In the beginning, man committed sin through the instigation of the woman; the stronger yielded to the weaker. Now the devil generally wages war against us in our weakest part, that part which is naturally inclined to the things of earth. The devil has this to his advantage: that the weaker and baser part of our nature inclines us to the very things that he desires of us. So he inflames these desires and inclinations by means of his suggestions, with the result that the passions, which could have been beneficial to us if rightly used and controlled, easily become a source of ruin and corruption. Hence arises the disordered love for honor from which ambition springs, the desire for money from which avarice springs, the longing for sensual delights which is the source of gluttony and other intemperate acts, the hatred and unrestrained anger against those who try to keep us from the enjoyment of sensate goods, the envy of those who possess things that we desire for ourselves, and every other kind of vice.

From what has been said, we can see that just as the defenders of a besieged city put all their strength and resistance at the weakest point, where the enemies are trying to make a breach in order to enter, so the true servant of God should understand that the Christian life is a perpetual battle and constant warfare. And since life is one long struggle and temptation, the profession of the Christian is to be a man of war. As a soldier constantly under siege, he will protect and defend this weakest point of his passions so that he will not be overcome.

CHAPTER 25 ✠
God's Image and Likeness

WE COME NOW to the consideration of the highest part of the soul, which is the intellectual and rational part. Man's rational soul is spiritual, like the angelic substance, and for that reason it is not localized in any bodily member or organ, as are the internal and external senses. It is, therefore, the rational soul that distinguishes us from brute creation and makes us like unto God and the angels. This was testified by the Creator Himself when at the creation of man He said: "Let Us make man to Our image and likeness."

Observe with what solemnity the Creator proceeded to the creation of man. In fashioning other creatures, He did nothing more than say: "Let it be made," and immediately it was made. But in the creation of man He used a different formula and statement, for He said: "Let Us make." This signifies that the three Persons of the Trinity were immediately concerned with the creation of God's noblest creature in this visible universe.

But something yet greater is to be noted, for God said: "Let Us make man to Our image and likeness." To be an image of God pertains only to men and angels. All other creatures, even the sun and moon and stars, are not called images of God, but vestiges or traces of God. Since men and angels manifest much more of the grandeur of the Creator, they are called images of God.

This truth is confirmed by another detail of the creation of man. When God, as Scripture tells us, had formed man's body out of the slime of the earth, He breathed into this body the spark of life. And since the breath proceeds from the interior of the one who breathes, God wished by this act to have us know that the soul is something that proceeds from the bosom of God Himself; not that it is part of the divine substance, as some heretics taught, but because in many ways it shares in the attributes of God, as we shall soon see.

One of the aspects of the soul that has aroused the admiration of all wise men and especially manifests the divine power is the diversity of its functions. The human soul is at once purely spiritual and the form of the material body to which it gives life. But there is such a great discrepancy between things which are purely spiritual and those which are material that the disproportion between them does not permit them to be easily blended and united. Therefore, it must be taken as one of God's great wonders that He could impart such power and efficacy to the human soul that it can understand lofty and immaterial things as does the angel and that it also enables men to reproduce themselves as do the animals. It is as if God had made a creature that is part angel and part animal, for in man we find the powers proper to each of these vastly different creatures. With good reason could St. Augustine say that of all God's marvelous works the greatest is the creation of man.

Let us examine the various reasons why man is said to be an image of God. If we understand this, we shall also grasp something of man's dignity and we shall realize more fully the debt of gratitude we owe to God for the many blessings we have received from Him. Moreover, the man who appreciates his dignity will be less inclined to disfigure the divine image by debasing himself with the things of the flesh.

In the first place, man is said to be an image of God by reason of the intellect and free will that he possesses, as do God and the angels. None of the creatures inferior to man possess the prerogative of liberty, for they are all natural agents that cannot cease to do that for which they have been given the faculties and powers. But man is free and is master of his deeds; consequently, he can do or not do as he wishes.

But it is not only man's freedom and liberty that distinguish him from brute creation; he is also an image of God by reason of his intellect, for God, too, is an intellectual substance, though in a much more eminent degree than is man. Man's likeness to God on the part of his intellect is especially evident in the works of art that he produces. It is said that art imitates nature as far as it can, but this is merely another way of saying that man imitates God in his manner of working. In all His works the Author of nature disposes the means to fit the end that He has in view; for example, He has fashioned the teeth to cut and to chew food, the hands to work, the feet to walk, and the framework of the skeleton to bear the weight of the body. Man observes the same rule in the production of the works of art, as we see in the cutting of the cloth for his clothing, the shoes that he makes to fit his feet, the house that he constructs as his dwelling place, and the ships that he builds for navigation. Each product is proportioned to the end for which it has been made.

We have already mentioned that the Creator takes care to combine utility with beauty in the works of His hands, as is evident in the human countenance with its nose, eyes, eyelids, and lashes. All these organs serve to beautify the human face at the same time that they perform the various functions that each was meant to fulfill, and if any of them were changed, the beauty and utility of the face would also be lessened. So also in the production of the works of art, man imitates God to the best of his ability by trying to make artificial things both useful and beautiful. Visit the homes of the wealthy and you will find that the furnishings of these homes are constructed to serve not only for utility but also for beauty and adornment. Walk through the streets of any large city and you will see that the numerous offices and buildings or the variety of ships and boats in its port serve the same double purpose. And if you were to end your tour by entering a church or cathedral, you would discover the beauty of religious art in the architecture of the building, the ornamentation of the altars, and the inspiring melodies of the chant that fills the church with God's praise. If you were to visit a country fair or city market, you would again find countless products of man's ingenuity and art that compete with the art and genius of nature herself, not only as to construction and beauty but also as to the variety of things made. God created the world and filled it with a wide diversity of creatures; human art, in imitation of God, has made another world of artificial things.

Dionysius mentions three attributes that are possessed by God and man alike: being, power, and operation. So intimate is the relationship among these three attributes that it serves as the basis for the following valid principle: As a being is, so is its power, and as its power is, so are the works that proceed from it. Consequently, from a knowledge of the works, we can know the power, and from a knowledge of the power, we can know the being. But if so great a similarity is manifested between the works of man and the works of God, we can thereby conclude to the similarity and likeness that exist between man and God.

It is also a singular perfection of God that He is present in all places, in the world and above and beyond the world. In its own way, our rational soul can also go to all parts of the world whenever it wishes. Although we may now be in Italy, says St. Ambrose, we can think of the things of the East and West; we can unite ourselves mentally with people of Persia or Africa; we can travel in spirit with those who travel; we can be present to those who are absent; we can even resurrect the dead, as it were, and speak with them as if they were living. We are to understand by this that it is not the bodily part of us that is made in God's likeness, but that part of us which enables us to see those who are absent, to travel across the ocean, to scrutinize what is hidden, to view all the parts of the world, to descend into hell or to rise to heaven, and even to be joined with Christ.

A still greater proof that our souls are made to the image and likeness of God is the fact that the human soul, in addition to being a spiritual substance, is the principle and cause of all the functions performed by the body wherein it dwells. God works in all the creatures of this vast universe, conserving them in being and giving them the power to perform the functions for which He made them, for as First Cause, He concurs in all these lower operations. In like manner, our soul has plenary power and jurisdiction over the body and its functions, so that the human body performs no operation of which the soul is not in some way the principle and origin and cause. This is evident from the fact that a dead person ceases entirely to operate because the soul is separated from the body.

As a simple and spiritual substance, the soul is the principle of all the functions and operations of life. It is the soul that sees through the eyes, hears through the ears, smells, tastes, and touches, digests food in the stomach, converts nourishment into blood and disperses it through the network of veins and arteries, and supplies energy to the nervous system throughout the body. The soul likewise paints the pictures that are found in the imagination, retains the millions of things in the memory, discusses and argues with the intellect, and loves or hates with the will. Nothing is so small or insignificant in our body that it does not have the soul as its cause and principle. But if the soul is removed from the body, all the functions and operations of the body cease.

David greatly marveled at this when he said: "Thy knowledge is become wonderful to me; it is high, and I cannot reach it."[164] The commentary of Theodoretus on that verse can be summarized as follows: When, Lord, recollected in spirit and freed from the cares of the world and external affairs, I enter into myself and contemplate my own nature, and especially the rational soul that Thou hast given me; when I consider the knowledge of which it is capable and the arts invented by it to make life more pleasant and easy; when I think of the infinite number of words that are preserved in it and easily recalled when necessary; when I see how this soul governs the entire body, how it entrusts to the eyes the office of distinguishing between colors, to the tongue the distinction of tastes and the transmission of concepts by words, to the nose the perception of odors, to the ears the discernment of sounds, and to the sense of touch the awareness of pain or pleasure; when I consider all these things and see how they concur in the general structure of man, with his remarkable blending of the mortal and the immortal, I am astonished at so great a miracle. And since the human mind cannot fathom anything so wonderful, I confess that I am overcome and am forced to break out into hymns of praise and to exclaim with the prophet: "Thy

[164] Ps. 138:6.

knowledge is become wonderful to me; it is high, and I cannot reach it."

But what is meant by the statement that man is made not only in the image of God but also in His likeness? To this St. Bernard and St. Augustine respond by saying that the soul is called an image of God in regard to all that it has received according to its nature and it is called a likeness of God in regard to that which it has received gratuitously. They mean that the soul is an image of God in respect to the faculties and powers of the natural order that were bestowed upon it for the exercises of the natural life that is proper to it. It is called the likeness of God by reason of the supernatural graces and virtues that were showered on it by God so that it could live the supernatural life and merit eternal life.

It would follow from this that the soul's image of God, based as it is on the natural order, can never be lost, although the soul itself be condemned to hell. But the soul's likeness to God is destroyed whenever the soul loses sanctifying grace through any mortal sin. It is a terrible calamity for a man to experience the loss of this divine likeness and to be inflicted with the likeness that takes its place. As the Psalmist tells us: "And man, when he was in honor, did not understand; he is compared to senseless beasts and is become like to them."[165] What is more lamentable than the horrible fall whereby man, who in the purity of his life bore the likeness of God, exchanges the divine likeness for that of the beasts? How much lower could human misery fall and to what greater depths could it descend? One can see from this how great is the malice of sin, which has caused such a grave misfortune.

---

[165] Ps. 48:13.

Consider also that while the Creator is infinite in every way, the human soul is infinite in its capacity, its duration, its understanding, and its wisdom. It is infinite in capacity because there is nothing that it cannot comprehend, except God Himself. It is infinite in duration because it is immortal and will live forever, as long as God is God. It is infinite in its ability to understand and in its wisdom, because it could never understand or comprehend so many things that there would not yet remain something for it to know, something yet to discover. And even after a man would have comprehended all the arts and sciences of which human ingenuity is capable, his intellectual powers would still not be exhausted, but could know infinitely more than had already been comprehended. Hence, the potentiality of the human intellect knows neither limit nor terminus, for a man can never learn so much that he cannot learn more.

O God, if all the causes and motives for love are summarized and centered in Thee to an eminent degree, why do I not love Thee with the full capacity of my love? If we were to see any one of these motives of love in any creature, we would love that creature with such abandon that we would gladly die for it. Why, then, Lord, are we not inflamed with Thy love? Why do we not melt with love and desire to suffer a thousand deaths for love of Thee? If we recall the benefits we have received from Thee, we shall realize that we owe Thee the greatest debt of gratitude. If we consider love itself, we shall see that no one loves us more than Thou. Who is more perfect than Thee, more good, more beautiful, more kind, more noble, more wise, more powerful, and more generous?

What is it, Lord, that prevents our hearts from running to Thee? What bonds could be so strong that they hold us captive and prevent us from reaching Thee? If it is a love for the things of this world, how can such fragile and passing things hold back the impetus of our love for Thee? Will a little blade of grass be sufficient to resist a stone that comes hurtling down a mountain side?

Some may say that although all the motives and causes of love are centered in Thee, there is no proportion between something so lowly as ourselves and something so lofty as Thou. Thou art most excellent; man is most base. Thou art a spirit inaccessible and incomprehensible; man is flesh, miserable flesh. But to whom could my soul bear greater likeness than to Thee, Lord, since I have been made in Thy image? To whom is my heart better proportioned than to Thee, since Thou hast created it for Thyself? My soul was made to be a vessel of election so that Thou couldst fill it with Thyself and no created thing could ever fill it completely. Thou art a spirit and our souls are spiritual; Thou art invisible and our souls are invisible; Thou art immortal and our souls are immortal; Thou dost possess an intellect and free will and our souls possess these qualities also. Thou art perfect goodness and holiness and power; if the devil does not erase the likeness we bear to Thee, our souls are likewise filled with virtue and goodness.

May Thy name be ever blessed for making us like unto Thyself and for making us for Thyself. So truly are we made for each other that we can exclaim with the spouse in the Canticle: "My Beloved to me, and I to Him." The fact that Thou art so lofty and we so lowly increases the motives for love. Much more lovable is the likeness that is accompanied by inequality than that which is in every way equal. Greater is the love of the father for his son and the wife for her husband than the love between brothers, who are equal in all things. More sweet is the harmony of two different voices blending in the one melody, than when both voices sing on the same note. Therefore, although there is a kind of likeness and equality between Thyself and us, the disproportion between us is a cause of greater love. When a thing is imperfect, it inclines to a greater love of the perfect so that it may partake of greater perfection. So it is, Lord, that in our lowliness we do not lose sight of Thee. In Thy light we see Thee as the true light, and although Thou art most powerful, Thou art no less good than Thou art great. Thy greatness and power make Thee supreme, but Thy goodness makes Thee merciful so as not to despise men.

But the reason why we do not love Thee as much as Thou shouldst be loved is because of that first sin, through which human nature was so inclined to itself that it tends to love all things for itself and direct everything to itself. Therefore, Lord, if Thou dost not heal our nature with Thy grace and dost not infuse in us the power of Thy charity through the Holy Ghost, we shall not be able to love Thee with the supernatural love with which Thou dost deserve to be loved. And since Thou dost command us, Lord, to love Thee with a love such as this, and yet we cannot do it without Thy help, give us Thy grace so that we can fulfill this sweet office. Grant that we may love Thee, if not as much as Thou dost deserve (for no one can do this but Thyself), at least to love Thee as much as we can, with all our heart and strength.

Grant that we may love Thee with a simple and disinterested love and love nothing else more than Thee; with a strong love that will refuse no effort or labor for Thee; with an affective and diligent love that will always be occupied with the things of Thy service; with a unitive love that will never cease to love Thee and will never depart from Thee; with a prudent love that will never exceed Thy laws by misguided zeal or fervor; with a well-ordered love that will love all things in Thee and Thee above all things; with a pure and chaste love that will love Thee for Thy sake alone; with a zealous love that will love only Thy glory; with a violent love that will tear our hearts from all things earthly and keep them fixed on Thee until, having passed through the desert of this life, we shall see the splendor of Thy beauty and shall love Thee eternally in the company of the blessed, who never cease to love and praise Thee, the King of kings.

CHAPTER 26 ✠
Man's Gratitude to God

ONE OF THE greatest impulses that move the heart to love is the recognition of benefits received. The reason, as the philosophers tell us, is that while good is of itself lovable, everyone is especially inclined to love his own good. Consequently, he who wishes to arouse his heart to the love of God should frequently consider the benefits he has received from God. These benefits are innumerable, but we can reduce them to a certain number for the greater facility of those who wish to practice this pious exercise.

What language and what writings could ever suffice to exhaust the deluge of God's blessings and mercies? Yet, how could we better employ our time and energy than in a consideration of such matters? In order better to understand the grandeur of the divine benefits, let us first consider the excellency of the Giver and our own lowliness, for a gift is the more esteemed and praiseworthy as the giver is more excellent and the recipient is more lowly.

The greatness of the divine Giver is manifested to us in many ways. If you raise your eyes to the heavens, the grandeur and beauty that you see there will tell you of the power of Him who brought forth the heavens merely by His wish and command. Even now, if He so desired, He could create another thousand heavens better than the one He has created and He could do it with greater ease than that with which you open and close your eyes. Or consider the excellence of His knowledge as it is manifested in the marvelous order and harmony of the universe as a whole and in each one of its parts, down to the most insignificant creature. For example, the structure of the body of a bee, a mosquito, or any other insect, however small, would fill you with admiration. The same could be said of the greatness of His goodness, majesty, beauty, mercy, sweetness, benignity, and clemency; they far surpass anything that could be said of them.

Yet this admirable Lord is He who from the heights of the heavens has fixed His gaze upon you, a lowly creature, and in His infinite charity has shown you so many mercies. If you consider who He is and what you are, then even if He were to give you a crumb of bread, He would be deserving of inestimable gratitude by reason of His divine excellency. In this spirit and with these sentiments the holy Job marveled at the generosity of God when he said: "What is a man that Thou shouldst magnify him? Or why dost Thou set Thy heart upon him?"[166] The mere fact that God is mindful of man and has a place in

[166] Job 7:17.

His love for a creature so lowly is a source of great wonder for anyone who realizes the greatness of God. What could He do for man that He has not done? And if it is a source of amazement that God should even think of man, how much more amazing it is that He should become man Himself and die on the cross for man's redemption.

Man should therefore consider well the following three points when reflecting upon the benefits he has received: Who bestows the benefits, to whom they are granted, and why they are granted. Who? God. To whom? Man. Why? Out of sheer love. God, who has need of nothing outside Himself and seeks for nothing outside Himself, has loved you from all eternity. He deigned to create you and to bestow innumerable blessings upon you so that He might enable you to share in His glory.

Consider how this great God brought you from non-existence to existence and made you in His image and likeness. Open your eyes to the dignity that is yours. You are not a mere vestige or trace of the Creator, as are other creatures; you are His very image and likeness. Like Him, you are an intellectual being; like Him, you have free will and knowledge, so that as you now resemble Him in your being and life and operation, you may later become a true likeness of His infinite beauty. And in order that your glory would not be transitory and cease with the passing of time, He made you immortal, so that you could be happy for all eternity. Other creatures have no more than a glimpse of the world and then they disappear. But you have come forth from non-existence to existence, never to return to your former nothingness but always to enjoy eternal life.

Understand your dignity and realize that you have such a capacity for happiness that no other creature could ever fill your desires. God alone can satisfy you. Therefore, seek only God as the spouse of your soul, as the fulfillment of all your desires, and as your ultimate end.

O marvelous dignity of our souls! The King whose beauty causes the sun and moon to pale, whose majesty the heavens and the earth revere, whose wisdom the choirs of angels praise, whose goodness all the blessed in heaven worship, that same King desires to dwell in you as in His palace. Prepare and adorn your temple, daughter of Sion, and receive your King, whose presence will gladden and enrich you. Recall the words of St. Bernard: "Blessed is the soul that each day cleanses her heart to receive her God. Blessed the soul in which the Lord finds rest and a dwelling place, so that it can now say: He who created me dwells in my tabernacle and He will not deny it the peace of heaven, because my soul has prepared for Him a dwelling place and a place of rest on earth."

Consider also the magnitude of the love that prompted God to bestow His gifts upon you, whether they be little or great. A father is prompted by no less love in giving his child clothing as when he gives it a rich inheritance, for both the great and the small proceed from the same love. So also, the same infinite love prompts the eternal Father to give to His children the small gifts as well as the great ones. Consequently, He should be loved in return, no less for the one than for the other. Realize, then, what you owe to God, who created you out of love, even though He knew how poorly you would return His love and how many things you would do contrary to His will. Give thanks to Him for His great benefits and realize that neither in heaven nor on earth will you find anyone who is as truly your father as He is.

Look back at the various stages of your life and you will begin to understand the countless blessings that you have received from God. When you were as yet in the womb of your mother, who was it that watched over you so that you would not die before you were born? It was the same one who has watched over you even until now, so that you can rightly say with the Psalmist: "From my mother's womb Thou art my God; depart not from me."[167] At the time of your birth, who protected you so that you would not be numbered among those infants that seem to have been born to die rather than to live? And since the day of your birth, how many dangers, diseases, and sudden misfortunes the Lord in His merciful providence has spared you, holding back the evils and harm that could have befallen you and of which you were not even aware?

I beg you not to dismiss this great blessing, for it is deserving of singular gratitude to God. What infirmity or wound does one man suffer that another man could not suffer equally as well? As descendants of Adam, we are all children of the same father. We are all conceived in original sin and we have all committed personal sins. Why is one man lame, another deaf, and another blind? Why do certain ones suffer from cancer, tuberculosis, or some other disease? Why does this or that person pass day and night in continual pain, knowing scarcely an hour of happiness or relief? Yet the Lord has exempted you from all such sickness and suffering so that you are master of your own body and can enjoy many peaceful hours. How much you owe to God for such a singular blessing! You are a sinner like the rest of men and equally deserving of affliction

[167] Ps. 21:11.

like the others, but God has spared you while others endure pain and suffering.

Nor can you overlook the daily care that the Lord has for you. Consider how difficult it is for some men to provide for their daily sustenance. Some earn their daily bread by the sweat of their brow; some, in the midst of great dangers to their soul; others, with constant effort and affliction to their spirit; and others, in peril of their life. Even at the cost of great efforts and dangers, some men are scarcely able to earn enough for their daily bread. But you, perhaps, each day find the table set and well provided with food and all that is necessary for your daily life.

If, moreover, you consider the creatures of this world, you will see that they have been made for your service and welfare. They are part of the heritage that your heavenly Father has left to you. How great, then, must be the divine goodness that has provided so many things for you who do not merit them, even after your many sins and faults whereby you deserve to lose them. How many times have you been frivolously playing or swearing or committing some sin at the very moment that He was bestowing His gifts upon you? And how many times have you used these very gifts in a sinful manner?

The creatures of this world are the servants through which God provides for your nourishment. Do not, then, be such a child as to be unmindful of the Father who brought you forth while you give all your love to the servants that care for you, for they would not serve you unless they had been commanded to do so. Abandon the things of this world in order to follow your true Father.

The very benefits that God has bestowed on other creatures have been given for man's benefit, and not for the creatures themselves. This is one of the most consoling truths in the created universe. The beauty and power of the sun, the moon, and the stars, and the beauty of trees and flowers and precious stones, to whom do they give more profit or delight than to man? The perfume and color and beauty of the rose, to whom are they more pleasing than to man? If you can appreciate this truth, then you will realize that all the beauties and perfections of creatures are for your benefit, because all of them were made for you. See, then, how much more you owe to God than you realize, because all the good that He has bestowed on creatures He has thereby bestowed also on you.

What a great spectacle is this visible world if you realize that all the creatures in it are gifts sent to you from God. Even more, they are messages addressed to you from the Creator. Here God is; here He speaks to you; here He teaches you and seeks to draw you to Himself. How is it, then, that in the midst of all these marvels and signs of His goodness, you do not know Him? How is it that in spite of such great benefits you do not love Him? Why is it that your heart never asks: "Who is this that has bestowed so many mercies on me? Who is this that in so many ways reveals Himself to me? Who is this that in such divers ways seeks to draw me to His love? Who is this that by so many testimonies and proofs seeks to make me know Him? Who is this that so loves me that He created all things for my service and benefit? Who is this that out of pure goodness and without any merits on my part, desired to be my Good Shepherd, the Lord of my house, the defender of my goods, the healer of my sickness and wounds, and the provider for all my wants?"

Why is it that in spite of so many blessings, God is not loved? Why, in spite of so many signs and testimonies, does

He remain hidden from us? He offers Himself to us through so many of His creatures, but we do not find Him. He works so many wonders for us, but we do not know Him. Such is the effect of sin's corruption that it makes us blind to His splendor and insensible to His love.

Perhaps you will say that these common benefits to mankind seem to be more the work of nature than the work of God. Then I reply that this is not the voice of a Christian, but that of a pagan. It is not even the voice of a pagan, but that of an animal, for we read the following admission in the works of the pagan philosopher Epictetus: "Perhaps you will say that nature has bestowed these benefits upon you. O ignorant one! Do you not realize that when you say this, you merely change the name of God? What is nature but God Himself, who is the principle of nature? Therefore, unfortunate man, do not excuse yourself by saying that you owe a debt to nature and not to God, for there is no nature without God. If you should receive a gift from Lucius Seneca and were to say that you felt obligated to Lucius and not to Seneca, the identity of the benefactor would not thereby be changed, but only his name."

Not only the obligations of justice but our very needs and poverty urge us to be mindful of the Creator if we wish to attain happiness and perfection. We know well that creatures are not generally born with their full perfection. The same cause that gave them their beginning and origin must also bestow on them their completion and perfection. Then realize, rational creature, that this is also your condition. You are not yet fully made and perfect, but much is lacking to your perfection. This should be evident to you from the constant longings of your very being, which feels the need for something more and yearns for greater perfection. God desired that you should hunger still and that your needs should bring you to Him. It is not because of His poverty and want that He did not perfect you at the beginning, but because of His love; not that you should be poor, but that you should be humble; not that you should be needy, but that He would always have you near Him.

If, therefore, you are poor, needy, blind, why do you not go to the Father who made you, so that He can supply what is wanting to you? Observe how David did this very thing: "Thy hands have made me and formed me. Give me understanding and I will learn Thy commandments."[168] It is as if David had said: "Thy hands, Lord, have fashioned all that I have and whatever is in me, but the work is not yet completed. From whom shall I seek that which is lacking to me, except from Him who has given me all that I possess? Grant me light, Lord; illumine the eyes of one blind from birth so that he may know Thee and may thus see completed what Thou hast begun in him."

God alone can create without defects, augment without confusion, enrich without ostentation, and give complete satisfaction without the possession of many things. Possessing God, man is poor and content, rich and naked, alone and happy, dispossessed of everything but master of all things. With good reason does the wise man say: "One is as it were rich, when he hath nothing, and another is as it were poor, when he hath great riches."[169] Wealthy indeed is the pauper who possesses God, as did St. Francis of Assisi; poor indeed is the rich man who lacks God, as do many of the lords of he world. Of what avail are all the power and wealth of many riches if, with all

[168] Ps. 118:73.

[169] Prov. 13:7.

that, you live a life beset with cares and torn with desires that you cannot fulfill, in spite of all your possessions? Of what value are gorgeous clothes and delicate fare if these things cannot appease the anxiety and longing of your heart and soul? During the night there are many restless turnings on the soft and comfortable bed of the rich man and they cannot be cured by a well-filled purse.

Chapter 27 ✠ *Creation of the Angels*

Infinitely happy and glorious in the vision of His own divine beauty, God is also magnificent and liberal. Since He is supremely good and diffusive of His goodness, He was not content to communicate His blessings merely to the creatures of this visible world. He likewise willed to create higher creatures to whom He could communicate the riches of His happiness and glory. It was as if God did not wish to be alone in His happiness and for that reason He created two excellent types of creatures in His own image and likeness that would be capable of receiving a share in His glory. Thus, God created the angels in heaven and men on earth. The angels are purely spiritual substances; men are spiritual substances united to bodies.

But the works of God are perfect, as He Himself is, and since He had created these two kinds of creatures for so noble an end, He also provided them with the powers and perfections necessary for attaining that end. Shabby and tattered men are not admitted to the palaces of kings, but only those who are neat and properly dressed. So also, sensual and carnal men cannot enter into the heavenly mansion of the King of kings, for they are spiritually shabby and tattered. Under one condition will the Lord grant admission to the kingdom of heaven: that men be faithful and obedient to Him and use well the graces and benefits received from Him. Then they can hope to obtain their sovereign good. But if they act otherwise, they will lose all because of their sin.

This same condition was placed upon all the angels after their creation. They were to enter into the divine presence and worship at the throne of God only after they had given proof of their obedience and submission to Him and had resolved to use their blessings and graces for His honor and glory. One group of angels, recognizing that all the goods and gifts they possessed were from God, gave thanks to Him, humbled themselves before Him, and with all their love offered to be His faithful servants forever and to obey His laws. These good angels were then confirmed in grace and raised to the beatific vision of the divine beauty and they shall possess it for all eternity.

Among the angels there was one who was especially perfect and beautiful and, according to St. Gregory, he was the most excellent of all the angels. Consequently, he should have been most grateful, most humble, and most obedient to the Creator who had so wonderfully exalted him. But he was not. Rather, enamored of his own beauty, he became puffed up with pride and sought by his own power to be like unto God. As a punishment for his ingratitude and pride, he was cast out of that glorious place where only the humble dwell. Likewise cast out was a multitude of angels who had followed Lucifer's example and counsel.

The evil angels were obstinate in their malice and since they despaired of ever returning to the position that they had forfeited by their pride, they cultivated a fierce hatred for the God who had condemned them to hell. As a result of their hatred, they work with all their art and knowledge to lessen His glory and to lead men from His service. Unable to earn a place in heaven, they strive to gain power on earth by deceiving miserable men. Thus, ignorant men are led to the worship of devils and idols, malicious men are gradually weakened until they become apostates from the true Church, and hundreds of new sects and religions are introduced into the world for the promulgation of false beliefs.

Not content with attacking and weakening the faith of men, the devils often persuade and convince them that the human soul is mortal and that there is nothing to life but birth and death. Once they have achieved this, they lead these wretched men into all manner of vices and baseness, as is evident in any nation that disregards God or denies His existence. Such men live like animals, for they seek nothing but the present and are interested only in those things that pertain to the body. This is the degeneracy to which men can fall when they heed the instigations of the devil, the father of lies, and forget completely that they have been made in the image and likeness of God and are capable of possessing Him for all eternity.

CHAPTER 28 ✠ *God's Care for All His Creatures*

WE SHALL CLOSE our meditations with a consideration of the general care and providence that God shows for all His creatures. At the outset we should note that there are two kinds of efficient cause: the one is sufficient to produce something, but once the effect has been produced, it exerts no more influence, as in the case of the architect who makes a house or the painter who paints a picture. The other not only produces the thing, but also preserves it in being after it has been made, as we see in the rays of light caused by the sun, for if the sun should become dark or cease to exist, the rays of light would also disappear.

Catholic faith teaches that the sovereign Lord is the cause of all created things because He gave them their existence and that He also preserves them in the being that He gave them. So great is the dependence of creatures on the Creator that if He were for a moment to turn away from them, they would immediately be annihilated and sink back into the nothingness from which they came.

Consequently, it is necessary that God be present in some way to all things that exist, sustaining them not only by His presence and power, but by His very essence. To understand this we should observe that all other causes produce their effects by virtue of the power they possess, as fire causes heat in other things by reason of the heat it possesses. But in God there is no distinction between His power and His essence, for in His lofty and exalted nature there are no accidents or properties in the strict sense of the word. Everything in God is God, without any admixture or composition. Moreover, wherever there is any part of God, it is all God, because His supreme simplicity does not permit any division whereby part of Him could be in one place and part in another. Lastly, cause and effect must in some way be united and be in contact with each other, and since being is the most universal and most intimate effect in created things, it follows that God is present in the most intimate part of all things. For that reason God is said to fill the heavens and the earth. He is entire in all the world and entire in each part of the world.

But God not only preserves the being of all creatures, He is also the cause of all their movements and activities. As a result, no created thing can move a hand or foot or open its mouth or open and close its eyes save by the power of God. He is, in a sense, more the cause of the movement than is the creature that moves. Avicenna taught that God does no more than assist in the order and movement of the heavens and that by means of the heavenly movements He governs all other things in the lower world. But Christian philosophy goes even farther and teaches that the First Cause, which is God, concurs in the movement and activity of all inferior causes. Consequently, all the effects of these inferior causes can be attributed more truly to the First Cause who made them than to those which immediately produce the effects. Similarly, it is more proper to say that the painter paints the picture rather than the brush with which he works.

If we consider our relationship with God from the aspect of our dependence on Him, we shall find that there are three ways in which some things can depend on others. Some depend on others for their creation or production, but after receiving existence, they no longer need an extrinsic cause for conservation in being, as is the case of a painting or any other artificial thing that comes from the hand of the artist. Other things depend on their causes in the same way that the life of the body depends on the presence and power of the soul, whereby it lives and continues in existence. Thirdly, some things depend on their causes for the perfection or plenitude of their being, as does the student on the professor who teaches him or the wife on the husband from whom she receives the necessities of life.

These three types of dependence create a close bond among the things that are interrelated and are at the same time the motive of great love. As a result, all effects have a natural love for the causes that produce them, sustain them, or from which they seek their full perfection. As a result of the first kind of dependence, we see the great love that children have for their parents and parents for their children. By reason of the second type of dependence, it is natural for the other members of the body to protect the head, which is one of the most vital members of the human body. And by reason of the third type of dependence, we see the great love that a wife has for her husband, for she receives from him many things that contribute to her perfection.

The same three kinds of dependence are to be found in our relationship with God, and in an eminent degree. Since He has given us existence, He ought to be loved by us as a father is loved by his children; since He conserves us in being, He should be loved as the head is loved by the members; and since He offers us the plenitude of perfection, he should be loved as the bridegroom is loved by the bride. Acknowledge these obligations and, knowing what you have been and what you are and what you hope to be, love Him who has done so much for you and will continue to do so much for you.

Grant that I may love Thee, Lord, for I am Thy creature and Thou art my Maker, from whom I have received my very being and existence. Let the waters run back to their source, let the effect return to the cause that produced it, and let the creature turn back to the Creator who fashioned it.

Do not let me be guilty of such treason, Lord, that I would surrender the keys of Thy mansion to anyone but Thee. I am Thine, Lord; I shall remain Thine and Thine I desire to be forever. Receive me as Thy own and do not reject that which Thou hast made for Thyself.

On whom shall I fix my eyes, Lord, and whom shall I love but Thee? For Thy hands have created me, Thy providence sustains me, and Thy creatures serve me. Through whose power do I exist and from whom do I have all that I possess, if not from Thee? Thou alone art the source of all my good and the storehouse of all my treasures.

Thou didst plant me by Thy hand when Thou didst create me and since Thou dost now conserve me in being by the care and watering of Thy divine providence, who but Thee shall harvest the fruit of this land? I am Thy acreage and soil and Thou art my Lord and Master. All the plants of this land—my faculties and powers—are for Thy service. For Thee are the flowers of my desires and the fruits of my good works. May my eyes bless Thee, my tongue praise Thee, my hands serve Thee, my feet walk along the path of Thy commandments, and my heart be inflamed with Thy love. May my memory never forget Thee, my intellect ever contemplate Thee, and my will delight only in Thee. Let such be the harvest and fruits of this land.

Surround it, Lord, with a wall of fire and close all its gates so that none but Thee can enter in. I adjure and command you, all created things, that you touch not anything in this land of His. Let all be Thine, Lord, and let all be used in Thy service. Let all other creatures die to this love and let me die to them.

May I love Thee, Lord, for Thou alone can finish the work Thou hast begun in me. Thou alone can give my soul its full perfection. May I love Thee, Lord, with an intimate and fervent love. May I have the arms of good desires and good affections with which to embrace Thee, sweet Spouse of my soul, from whom I hope for all good.

The ivy embraces the tree in so many parts that the whole vine seems to be made up of arms whereby it can be more firmly attached to the tree and can climb upward until it reaches its full perfection. Thou art the tree, Lord, that I desire to embrace and cling to, so that I may attain that which is still lacking to me. Let my soul grow like the ivy in virtues and graces when it embraces Thee. Let me be all arms so that I may embrace Thee in every part.

Help me, Lord, and lead me far along Thy path, for the weight of my mortality impedes my progress. Thou, Lord and Savior, who didst ascend to the height of the Cross in order to draw all things to Thyself, Thou who in Thy great love didst unite two natures in one Person to become one with us, deign to unite our hearts with Thee in such a strong bond of love that they will become one with Thee.

In Thy hands, Lord, are all my days, past and present and future. In the past I received from Thee the being that I now have; in the present Thou dost preserve me in life, as the sun does the rays of light that emanate from it; and in the future must come from Thy hand my final perfection and the fulfillment of all my desires, when my soul will find perfect rest and be united with Thee to share in the happiness for which Thou hast created me.

Look down upon me, Lord, with Thy merciful and paternal gaze and infuse into my soul the rays of Thy mercy and love so that, raising my eyes to Thee in humility and reverence, I may receive the blessing of Thy light. Looking to Thee, I repeat with the Psalmist: "My eyes are ever toward the Lord, for He shall pluck my feet out of the snare. Look Thou upon me and have mercy on me, for I am alone and poor."[170]

In the same spirit let us all say: "To Thee have I lifted up my eyes, who dwellest in heaven. Behold, as the eyes of servants are on the hands of their masters, as the eyes of the handmaid are on the hands of her mistress, so are our eyes unto the Lord our God, until He have mercy on us."[171]

---

[170] Ps. 24:15–16.

[171] Ps. 182:1–2.

Appendix ✠

Prologue: *Guía de pecadores,* prologue; *Memorial de la vida cristiana,* prologue.

Chapter 1: *Introducción al símbolo de la fe,* Part I, chapter 3.

Chapter 2: *Compendio de la "Introducción al símbolo de la fe,"* Part I, chapter 2.

Chapter 3: *Introducción al símbolo de la fe,* Part I, chapter 38.

Chapter 4: *Introducción al símbolo de la fe,* Part I, chapter 2.

Chapter 5: *Guía de pecadores,* Book I, Part I, chapter 1.

Chapter 6: *Adiciones al "Memorial de la vida cristiana,"* Part II, chapter 22.

Chapter 7: *Adiciones al "Memorial de la vida cristiana,"* Part II, chapter 22.

Chapter 8: *Adiciones al "Memorial de la vida cristiana,"* Part II, chapter 22.

Chapter 9: *Memorial de la vida cristiana,* Treatise V, chapter 4; *Manual de diversas oraciones.*

Chapter 10: *Compendio de la doctrina cristiana,* Part I, chapter 4.

Chapter 11: *Introducción al símbolo de la fe,* Part I, chapter 36.

Chapter 12: *Guía de pecadores,* Book I, Part II, chapter 6.

Chapter 13: *Introducción al símbolo de la fe,* Part IV, dialogue 3; *Compendio de la doctrina cristiana,* Part I, chapters 3 and 5.

Chapter 14: *Introducción al símbolo de la fe,* Part I, chapters 3 and 38.

Chapter 15: *Introducción al símbolo de la fe,* Part I, chapter 5.

Chapter 16: *Introducción al símbolo de la fe,* Part I, chapter 8.

Chapter 17: *Introducción al símbolo de la fe,* Part I, chapter 8.

Chapter 18: *Introducción al símbolo de la fe,* Part I, chapter 10.

Chapter 19: *Introducción al símbolo de la fe,* Part I, chapters 11 and 12.

Chapter 20: *Introducción al símbolo de la fe,* Part I, chapters 18–21.

Chapter 21: *Introducción al símbolo de la fe,* Part I, chapters 13 and 38.

Chapter 22: *Introducción al símbolo de la fe,* Part I, chapters 25 and 26.

Chapter 23: *Introducción al símbolo de la fe,* Part I, chapters 27. 30, 31.

Chapter 24: *Introducción al símbolo de la fe,* Part I, chapter 33.

Chapter 25: *Adiciones al "Memorial de la vida cristiana,"* Part II, chapter 22; *Introducción al símbolo de la fe,* Part I, chapters 24–25.

Chapter 26: *Guía de pecadores,* Book I, Part I, chapter 2; *Adiciones al "Memorial de la vida cristiana,"* Part II, chapter 22.

Chapter 27: *Compendio de la "Introducción al símbolo de la fe,"* chapter 8.

Chapter 28: *Adiciones al "Memorial de la vida cristiana,"* Part II, chapter 22; *Introducción al símbolo de la fe,* Part I, chapter 38.